LEGACY ON STONE

Rock Art of the Colorado Plateau and Four Corners Region

Sally J. Cole

Johnson Books • Boulder

Cover design by Molly Gough
Cover photo by Sally J. Cole

Credits:
Maps were prepared by Margaret Stone. Rock art illustrations were drawn from projected photographic slides, photographs, and field sketches by Margaret Stone, Barbara Blackshear, and Sally J. Cole.

Produced with the support of the Colorado Endowment for the Humanities, Denver, Colorado, a grantee of the National Endowment for the Humanities.

Library of Congress Cataloging-in-Publication Data
Cole, Sally.
    Legacy on stone: rock art of the Colorado plateau and Four Corners region / Sally Cole.
        p.   cm.
    Includes bibliographical references and index.
    ISBN 1-55566-074-6
    1. Indians of North America—Colorado—Antiquities. 2. Indians of North America—Southwest, New—Antiquities. 3. Petroglyphs—Colorado. 4. Petroglyphs—Southwest, New. 5. Pictographs—Colorado. 6. Pictographs—Southwest, New. 7. Colorado—Antiquities. 8. Southwest, New—Antiquities. I. Title.
E78.C6C6 1990
709'.01'130979—dc20   90-45715
                                                                                            CIP

Printed in the United States of America by
Johnson Publishing
1880 South 57th Court
Boulder, Colorado 80301

Contents

Acknowledgments

During fourteen years of research on the Colorado Plateau and in the Rocky Mountains, many people including fellow archaeologists, ranchers and farmers, and numerous individuals who explore the canyons and mountains of this region have shared information about rock art and have helped with documentation. I am grateful to all of you for your professionalism, generosity, and insights. I wish to identify certain organizations and individuals that have supported research for this book and its publication. First, I wish to acknowledge financial assistance provided by a research and publication grant from the Colorado Endowment for the Humanities and thank the staff for their helpfulness throughout the project. In support of the grant, I received an in-kind contribution of technical assistance from the Colorado State Office of the Bureau of Land Management. I appreciate their willingness to support the project and the efforts of Frederic J. Athearn, manager of the Cultural Resources Program.

I also wish to acknowledge in-kind support for the grant from individuals who helped me gather information and materials from files and in the field. These people donated time and knowledge and, in some instances, the use of their homes: Douglas W. Bowman, Archaeologist for Ute Mountain Ute Tribe; Henry S. Keesling, Craig District Archaeologist for the Bureau of Land Management; Brian Naze, Little Snake Resource Area Archaeologist for the Bureau of Land Management; Kristie Arrington, San Juan Resource Area Archaeologist for the Bureau of Land Management; Michael Selle, White River Resource Area Archaeologist for the Bureau of Land Management; Robert H. Nykamp, Routt National Forest Archaeologist; James S. Truesdale, Archaeologist for Dinosaur National Monument; Jack Smith, Chief Research Archaeologist for Mesa Verde National Park; Victoria Atkins; and Joanne and Edward Berger.

Preparation of the manuscript was aided by the talents of a number of people. I wish to thank Margaret Stone and Barbara Blackshear for their work on illustrations and dedication to accuracy. I thank Glenn Stone for commenting on the text and for sharing field sketches and photographs. I thank Hartley and Lynn Bloomfield and Harley Armstrong for their field sketches. Henry Schoch and Bill Harris provided photographs, and I thank each of them. Carl Weaver worked long hours to produce quality black and white prints of often difficult subject matter, and I appreciate his efforts. I also appreciate professional word processing by Louise Wagner. I wish to acknowledge the expertise of Rebecca Herr, Editorial Director at Johnson Books. She has made this complex project work smoothly.

Finally, I wish to acknowledge the consistent support of my husband, Chuck, who has visited rock art sites with me from California to East Africa and who shares my enduring fascination with the Colorado Plateau.

Sally J. Cole
Grand Junction, Colorado

List of Maps

INTRODUCTION

The focus of this study is Indian rock art in western Colorado and neighboring areas of the Colorado Plateau and Rocky Mountains. The region is characterized by geologic and environmental diversity and has had significant cultural diversity over time. This is emphasized by two national parks located near the southern and northern boundaries. Mesa Verde National Park to the south in the arid Four Corners area of Colorado, Utah, New Mexico, and Arizona is renowned for cliff dwellings, basketry, ceramics, and other art of the Anasazi tradition. Dinosaur National Monument, located in the Uinta Mountain Basin near the borders of Colorado, Utah, and Wyoming, preserves ruins and art of the Fremont culture, a northern neighbor of the Anasazi.

These parks and surrounding areas have archaeological evidence of other cultural traditions, such as the Archaic, distinguished by prehistoric hunters and gatherers who roamed the region in seasonal cycles for thousands of years, and historic nomads such as the Ute, Eastern Shoshoni, and Navajo. How various indigenous cultures developed and interacted with each other and with Euro-American groups over time and space is important to an understanding of the cultural history of this region and for explaining archaeological remains such as rock art. The study area lies within the Colorado Plateau, Rocky Mountains, and Wyoming Basin (Hunt 1967; Baars 1983). Land forms include deep and colorful canyons, river valleys, rock spires, and monoliths as well as mesas, plateaus, plains, and mountains with dense forests, lush meadows, and perpetual snow fields. Major rivers of western North America such as the Colorado, Green, Gunnison, Yampa, San Juan, and Dolores, originate in and flow through the region. These great rivers have provided corridors for the movement of people, objects, and ideas throughout the study area and beyond.

The area has had much to offer prehistoric and historic aboriginal peoples, peoples who for several thousand years gathered wild plants; hunted a variety of wild game; fished; farmed; camped; built structures of wood, stone, and earth; made tools; and performed ceremonies. Evidence of these activities is found in archaeological remains scattered throughout the area. The remains are material and ideological in nature. The latter include art forms, images that occur on natural rock surfaces, structure walls, pottery, basketry, skins, and cloth. Of primary importance to this study is rock art, symbolism depicted on natural rock surfaces. Rock art is found in places used by ancient and historic peoples for a variety of purposes. These original settings and associated artifacts provide clues for interpreting the art.

Indian rock art, in the forms of *petroglyphs* (pecked, stipple and solid; ground; incised; abraded; and scratched) and *rock paintings* and *drawings* (often called pictographs), in monochrome and polychrome, occurs on canyon walls, in rock shelters, and on boulders. Mineral pigments such as hematite, limonite, azurite, and gypsum taken from surrounding soils and clays and charcoal produced long-lasting liquid and solid paints in a variety of colors. It is probable that less durable vegetable dyes were also used, but these are more subject to fading and removal by water. Binders used to make paints include organic substances such as animal fats and vegetable oils and mineral substances such as gypsum (Wellmann 1979). Smith (1952) provides a thorough discussion of pigments used in prehistoric Hopi kiva murals that is useful for the study of rock paintings. During the historic period, after A.D. 1880, Ute artists in southwest Colorado used commercial dyes manufactured for marking sheep. Rock paintings made with these dyes remain quite bright in protected areas and are faded or have been erased in areas that are directly exposed to sunlight and water.

River corridors and tributary canyon networks are the locations of most of the region's rock art, but some sites are found in mountainous areas (Plates 1 and 2). *Petroglyphs* are found on rock surfaces coated with "desert varnish," of iron- and manganese-oxides and other minerals; the intensity of the stain varies with rock composition and exposure to moisture and sunlight. More recent petroglyphs may be seen in sharp contrast to the background rock because they have been formed by the removal of surface patina, and the new surface has not had sufficient time and conditions to darken. Presently, most *rock paintings* and *drawings* made with liquid and solid pigments are confined to rock shelters and other protected areas, although it is probable that paintings and drawings once existed in more exposed situations. The original scope of rock art will probably not be known since weathering has removed pigments in exposed locations as well as entire rock surfaces

Plate 1. *Sandstone canyon and rock shelter north of the San Juan River in southeastern Utah near the Colorado border. Ancient and historic Indian cultures of the Colorado Plateau occupied such locations and used them for making rock art.*

Plate 2. *Mountainous area of northwestern Colorado near the Utah border. Sandstone canyon walls and rock outcrops in this area exhibit rock art, and the area was occupied by prehistoric and historic Indian cultures. The Fremont masonry structure seen on the promontory of rock has been dated approximately A.D. 1500 (Creasman and Scott 1987:11).*

that exhibited petroglyphs and paintings. This geological process is taking place at the present time, a fact that was clearly demonstrated by the 1988 loss of rock art at a site in Rio Blanco County, Colorado. At this site, rock paintings were removed by exfoliation of sandstone surfaces, probably due to moisture within and outside the host rock (Plates 3 and 4).

Vandalism and land development have also taken a heavy toll on rock art and related archaeological sites since the settlement of the study area by Euro-Americans in the late 1800s. Rock art has been removed by graffiti carved on the rocks, gunfire, saws, bulldozers, and by being buried beneath reservoirs of water. Archaeological sites that may have provided information for the interpretation of rock art and other aspects of the past have been destroyed by "pot hunting" or digging that destroys the archaeological context of sites and leaves an inadequate record of artifacts and associations. Despite its ongoing destruction, Indian rock art remains highly visible throughout the study area and is an enduring record of past ideas and practices. This record, viewed from archaeological, historic, and ethnographic contexts, presents an opportunity to interpret the past and contributes to the overall effort by archaeologists to explain cultural and social dynamics over time.

Significant archaeological investigations have been undertaken since the early part of the twentieth century, and an increasing awareness of the importance of rock art to archaeological interpretation has developed. A number of studies have been made of Colorado Plateau and Rocky Mountain rock art (Jeancon 1926; Huscher and Huscher 1940; Gebhard and Cahn 1950; Wormington and Lister 1956; Wenger 1956; Buckles 1971; Schaafsma 1963, 1971, 1972, 1980; Fetterman 1976; Rohn 1977; Toll 1977; Conner and Ott 1978; Castleton 1978, 1979; McKern 1978; Creasman 1981, 1982; Hendry 1983; Cole 1987, 1988, 1989c; Noxon and Marcus 1985; Walker and Francis 1989; and others). This volume provides an overview of rock art in the study area and a synthesis of previous work.

The first chapter in this volume briefly describes the physical and environmental settings for rock art in the study area and outlines the cultural history. The second chapter discusses the nature of rock art and how it is dated and cultural affiliation determined. Subsequent chapters provide descriptions and analyses of rock art, including generalized location maps and illustrations. Site locations are given in approximate terms only to protect rock art and related archaeological sites from vandalism.

In an appendix, a list of numbered sites used in the preparation of this volume is provided as a reference for rock art research. The num-

Plate 3

Plate 4

Details of Barrier Canyon Style rock paintings at site 5RB106, White River drainage, northwestern Colorado. Plate 3 was taken before 1987, and Plate 4 was taken after 1987. Damage to the right portion of the panel resulted from natural deterioration of the sandstone surface. Plate 4 is courtesy of the Bureau of Land Management, Frederic J. Athearn, photographer.

bering system is keyed to records held by state and federal agencies responsible for inventorying and protecting sites in the study area.

Rock art is described as it is related to styles that are identified for the Colorado Plateau and Rocky Mountain areas beginning with that of earlier cultures. All rock art examined for the study region does not cleanly fit within existing style categories for a variety of reasons, including cultural differences that affect the symbolism of a given area. Nevertheless, style categories provide a general framework for comparison and enable us to see cultural relationships, change, and continuity as reflected in the symbolism of a region over time.

A special emphasis of this study is rock art of the Ute Indians, historic aboriginal people of western Colorado and adjoining Utah. The final section in this volume analyzes Ute rock art utilizing historic and ethnographic information. Ute iconography and symbolism from the A.D. 1600s to the mid-1900s is viewed from the perspective of Ute culture before and during the reservation period. This information identifies how rock art has been used by one aboriginal group during the historic period and, accordingly, offers insights into the making of ancient rock art, vividly connecting the activities of the present with the past.

THE LAND
AND CULTURES

The general study area is located in the Colorado Plateau and adjacent Rocky Mountains. The Colorado Plateau is part of the Great Basin Desert Province that lies east of the Wasatch Mountains and west of the Continental Divide. Streams and rivers of the plateau are part of the Colorado River drainage system flowing from Colorado and Wyoming to the Gulf of California. Geological formations of the land are composed of ancient erosional sediments carried by air and water and volcanic deposits (Baars 1983). These formations are exposed in mountains and canyons that have been uplifted, eroded, and downcut by rivers and tributary streams. Striking examples of geologic formations are rock outcrops, canyon walls, and boulders composed of reddish-brown and tan sandstones and gray to black basalts. These have long provided suitable surfaces and overhangs for making and sheltering aboriginal rock art.

Environmentally, the study region is semiarid and is included within the Upper Sonoran life zone. Elevations within the region range from approximately 4,000 feet above sea level in valley floors to more than 14,000 feet on the peaks of mountains. Individual environments within the region include desert plant communities with Indian rice grass, sage, salt bush, and *chamisa*; riparian vegetation such as cottonwood trees, willows, rushes, and cattails; pinyon and juniper woodlands; subalpine and alpine forests; and tundra. Modern fauna include elk, mule deer, black bear, desert and mountain bighorn sheep, pronghorn, mountain lions, coyotes, rabbits, prairie dogs and other rodents, a variety of fish, reptiles, and amphibians. Birds include raptors such as eagles, hawks, buteos, and owls; scavengers such as vultures, ravens, and magpies; herons, Sand Hill cranes, egrets, and other wading birds; ducks, coots, geese, and other waterfowl; and a variety of songbirds.

The southern portion of the study region, which includes southwest Colorado and adjacent portions of New Mexico, Arizona, and
Utah (the Four Corners), is characterized by broad valleys and mesas,
such as Mesa Verde, and laccolithic mountains (bowed up by igneous
rock within the earth's crust), such as Sleeping Ute Mountain and the
Abajo Mountains in the west, and major mountain ranges and valleys
associated with the southern Rocky Mountains in the east. Of these,
the San Juan and La Plata mountain ranges rise to heights of more
than 14,000 feet above sea level and give rise to the Dolores River and
its tributary, the San Miguel River, and to the San Juan River and its
tributaries, the Animas, La Plata, and Piedra rivers. The San Juan River
and its tributaries flow south and west from Colorado into New Mexico, Arizona, and Utah before joining the Colorado River. The
Dolores and the San Miguel flow north and west, away from the San
Juan River basin, to join the Colorado River. South of the Four Corners, the Little Colorado River flows from the Mogollon Plateau of
Arizona and New Mexico to join the Colorado River at the eastern
edge of the Grand Canyon.

Archaeological sites of the San Juan River drainage have been
extensively investigated since the latter part of the 1800s and initially
served to define the Anasazi culture. The sites have contributed significantly to knowledge about the prehistory of the Four Corners area and
the southwestern portion of North America. In an archaeological context, the best known physical and geologic feature is the Mesa Verde,
location of spectacular Anasazi ruins administered by Mesa Verde
National Park and the Ute Mountain Ute Tribal Park.

West central Colorado and adjacent portions of Utah lie to the
north of the San Juan River drainage and are bounded by the Book
Cliffs, the Roan Plateau, and the Flattop mountain ranges on the
north. The area is dominated by high mountains in the east, including
Grand Mesa and Battlement Mesa, and the northern San Juan, the
West Elk, and Elk mountain ranges. In the west, the land is marked by
the laccolithic Henry, La Sal, and Abajo mountains, Navajo Mountain,
and by the San Rafael Swell and Uncompahgre Plateau. Broad river
valleys and canyon systems of Canyonlands National Park, Arches
National Park, and Colorado National Monument surround the
mountain areas. Three rivers, the Gunnison and its tributary, the
Uncompahgre, and the Little Dolores, originate in the higher elevations of the area and ultimately join the Colorado River near the Utah
and Colorado boundary. Somewhat to the south, the confluence of
the Dolores and Colorado rivers takes place, also near the Utah and
Colorado boundary.

Rock art of west central Colorado and adjacent Utah is visible along the various river corridors and has been reported since the early part of the twentieth century. Significant archaeological studies in west central Colorado and adjacent Utah have been concentrated in the vicinity of the Uncompahgre Plateau, the La Sal Mountains, Abajo Mountains, and the Book Cliffs. These studies have contributed to knowledge of Archaic, Anasazi, Fremont, and historic Ute cultures.

Northwestern Colorado and adjacent portions of Utah and Wyoming are generally mountainous. The area lies north of the Book Cliffs, Tavaputs Plateau, and Roan Plateau, and the northern portion includes the Uinta Mountain Basin and arid plains and mountains of Colorado and Wyoming that are drained by the Green and Yampa rivers. High mountains dominate the east and give rise to the White, Yampa, and Elk rivers and to the Colorado River that shares its name and water with a major portion of the southwestern United States. The Uinta Basin contains large mountain valleys and canyon systems that feed the Green, Yampa, and Uinta rivers. Both the Yampa and Green rivers flow through Dinosaur National Monument. The Green, the Yampa, and the White River drainages all have considerable archaeological significance, including evidence of the Fremont culture. River canyon systems throughout the Uinta Basin are renowned for aboriginal rock art.

THE CULTURAL HISTORY

Paleo-Indian Tradition

The earliest cultural remains of western Colorado and adjacent areas are from the Paleo-Indian period dated from approximately 10000 to 5500 B.C. The characteristic lifeway of this period is big game hunting and the pursuit of large, now extinct, mammals that were present in North America during a period of cooler and wetter climate associated with the Pleistocene era (Eddy, Kane, and Nickens 1984; Grady 1984; Guthrie et al. 1984; Reed 1984). Presently, relatively little archaeological information is available about Paleo-Indian peoples, and no rock art in the study region has been assigned to that culture stage. It is possible that Paleo-Indian rock art exists on ancient and well-preserved rock surfaces, but it is difficult to make associations without precise dating techniques. This is particularly true in areas where rock art of later cultures may occur at the same sites.

Archaic Tradition

It is to hunting and gathering peoples of the Western Archaic cultural tradition that the earliest rock art of the study area is ascribed.

The hunting and gathering lifeway is generally dated from approximately 5500 B.C. to A.D. 1 in western Colorado (Eddy et al. 1984; Grady 1984; Guthrie et al. 1984; Reed 1984) when more sedentary village and farming groups known as Formative cultures appeared in the western Colorado area. However, it is very possible that hunting and gathering groups were in the region continuously until the historic period and may have coexisted with more sedentary farming peoples. After approximately A.D. 1150–1300, tools identified with Numic-speaking peoples (hunters and gatherers of the Great Basin), such as the historic Ute and Eastern Shoshoni, are found in western Colorado.

Western Archaic lifeways adapted to desert, mountain, and plains environments have been associated with the area (Wormington and Lister 1956; Jennings 1957, 1964, 1978; Irwin-Williams 1967, 1973; Buckles 1971; Eddy et al. 1984; Grady 1984; Guthrie et al. 1984; Reed 1984; Black 1986). The Western Archaic lifeway is recognized as being essentially nomadic, with annual rounds undertaken for the procurement of food and material goods. Small extended family groups or otherwise related bands of hunter-gatherers probably traveled seasonally to locations where staple foods, such as pinyon nuts, juniper berries, and rice grass, could be harvested and processed and where larger animals such as bighorn sheep, pronghorn, mule deer, and bison could be successfully hunted. It is likely that major hunting and gathering events involved bands representing more than a single extended family and were marked by ceremonial and social occasions of which rock art may have been a part.

Archaic people utilized open sites, caves, and rock shelters for seasonal camps. Evidence that Archaic peoples also built living structures, including pit houses and superstructures of mud, stone, and brush, has been reported by Gooding and Shields (1985) and Metcalf and Black (1988). Archaic structures in the mountains of Colorado and the northern Great Basin suggest the presence of substantial living structures as early as eight thousand years ago. The Yarmony Pithouse site (5EA799) in western Colorado, six meters in diameter, is proposed to have been of sufficient size to shelter a single extended family and was probably used seasonally over a number of years (Metcalf and Black 1988).

The long Archaic lifeway produced many archaeological remains, including chipped and ground stone artifacts; implements of horn, antler, wood, bark, and fiber; baskets; netting; matting; sandals; moccasins; rabbit fur blankets; unfired clay, stone, and vegetal figurines; reed duck decoys; atlatls or spear throwers; jewelry of bone, stone, and shell; bone gaming pieces; string and feather ornaments; and rock art (Irwin-Williams 1979; Aikens and Madsen 1986). Archaic rock art of the study area has been described by Buckles (1971), Schaafsma (1971; 1972; 1980), Turner (1963, 1971), Castleton (1978, 1979), Cole (1987, 1989c), and others. Thus, despite the destructive effects of time, important remains are available for interpreting this remote culture and its rock art.

Regionally adaptive phases of the Western Archaic lifeway that may have been represented in western Colorado during Early, Middle, and Late Archaic periods are discussed by Eddy et al. (1984), Grady (1984), Guthrie et al. (1984), and Reed (1984). Gooding and Shields (1985) provide a chronology for the northern Colorado Plateau based on radiocarbon (Carbon 14 measurement) dates from western Colorado and adjacent areas. The chronology spans the period from approximately 7000 B.C. to the historic present and indicates at least five thousand years of continuous occupations in western Colorado.

A specific manifestation or cultural unit of the Archaic, the Uncompahgre Complex, has been identified on the Uncompahgre Plateau and to the east along the Colorado River in west central Colorado (Wormington and Lister 1956; Buckles 1971; Reed 1984; Gooding and Shields 1985). The Uncompahgre Complex is dated from approximately 7000 B.C. until just prior to the historic period, A.D. 1300 or later (Buckles 1971). Hunters and gatherers of the Uncompahgre Complex probably coexisted with neighboring peoples who were more sedentary and practiced agriculture: the Anasazi and Fremont. Rock art of the Uncompahgre Complex has been described by Wormington and Lister (1956), Buckles (1971), and Cole (1987, 1989c).

The Uncompahgre Complex (Wormington and Lister 1956) was originally described as a variant of the Desert Culture as defined by Jennings (1953). Buckles (1971) renewed investigations and defined nine phases for the Uncompahgre Complex that he described as a "technocomplex" or cultural convergence within a common environment (Clarke 1968) that endured for several thousand years as part of the Western Archaic lifeway. "The Uncompahgre Complex appears to represent an adaptation to the varied environments of the Uncompahgre Plateau which has great time depth," wrote Buckles. "The complex could, I think, be considered as evidence of a representative of a generalized culture with the potential to adapt to a large number of environments in specific ways by changing artifact frequencies and the frequencies of attributes" (Buckles 1971:1357).

Black (1986) includes the Uncompahgre Complex in the Mountain Tradition. He outlines a culture history of the Colorado mountains and concludes that an Early Archaic presence was a result of an eastern migration of Great Basin–based populations that arrived at least 9,500 to 9,000 years ago. Following that migration, an Archaic Mountain Tradition dated between approximately 7500 B.C. and A.D. 1300 developed and came into seasonal competition with neighboring desert and plains-based groups. A result of this competition was a diversity of archaeological remains typical of a technocomplex.

In the Four Corners area, including southwest Colorado, phases and complexes of the Oshara Tradition (dated about 5500 B.C. to A.D. 400) have been identified (Irwin-Williams 1979; Nickens and Hull 1982). The Oshara Tradition is defined as "a long-term continuous development within the Archaic spectrum, which culminated ultimately in the formation of the central core of the relatively well-known sedentary Anasazi (Pueblo) culture" (Irwin-Williams 1979:35).

Farming Cultures

The Anasazi Tradition

Southwest Colorado and adjacent areas have numerous Anasazi sites. The Anasazi cultural tradition is found in the Four Corners area of Colorado, New Mexico, Utah, and Arizona and is within the northern portion of the North American Southwest culture area (Cordell 1984). Early traditions that probably influenced the Anasazi are the Hohokam and Mogollon, cultures that built villages and practiced agriculture in geographic regions to the south for approximately two thousand years, from 300 B.C. to A.D. 1500. The Anasazi tradition generally spans a period from 100 B.C. and earlier to approximately A.D. 1540 when the Spanish entered the Southwest (Ortiz 1979). Traits of the prehistoric tradition continue to be represented among historic Pueblo Indian groups in northeast Arizona and in New Mexico. Western Pueblo people living on the Colorado Plateau in Arizona and New Mexico are the Hopi and Zuni. Farther east at Acoma and along the Rio Grande in New Mexico are additional Pueblo groups.

As noted in the introduction, sites of the San Juan River drainage originally served to identify the semisedentary and sedentary agricultural tradition known as Anasazi. The tradition is divided into six major branches, or variants, that are more specifically described by regional and local phases characterized by pottery, architecture, food products, and other materials. The six branches are: Mesa Verde, Chaco, Kayenta, Virgin, Winslow or Little Colorado River, and Rio Grande (Cordell 1984). The Mesa Verde branch dominates southwest Colorado and adjoining portions of New Mexico and Utah. Sites associated with the Chaco branch also occur in that area. Interaction with the Kayenta branch of northeast Arizona is suggested by pottery and rock art found in southeast Utah and southwest Colorado.

Stages of Anasazi cultural development are generally described according to the Pecos Classification system (Kidder 1927) based on the presence of traits identified from excavated cultural materials, primarily architecture and ceramics of the San Juan Anasazi. All of the stages within the system are not assumed to have uniformly occurred throughout the Anasazi area, and dates associated with each culture stage vary according to regional and local developments. It is generally accepted that the Anasazi developed from indigenous Archaic populations of the Four Corners region. Culture stages of the Pecos Classification (adapted from Cordell 1984:55) with generalized dates appropriate to western Colorado (Jennings 1978:97; Nichols and Smiley 1982:94; Eddy et al. 1984) are given below:

1. **Basketmaker I**: (traits now generally attributed to the late Archaic stage).
2. **Basketmaker II**: Evidence of agriculture; atlatl or spear-thrower present; no pottery; no cranial deformation; pre–A.D. 1 to 500–700. Early Basketmaker II sites south of the San Juan River are generally dated between 200 B.C. and A.D. 200.
3. **Basketmaker III**: Pit house or slab house dwellings; pottery (undecorated cooking ware); no cranial deformation; A.D. 450 to 750–800.
4. **Pueblo I**: Aboveground villages of true masonry; neck-banded cooking ware; cranial deformation; A.D. 750 to 900–1000.
5. **Pueblo II**: Widely distributed small villages; corrugated cooking ware; A.D. 850 to 1100–1150.
6. **Pueblo III**, or **Great Pueblo**: Large communities; artistic elaboration and craft specialization; A.D. 1100–1300.
7. **Pueblo IV**, or **Proto-Historic**: Artistic elaboration declines; plain wares replace corrugated cooking wares; after A.D. 1300, sites on the northern Colorado Plateau and in the western Colorado area were abandoned.
8. **Pueblo V**, or **Historic**: A.D. 1540 to present on the southern Colorado Plateau and in the Rio Grande drainage.

Items associated with the Anasazi through time include: corn; beans; squash; basketry; plain, corrugated, and decorated pottery; villages; pit houses; aboveground masonry and adobe or *jacal* structures, including multistory masonry buildings, courtyards, *kivas* or partially subterranean ceremonial rooms, and towers; water-control features; anthropomorphic (humanlike) and other clay figurines; basketry shields; matting; wood implements; flutes; wood, stone, clay, and feather ceremonial objects; shell, wood, and stone jewelry; turkeys; dogs; turkey feather blankets; woven cotton blankets and sashes; fiber aprons; atlatls or spear throwers; bows and arrows; and rock art (Amsden 1949; Plog 1979; Cordell 1979; Eddy et al. 1984; Morris and Burgh 1941; Morris 1980). Anasazi rock art has been described by Kidder and Guernsey (1919), Guernsey and Kidder (1921), Turner (1963), Pilles (1975), Schaafsma (1972, 1980), Grant (1978), Castleton (1979), Cole (1987, 1989a, 1989b), and others.

The abandonment of the northern Anasazi area (the Colorado Plateau north of the San Juan and Colorado rivers) after A.D. 1300, including all of western Colorado, has been explained as a result of environmental changes affecting agriculture; pressures from nomadic groups such as the proto-Navajo and Apache, Ute, and Southern Paiute; and social and political reorganization (Cordell 1984). It is likely that no single explanation accounts for the movements south and east, but it is clear that traits of the Anasazi tradition (as well as those of the Hohokam and Mogollon) remain in historic Pueblo Indian culture (Reed 1946, 1948; Johnson 1965).

The ruins and rock art of the San Juan Anasazi (including those of the upper Dolores River) have been extensively researched, and the Anasazi culture is clearly the most thoroughly described and analyzed of all the ancient cultures in the study area. As a result, materials and rock art of the Anasazi are frequently used for comparison with those of other cultures such as the Archaic and neighboring Fremont to determine cultural and chronological relationships.

In southwest Colorado and the generalized Four Corners area, Anasazi sites are generally typical of the tradition as defined for the San Juan region. More specifically, following the Basketmaker II period, the Mesa Verde Anasazi are described by six phases dated between A.D. 500 and 1300 (Hayes 1964; Wade 1979): La Plata (500–700); Piedra (700–900); Ackmen (900–975); Mancos (975–1075); McElmo (1075–1150); and Mesa Verde (1150–1300). Pit house villages, cliff dwellings, mesa top structures, distinctive ceramics, and other materials of Mesa Verde National Park and the Ute Mountain Tribal Park characterize these phases (Plate 5). Similar sites and materials are found in the nearby upper Dolores River area just north of the San Juan drainage, on Cedar Mesa in Utah, and along the San Juan River in northwest New Mexico and southeast Utah.

Anasazi sites outside the San Juan River drainage to the north, in the Canyonlands area of west central Colorado and adjacent Utah are much less well known and evince interaction with the Fremont culture and with local hunters and gatherers. Material evidence of the Anasazi is strong in certain areas and less definitive in others. Material evidence

Plate 5. *Cliff Palace, a large Anasazi cliff dwelling in Mesa Verde National Park, Colorado. Similar types of masonry structures, within and outside of rock shelters, were built throughout the Four Corners region during the late Pueblo II and Pueblo III periods, A.D. 1000-1300.*

of the Fremont is sparse throughout the area, and the role of local hunters and gatherers is poorly understood. Rock art in this region has a unique blending of style traits associated with the San Juan Anasazi, the Fremont, and the Archaic.

The Anasazi of this northern region have been described as Canyonlands Anasazi (Noxon and Marcus 1985) in recognition of their cultural distinctiveness. However, to date they are generally described as part of the Mesa Verde branch and are considered a northern extension of the San Juan Anasazi. Sites are located in canyon areas surrounding the Uncompahgre Plateau and the La Sal, Henry, and the northern Abajo mountains and are in the drainages of the Colorado, Green, and lower Dolores-San Miguel rivers.

Pierson (1981) discusses northern Anasazi populations of the Abajo and La Sal mountain areas in east central Utah and adjacent Colorado. He observes that the Fremont were possibly present in the same area and that hunters and gatherers may have controlled the higher mountain areas. For the north slope of the Abajo Mountains, including the Needles District of Canyonlands National Park and Indian Creek, Pierson (1981:53) observes: "The picture that evolves of the inhabitants of the Abajo Mountain area is of an early population of hunting-gathering types that either had lived in or about the area for some time or had moved into it periodically to use it. The population appears to have been sparse until Basketmaker times, when a small resident population began to grow crops of corn in the area. . . . The Pueblo pattern of small and medium-sized masonry villages with religious centers in the form of circular below-ground kivas and outlying farm and storage facilities was well established by Pueblo II times in the Abajo Mountain area."

The Abajo Mountains Anasazi are assigned to the Mesa Verde branch of the San Juan Anasazi, but the cultural picture is not typical of Mesa Verde population centers. However, Pierson views the Abajo Anasazi as more typical of the overall San Juan Anasazi pattern than the La Sal Mountains Anasazi.

Tipps and Hewitt (1989:136) report Anasazi materials of the Basketmaker III–Pueblo I period (dated approximately A.D. 575–900), Pueblo I–II period (A.D. 900–1100), and the late Pueblo II–III period (approximately A.D. 1000–1250) at sites in the Needles District of Canyonlands National Park. The primary occupation of that area is viewed as being during the late Pueblo II–III period, and immigration into the area is suggested by a relatively rapid population expansion. Ceramics of the area indicate a Mesa Verde branch affiliation for the occupants. Despite the presence of Fremont style rock art, similar to that of the Fremont, Fremont occupation is not indicated.

Along with agricultural pursuits, the Abajo Anasazi continued a Basketmaker-like practice of hunting and gathering. Sites in Canyonlands National Park and surrounding areas of pinyon and juniper woodlands include population centers consisting of pit houses and masonry pueblos and cliff dwellings that are classified as Basketmaker-Pueblo III. Early populations appear to have been sparse, and during the Pueblo II period a population explosion occurred. The heaviest population of the area appears to have been between A.D. 1000 and 1150 (Thompson 1979). The Abajo Mountains area was probably abandoned by 1250 (Pierson 1981:51).

Fremont activities in the Abajo Mountains area are not strongly indicated from the material record, but rock art similar to that of the Fremont is frequently associated with late Pueblo II–III Canyonlands Anasazi sites. Noxon and Marcus (1985) have identified Canyonlands Anasazi Style and Southern San Rafael Fremont Style rock art in the area. "Faces motif" rock art similar to Fremont anthropomorphic clay figurines described by Morss (1954), "shields," and shield-figures (images showing an anthropomorph with a shieldlike form in front of the body) known from Fremont rock art styles are examples of Fremont-like imagery. Tipps and Hewitt (1989) recognize the presence of a Faces Motif Anthropomorphic Style in the Needles District of Canyonlands National Park but argue that the Canyonlands Anasazi Style appears to be broadly defined and lacks clear diagnostic traits.

Sharrock (1966) has suggested that the Anasazi borrowed symbolism from the Fremont. This may have also been true (but to a lesser extent) for Anasazi in the San Juan River area. Evidence for this exists in Fremont-like anthropomorphs painted on the plastered wall of a late Pueblo II–III structure in Natural Bridges National Monument (Hobler and Hobler 1978) and the presence of shields and shield-figures at Pueblo III sites in Utah and Arizona. Schaafsma (1971) has discussed the possible transmission of shield representations from the Fremont to the Anasazi.

Pierson (1981) notes that Anasazi sites in the La Sal Mountains area (Arches National Park, Mill Creek, and Kane Creek near Moab, Utah, and various canyons near the confluence of the Dolores and Colorado rivers) are sparse and problematical and that a Fremont presence cannot be ruled out. Masonry sites in the vicinity of Paradox Valley along the lower Dolores River in Colorado are cited as the best evidence of an Anasazi presence and the most like those of the Abajo Mountains. These sites may have been abandoned by A.D. 1150 (Gleichman, Eininger, and Scott 1982). Some sites near Moab, Utah, also have clear Anasazi cultural affiliations (Pierson 1981). La Sal Anasazi sites are estimated to date from the Basketmaker II to Pueblo III period.

Pottery and perishables indicate that most La Sal Anasazi sites date during the Pueblo II–III period (Pierson 1981:62). Early La Sal Mountains Anasazi were likely to have been nomadic; later groups lived in pit house villages near the confluence of creeks and rivers and utilized circular masonry structures that occur isolated on hilltops, possibly for defense or religious reasons. A strong emphasis on hunting and gathering is typical of the La Sal Anasazi.

Material evidence of contact between the La Sal Anasazi and the Fremont is present in the La Sal Mountains area (Pierson 1981; Gleichman et al. 1982), and Fremont style rock art similar to that at sites in the Uinta Basin and Capitol Reef National Park also occurs in the area. Pierson (1981), like Sharrock (1966), concludes that certain rock art, such as triangular anthropomorphs and shield-figures, occurs as the result of contact with Fremont peoples. The Canyonlands area is culturally complex, and that complexity is represented in the material culture as well as in the rock art. Evidence indicates that the area was one of interface, not only between Anasazi and Fremont but also between these more sedentary peoples and groups of hunters and gatherers. For example, based on settlement and subsistence patterns, Toll (1977) proposes that Paradox Valley–Lower Dolores sites are Fremont rather than Anasazi. Hunt (1953) argues for a Fremont occupation in the La Sal Mountains, but this remains in question (Lindsay 1976; Thompson 1979). And Pierson (1981) reports a marked similarity between some sites and burials in the Moab area and the Turner-Look Fremont site to the north reported by Wormington (1955).

Gleichman et al. (1982) conclude that Anasazi and Fremont peoples are likely to have temporarily used the La Sal Mountains and lower Dolores River and San Miguel River areas of west central Colorado and probably traded with local Uncompahgre Complex hunters and gatherers. Between A.D. 700 and 1150, local groups adopted architectural and horticultural attributes of the neighboring peoples and traded for ceramics: "This timespan covers the period of Pueblo I and II of the Southwest and more specifically the Fremont era of eastern Utah . . . . The stone structures are similar to those of the Fremont, the ceramics are for the most part derived directly from the Anasazi to the South, and the projectile points are Uncompahgre in style" (Gleichman et al. 1982:492).

After a review of the archaeological data from the southern portion of the west central Colorado region, Reed (1984:35) concludes that the "architectural and artifactual variation seems too great to support the presence of a *bona fide* Anasazi occupation of the project area." Likewise, Reed does not see evidence of a regional variant of the Fremont culture in west central Colorado. Instead, he suggests a regional sedentary or Formative Stage population that developed out of the local Archaic and maintained cultural interaction with neighboring Anasazi and Fremont groups (Reed 1984).

Fremont Culture

The Fremont culture has been variously classified in the literature and has been associated with Southwest, Great Basin, and Plains cultural traditions (Aikens 1966; Gunnerson 1969; Breternitz 1970; Marwitt 1970, 1986; Madsen and Lindsay 1977; Jennings 1978; Lipe 1978; Madsen 1979, 1989; Cordell 1984). The Fremont culture is believed to have developed from indigenous Archaic populations and is generally dated between approximately A.D. 400 and 1500 in the study area (Marwitt 1970; Creasman and Scott 1987). Stages of cultural development such as those of the Anasazi tradition are not generally recognized, although a Basketmaker-like Fremont stage has been recognized by some archaeologists (Burgh and Scoggin 1948; Burgh 1950; Gillin 1955; Berry and Berry 1976), and correspondences between eastern Fremont rock art and San Juan Basketmaker art are well documented (Morss 1931; Schaafsma 1971). Jennings (1978:155–156) considers the initial development of the Fremont from indigenous Archaic populations to have been triggered by the same early Mogollon or Hohokam influences that triggered the Anasazi development.

The Fremont are viewed as sedentary and semisedentary agricultural groups that relied less on agriculture and more on hunting and gathering than the Anasazi. Certain groups were clearly more sedentary than others; overall, the culture can be seen as highly diversified.

Five regional or geographic variants of the Fremont have been described by Marwitt (1970, 1986) and Jennings (1978). Variants of the western Fremont are identified for the Great Basin and eastern variants for the Colorado Plateau–Uinta Basin area. Uinta Fremont sites are typically located in the drainages of the Green and Yampa rivers, and San Rafael Fremont sites typically occur in drainages of the Green, Colorado, and Escalante rivers. Phases and dates for Fremont culture variants based on Jennings (1978) and Cordell (1984:97) are given below:

Great Salt Lake:	Levee phase	A.D. 1000–1350+
	Bear River phase	A.D. 400–1000
Uinta:	Whiterocks phase	A.D. 800–950
	Cub Creek phase	pre-A.D. 800
San Rafael:		A.D. 700–1200
Sevier:		A.D. 780–1260

Parawan: Paragonah phase   A.D. 1050–1300
                      Summit phase   A.D. 900–1050

Marwitt (1986:169) proposes beginning dates of approximately
A.D. 650 for the Cub Creek phase of the Uinta Fremont and extends
the San Rafael Fremont period to A.D. 1250. More recently, Truesdale
(personal communication) reports estimated radiocarbon dates for
Cub Creek phase pit houses in Dinosaur National Monument at
approximately A.D. 600–700. Additional information and radiocarbon
dates from Dinosaur National Monument indicate that the Fremont
emerged from a local Archaic population and that the heaviest occupation of the area was between approximately A.D. 600 and 1000 (Truesdale, personal communication). Tree ring dates ranging between A.D.
1010 and 1330 from two sites in Dinosaur National Monument indicate later occupation of the area, possibly associated with late Fremont
occupations in nearby areas of Utah and Colorado (Creasman and
Scott 1987).

A radiocarbon date of approximately A.D. 1350 is associated with a
structure site at McConkie Ranch in the Dry Fork Valley, west of
Dinosaur National Monument, near Vernal, Utah. The site contained
Fremont pottery and is located just below a cliff with extensive panels
of Fremont style rock art.

In the White River area of northwestern Colorado, Creasman
(1981) proposes that the Fremont of Cañon Pintado National Historic
District on Douglas Creek developed out of a local Archaic base as
early as A.D. 450–500 and are most closely associated with the San
Rafael Fremont variant. Sites of the area include farmsteads located on
rises just above arable land and stone structures that are often located
on prominent rock outcrops within and overlooking canyons. One
such overlook site (Plate 2) has yielded a radiocarbon date of approximately A.D. 1500 (Creasman and Scott 1987:11). Based on this and
other late Fremont dates in Utah and Colorado, it is suggested that
the Fremont may have remained until the late prehistoric period and
may have interacted with Numic-speaking Ute and Shoshoni groups
(Liestman 1985).

Archaeological remains of the San Rafael and Uinta Fremont
include chipped and ground stone artifacts, including long "Fremont
blades"; distinctive one-rod-and-bundle basketry; distinctive maize or
corn; plain and decorated pottery; shallow pit houses; aboveground
masonry and adobe structures; villages; gourds; moccasins; anthropomorphic and zoomorphic clay, stone, and vegetal figurines; jewelry of
bone, shell, and stone; bone gaming pieces; stone balls; bone and
antler tools; and rock art (Wormington 1955; Aikens 1978; Grady

1984; Marwitt 1986). Rock art of the Fremont has been described by Gunnerson (1969), Schaafsma (1971, 1980), Castleton (1978, 1979), and others.

Unlike the situation with the Anasazi and historic Pueblos, it is not clear which ethnic groups received cultural input from the Fremont following the disappearance of the culture. It may be that more than one group in different geographic areas was involved. Aikens (1978: 153) notes that the southern Fremont variants (San Rafael and Parowan) are most like the neighboring Anasazi while the northern variants (Sevier, Great Salt Lake, Uinta) more closely resemble neighboring cultures of the western and northwest Plains. Lipe (1978: 481–482) has suggested that Fremont groups moved south prior to A.D. 1300 in a manner similar to the Anasazi and perhaps in response to similar pressures.

Ancestral connections have been proposed between the Fremont and northwestern Plains groups (Aikens 1966) and the Numic-speaking Shoshoni, Ute, and Southern Paiute (Gunnerson 1969). None of the proposals for intrusions of Fremont culture has been clearly demonstrated by archaeological data, although certain material and rock art evidence clearly link the Fremont with Numic-speaking groups (Keyser 1975, 1977, 1984; Liestman 1985; Shimkin 1986) and with the Anasazi (Hobler and Hobler 1978; Noxon and Marcus 1985; Marwitt 1986).

Madsen (1989:14–15) has written:

> I, for one, think that the sudden replacement of classic Fremont artifacts including basketry, pottery, and figurines by other types historically associated with Utah's native inhabitants, suggests that Fremont people were, for the most part, pushed out of the region and were replaced rather than integrated into Numic-speaking groups. This interpretation is strengthened by the fact that the most recent Fremont or Fremont-like materials, dating to about 500 years ago, are found at the northern and easternmost fringes of the Fremont region in the Douglas Creek area of northwestern Colorado and on the Snake River Plain of southern Idaho; areas at maximum distance along the postulated migration route of Numic-speaking populations.

Protohistoric and Historic Cultures

The combined Protohistoric (aboriginal) and Historic (Euro-American documented) periods in western Colorado and adjacent areas are dated between approximately A.D. 1250 and 1880–1882, after which Indians in the region were assigned reservations in western Colorado, western Wyoming, and eastern Utah (Jennings 1978; Eddy et al. 1984; Grady 1984; Guthrie et al. 1984; Reed 1984; Shimkin 1986). Proposed inhabitants of the study region during the Protohistoric period, between approximately A.D. 1250 and 1600, include hunting and gathering peoples, such as the Numic-speaking Ute and Eastern Shoshoni (Buckles 1971; Shimkin 1986). How early the Numic-speaking peoples were in the region has not been clearly demonstrated from excavated materials, but it is likely that they arrived between A.D. 1150 and 1400 (Schroeder 1952:10; Buckles 1971; Creasman 1981; Gordon et al. 1983; Grady 1984; Reed 1984; Liestman 1985; Shimkin 1986). Archaeological remains of Numic-speaking groups are likely to be very similar to those of other hunting and gathering peoples who were part of the long Archaic tradition described above. Therefore, a precise identification of prehistoric Numic items is often difficult. It is possible, however, that remains will be identified based on associations with datable materials and continuities with historic subjects.

After A.D. 1600, Numic-speaking peoples from the Great Basin, the Ute and Eastern Shoshoni, along with Athapaskan-speaking Navajo people, are historically as well as archaeologically identified in the area (Lischka et al. 1983; Shimkin 1986; Eddy et al. 1984; Grady 1984; Reed 1984; Ute Mountain Ute Tribe 1985a). The Ute people are identified as two major groups, eastern and western, that were divided into bands. The eastern Ute occupied western Colorado and adjacent portions of Utah and New Mexico, and the western Ute lived farther west in Utah. The Eastern Shoshoni include the Wind River Shoshoni and the Comanche-Shoshoni. Both groups were probably in western Wyoming and adjacent portions of northern Colorado, generally north of the Yampa River, before 1800 (Dean 1969; Stewart 1966; Grady 1984; Lischka et al. 1983; Shimkin 1986). The Comanche began to move onto the plains after A.D. 1700, and eventually left the area (Grady 1984:48), but the Wind River Shoshoni remained. The following discussion of these groups will begin with the Navajo, followed by the Eastern Shoshoni, and concluding with the Ute, who continue to live in western Colorado and eastern Utah.

Archaeological evidence indicates that the Navajo arrived in northern New Mexico in approximately A.D. 1640 (Eddy et al. 1984: 95–101). The Athapaskan-speaking Navajo and Apache had previously hunted, gathered, and practiced horticulture in the southern plains of Colorado. The Navajo migrated into the upper San Juan River drainage of northwest New Mexico and southwest Colorado in A.D. 1700 and left in approximately 1775 after raiding pressure from the

Ute, Comanche, and the Spanish. Spanish records document the presence of the Navajo and the Ute.

The Navajo of the upper San Juan River drainage of Colorado and New Mexico, the Gobernador District, are archaeologically and historically described by a series of phases dated between A.D. 1640 and 1868. A period of upper San Juan River occupation, A.D. 1700–1775, is known as the Gobernador Phase. Neighbors and allies of the Navajo during this period were Jemez and other Rio Grande Pueblo Indians who were seeking refuge following the Pueblo revolt of A.D. 1680–1692 against the Spanish (Eddy et al. 1984). Since 1868, the Navajo have occupied reservation lands presently located in Arizona, Utah, and New Mexico, and they have continued to use adjoining areas. Navajo sweat houses have been found as far north as the San Miguel River drainage of west central Colorado, some located near modern uranium mines (Gleichman et al. 1982). Possible examples of Navajo rock art are present in southwest and west central Colorado where Navajo people have worked and lived off the reservation.

This study will be limited to Gobernador Phase rock art and examples that are stylistically related. Navajo rock art from that phase has been described by Schaafsma (1963, 1972, 1980) and Grant (1978) for the Gobernador District and other areas of northwest New Mexico and for Canyon de Chelly National Monument in Arizona.

Gobernador Phase Navajo: 1700–1775

Archaeological remains of the Navajo during the Gobernador Phase adapted from Eddy et al. (1984) include forked stick hogans; Pueblitos; ramadas; fortified sites; pictographs and petroglyphs; Dinetah Utility pottery; Gobernador Indented pottery; Pueblo trade wares; chipped artifacts; basketry; ye'i, or Twin War God deities; sheep and horses; dance paddles; macaw fetishes; distinctive types of corn and beans; stone masonry hogans; sweat lodges; metal; and glass beads.

During the Gobernador Phase, the Navajo underwent profound culture change in the areas of economy and religion (Eddy et al. 1984:98). The Navajo hunted and gathered and practiced limited horticulture and sheep herding prior to this period. Afterward, the Navajo increasingly used the horse for bison hunting on the plains and for raids on Spanish settlements. The Navajo also intensified sheep herding and trade (Eddy et al. 1984).

Gobernador Phase religious symbolism, including that in rock art, began to show influences of Pueblo masked dances, mythic heroes, and deities (Schaafsma 1972; Eddy et al. 1984). These influences appear in the *Yeibichai* or *ye'i*, supernaturals personated by masked dancers and in the mythology of the War Twins. These supernatural beings are central to important curing ceremonies of the Navajo (Reichard 1950; Newcomb 1964; Zolbrod 1984).

Eastern Shoshoni: A.D.? 1500–1850

The Wind River Shoshoni and Comanche-Shoshoni are included in this study because of the possibility that these protohistoric and historic Numic-speaking groups made rock art south of their traditional homeland, in northwest Colorado and adjacent Utah, that is distinct from that of the Ute and can be identified despite parallels in lifeways and archaeological materials. Other Numic-speaking peoples classified as Northern Shoshoni and Western Shoshoni (D'Azevedo 1986) may have also been in the western Colorado area, but their historic territories are geographically more remote. Linguistic differences between the Numic-speaking groups (Miller 1986; Shimkin 1986) and other cultural differences reported in ethnographic studies (Lowie 1924; Hultkrantz 1986; Shimkin 1986) support the possibility that there were differences between the symbolism and art styles of the Shoshoni and Ute. Eastern Shoshoni rock art has been described by Gebhard and Cahn (1950), Gebhard (1951, 1969), Keyser (1975, 1977, 1984), and Hendry (1983). Keyser (1975) has suggested that the Fremont may have contributed the shield-bearing-warrior motif to the Eastern Shoshoni, who introduced it to other Plains groups after A.D. 1300. Contact between these peoples is likely to have taken place in northeast Utah and northwest Colorado.

The Eastern Shoshoni are believed to have arrived in the mountains and basins of western Wyoming and adjoining areas at approximately A.D. 1500 or earlier and are believed to have practiced a hunting and gathering lifeway typical of other Great Basin prehistoric peoples (Aikens and Madsen 1986; Shimkin 1986). Before and after historic contact and acceptance of the horse, the Shoshoni, like the Ute, adopted practices of Plains Indians, such as plains buffalo hunting and raiding for women, horses, and other goods. Unlike the Ute, the Shoshoni apparently maintained a high level of political and social organization and were involved in formal warfare and related activities of Plains Indians. Nevertheless, the Shoshoni retained a Great Basin cultural identity (Shimkin 1986).

Following the movement onto the plains after A.D. 1700, the Comanche came to share specific Plains cultural attributes that distinguished them from other Great Basin groups such as the Shoshoni and Ute (Lowie 1954). In 1868, the Wind River Shoshoni were assigned by treaty to the Wind River Reservation in western Wyoming.

According to Shimkin (1986:309),

> Eastern Shoshoni protohistory and history since about 1500 can be described in seven phases, beginning with pre-horse penetration of the High Plains and adoption of large-scale buffalo hunting, 1500–1700. During this period, the Comanche-Shoshoni attained high competence as a militaristic, buffalo-hunting people. With the acquisition of horses came the second phase, of widespread raiding throughout the plains, 1700–1780. In this period, it is certain that strong chiefly leadership and considerable protocol and sumptuary rights prevailed. The third period, 1780–1825, was marked by defeat by the Blackfeet, who had firearms, by smallpox, and by retreat to the west, with some cultural reorganization but much instability. A key development, about 1800, was the introduction of the Sun Dance by the Comanche Yellow Hand. . . . The fourth period, 1825–1880, was one of White alliances and renewed tribal vitality under Washakie.

Religion among the Wind River Shoshoni in the mid-nineteenth century was directed at two complimentary concerns. One was personal success and survival, and the other was community well-being. The first was accomplished by individuals acquiring supernatural powers from dangerous spirits and complying with taboos, including contact between fetishes and blood, especially menstrual blood. The second was accomplished by warding off disasters with group ceremonials, such as the Shuffling Dance and Sun Dance, led by individuals with supernatural power such as shamans who were believed to acquire power by supplication and dependency on powerful spirits. Shamanism was practiced for the purpose of curing illness (Shimkin 1986).

The quest for individual power could come from participating in ceremonies or by sleeping in sacred places to gain a vision of *poha*, powers manifested as mythological beings and animations of nature. Shimkin (1968:325) writes:

> The most sacred of places are the sites of pictographs (*poha kahni*, "house of power"), particularly in the vicinity of Din-woody Canyon, on the Wind River Reservation. There are hundreds of pictographs, clearly accumulated over a long period . . . They include large panels representing the feared Water Ghost Beings and Rock Ghost Beings.

Lowie (1924) describes the war practices of the Shoshoni as showing influences of Plains Indians most clearly. The emphasis of war was on stealing horses, but guns and other items were also stolen. Scalping was practiced but was not considered heroic, and it is not clear whether counting coup (the touching of an enemy's body with the hand or with a special stick) was practiced, although enemies may have been punished with a long stick.

War scouts carried wolf hides and walked with the aid of two sticks. When warriors returned to camp with scalps on sticks, they sang war songs, and the women rode out to meet them and took the scalp sticks. Other body parts of enemies, such as hands, were taken and used in dances held in the evening and days following the return of the war party (Lowie 1924).

Over time, the Shoshoni had horses and tack; tipis; baskets; bows and arrows; metal; guns; buffalo hide quivers and bow cases; spears (twelve feet long); and buffalo hide shields. Like those of the Ute, shield decorations included the addition of hide covers with painted designs, and feathers (Lowie 1924).

Ceremonial items of the Shoshoni included headdresses and other clothing, bird (crane) head wands, feather fans, forked dance sticks, drums, and flutes. The Shoshoni made hide paintings depicting scenes related to ceremonies such as the Sun Dance, buffalo hunting, and warfare (Shimkin 1986).

The Historic Ute: A.D. 1600–1880

The Ute generally lived to the north of the Navajo, north of the San Juan River in Colorado, New Mexico, and Utah, and to the south of the Shoshoni, south of the Yampa River in Colorado. Utes were organized into extended family groups and inclusive bands that practiced a mobile hunting and gathering way of life in the deserts and mountains, a lifeway similar to Archaic patterns previously discussed. Leadership among Ute groups and bands was generally based on special knowledge and skills of individuals. Leaders or chiefs, shamans, and other spiritual leaders were respected and functioned within the small groups as well as during seasonal events when members of bands came together for hunting, gathering, curing, and ceremonies. Leadership was not formalized, and leaders did not always have general recognition or power even within the smaller groups (Stewart 1942; Ute Mountain Ute Tribe 1985a, 1986a).

During the 1600s, Ute social organization became more complex and the groups and bands larger and more mobile. This is particularly true of those using the horse, although Ute society was generally not as organized as Plains Indian groups. Leading chiefs, or chiefs of entire bands, became recognized during this period and led buffalo hunts onto the plains and raiding parties (Ute Mountain Ute Tribe 1985a, 1986a).

Historic contact with the Ute was made during the 1765 expedition of Juan Rivera and the 1776 expedition of Father Escalante and Father Dominguez from Santa Fe into what is now western Colorado and eastern Utah. However, the Spanish had prior knowledge of the Ute (possibly by 1640) as a result of activities taking place between various Indian groups and the Spanish (Bolton 1972; Ute Mountain Ute Tribe 1985a; Smith 1974). Escalante and Dominguez recorded names of Ute bands in western Colorado and eastern Utah. Specific Ute bands identified in western Colorado include the Capote and Mouache of the southeast; the Wiminuche (Weeminuche) of the Uncompahgre Plateau in west central Colorado; the Tabeguache and Parimuche (Sabaquanas) of the Colorado River and White River, and the Yamparica Utes of the Yampa River area in northwest Colorado.

The Weeminuche band is also associated with southwest Colorado and adjacent Utah north of the San Juan River, and the Tabeguache or Uncompahgre Band is also associated with the Uncompahgre Plateau in west central Colorado. These bands are reported to have been living in those areas of western Colorado between 1800 and 1880 (Smith 1974; Ute Mountain Ute Tribe 1985a). Undoubtedly, the Ute bands adjusted their territorial boundaries over time, and a significant amount of interaction between the various Ute bands and neighboring Indians, such as the Navajo, is indicated in historic records (Eddy et al. 1984; Ute Mountain Ute Tribe 1985a).

Escalante and Dominguez (Bolton 1972) note that the Ute were in possession of the horse, and Smith (1974) proposes that the Ute had the horse by A.D. 1640. However, Stewart (1966) notes that the mounted Ute coexisted with Utes on foot after 1776, providing a contrast in life-styles and social structures for the historic Ute; that is, small family bands on foot with larger and more mobile bands or specialized groups on horseback. Stewart (1966, 1982) proposes that the eastern Ute or Colorado (and adjacent areas of Utah) Ute had the horse earlier than the more western Ute and that it played a greater role in their cultural and social development.

Between approximately 1600 and 1700, some aspects of Ute culture underwent drastic change related to the adoption of Plains Indian culture and the use of the horse. Examples of activities related to these changes are plains bison hunting and geographically far-reaching trading and raiding expeditions to the south and north. Clothing, ceremonies, and ceremonial items of the Ute often duplicated those of historic Plains Indians (Smith 1974; Marsh 1982; Pettit 1990; Callaway, Janetski, and Stewart 1986). However, Smith (1974) cautions that the use of horses by the Ute was not universal, and the veneer of Plains Indian culture often associated with the Ute did not change the basic Great Basin culture that the Ute shared along with other Shoshoneans or Numic-speaking Indians. "Mythology in all its aspects is equivalent among all Ute groups and is sharply marked off from the mythologies of the Plains' tribes, the Apache, Navajo, and Pueblo; all of the Ute mythology relates to the Great Basin area, as does most of Ute culture" (Smith 1974:19).

Over time, the Ute utilized the horse, trade beads, shields, the bow and arrow (the gun during the later period), chipped and ground stone artifacts, metal, baskets, pottery, brush wickiups, and tipis (Plate 4). Additional items used by the Ute included horse tack, jewelry, robes, and other traditional and European-style clothing, feather headdresses, stone pipes, feather fans, flutes, and notched rasps used for music during ceremonies. Hide and cloth paintings with ceremonial and mythological scenes were made by the Ute (Buckles 1971; Callaway et al. 1986). Rock art associated with the Ute has been described by Buckles (1971), McKern (1978), and Cole (1987, 1988).

Ethnographic information indicates that Ute religion was centered around shamanism and personal guardian spirits sought by shamans and other individuals (Stewart 1942; Smith 1974). Males and females acted as shamans and were called upon for spiritual leadership, curing, and the interpretation of dreams. Powers were believed to be passed to shamans by natural dreams and by visions sought in isolated mountain places. Individuals gained personal guardian spirits and knowledge of especially "powerful paint" by dreams and visions sought in isolation and by fasting. Paints or pigments with power were used to decorate bodies, clothing, and shields and to make hide and cloth paintings. Charms were used to control power, and imitative magic was used to kill a person or animal by shooting an image with an arrow (Stewart 1942).

The Ute participated in group ceremonial dances, some of which were borrowed from Plains and other Indian groups. Examples of borrowed dances are the Sun Dance, which is concerned with buffalo hunting, warfare, and health, and the Scalp Dance, which is concerned with warfare (Smith 1974). One ceremony that is believed to be aboriginal Ute is the Bear Dance, which is recounted in Ute mythology (Smith 1974; Jorgensen 1986). The Bear Dance was an occasion in which family groups and bands came together at the end of winter. This ceremony served as an occasion for women to choose male partners and allowed Ute women and men from various family groups to perform music, dance, and socialize for approximately ten days. The Bear Dance was "performed to propitiate bears, to make Ute hunters more successful, and to make men and women successful in their sex lives. It was also used as the public announcement of the completion of the girls' puberty ritual" (Jorgensen 1986:663). Shamans practiced curing during the Bear Dance ceremony. For a period after 1876, the Bear Dance was apparently altered to emphasize spiritual power and good health (Jorgensen 1986). The Bear Dance and the Sun Dance are viewed as having been important to the maintenance of Ute society (Callaway et al. 1986).

Warfare appears to have been practiced for various reasons by the Ute, including "just for fun"; for stealing women, horses, food, and other goods; for protection; for revenge; and for war honors or status. Certain items associated with warfare included bows and arrows; guns; war bonnets; hide caps; hair feathers; buffalo hide shields decorated with hide covers, feathers, and paint; feathered lance standards; body paint; breechcloths; scalps (displayed on poles and tied on the heads of horses); and the hearts of enemies (Stewart 1942:301; Callaway et al. 1986:350).

Ute people living in Colorado prior to 1880 were identified as a group (tribe) by non-Indians, although the various Ute bands did not view themselves in this manner and continued to function as separate social groups. Ute bands living in the south and north were ultimately assigned to three reservations located in eastern Utah and southwestern Colorado. Utes of the Tabeguache or Uncompahgre band from west central Colorado and those of the Parimuche and Yamparica of the Colorado, White, and Yampa rivers to the north were moved to what is now the Uintah and Ouray Indian Reservation in northeastern Utah. Mouache and Capote bands of southern Colorado and adjacent New Mexico were moved to the present-day Southern Ute Indian Reservation, and the Weeminuche band was moved to the Ute Mountain Ute Indian Reservation on the Mesa Verde of southwest Colorado.

Various historic and ethnographic records have been written with regard to the Ute reservation period (Reed 1896; Stewart 1942, 1966; Smith 1974; Conetah 1982; Marsh 1982; Pettit 1982; Callaway et al. 1986; Ute Mountain Ute Tribe 1985a, 1986a), some of which have been previously cited. For the purpose of rock art study, this volume will concentrate on reservation period rock art of the Ute Mountain Utes.

Four important reasons have led to the emphasis on Ute Mountain Ute rock art. One reason is that the Ute Mountain Ute reservation area was settled by a single Ute band, the Weeminuche, rather than a group of bands that by necessity would have shared land, activities, and ideas, all of which may have influenced rock art. It is more likely that Ute rock art that is associated with the history of a single band can be identified as to artist(s) and meaning. A second reason, related to the first, is that the Weeminuche band lived to a great extent in isolation during the early reservation period and continued to depend on traditional lifeways for survival.

A third reason for the study of Ute Mountain Ute rock art is that the Weeminuche band was led by a series of traditional chiefs from the onset of the reservation period until the recent past, and the last traditional chief, Jack House, is credited with making rock art.

The fourth and final reason for the emphasis on Ute Mountain Ute rock art is the location of the reservation on the Mesa Verde, a location that has a significant tradition of Anasazi occupation and one that exhibits numerous panels of Anasazi rock art discussed in this volume. Thus, historic Ute rock art and Anasazi rock art exist in a single general location, often on the same panels. This provides a rare opportunity to compare and contrast historic images with more ancient ones, something that has also been done with Navajo and Anasazi rock art in the Gobernador District (Schaafsma 1963, 1972). A brief history of the Ute Mountain Ute Reservation and its people is provided below.

Ute Mountain Ute Reservation: A.D. 1850–present

The first treaty between the Ute people and the U.S. government that allowed entry into Ute lands by non-Indians was signed in 1850. The treaty had little effect upon the Weeminuche band located north of the San Juan River in Utah, Colorado, and New Mexico, far from government agency posts (Ute Mountain Ute Tribe 1985a). Additional treaties were made between the Ute and the United States in 1864 and 1868, and an agreement concerning the removal of Utes from the mining area of the San Juan Mountains was made in 1874 (Ute Mountain Ute Tribe 1985a). This agreement significantly impacted the Weeminuche band by denying them access to the mountainous area in which they hunted and gathered during the summer season. In 1880, the southern Utes, Mouache, Capote, and Weeminuche bands were restricted to reservation lands in southwest Colorado, but there was a continual push from Colorado to move the southern Utes out of the state (Ute Mountain Ute Tribe 1985a). In 1885, a bill provided for allotments of land to individuals in the eastern portion of the Southern Ute Reservation. The Mouache and Capote bands participated in this program, but the Weeminuche refused to do so and moved to the western portion of the reservation (Mancos Canyon–Mesa Verde area) as a group, surviving on government rations and a traditional hunting and gathering lifeway (Ute Mountain Ute Tribe 1985a).

In 1897, the Ute Mountain Ute Reservation, the western portion of the former Southern Ute Reservation, was established for the Weeminuche band. White Mesa or Allen Canyon Utes living in nearby Utah, who had familial and traditional ties with the Weeminuche band, are officially associated with the Ute Mountain Ute Reservation (Ute Mountain Ute Tribe 1985a).

Sheep herding and cattle raising were practiced by the Ute Mountain Utes, with cattle raising being favored. Horses, traditionally important to the Ute, continued to be raised by individual Weeminuche people. Traditional ceremonies of the Weeminuche, such as the Bear Dance and Sun Dance, were maintained, but many cultural changes resulted from reservation life that prevented the Weeminuche from continuing to practice a nomadic lifeway that had sustained them for centuries.

In 1934, a tribal government was established for the Weeminuche band, and it is today officially known as the Ute Mountain Ute Tribe. After 1885, during the period the Weeminuche lived on the Southern Ute Reservation with the Capote and Mouache bands, the Weeminuche were led by a "chief among the chiefs," or leading chief, known as Ignacio (Ute Mountain Ute Tribe 1986a:8). Ignacio's leadership continued after the Ute Mountain Ute Reservation was established, and he served as an Indian policeman to keep the local peace. Ignacio and his followers resisted various acts by the U.S. government that he believed were a threat to traditional band values. Ignacio remained the most influential chief until his death in 1913.

After Ignacio's death, Mariano (1846–1925?) became the leading chief. Other chiefs, such as Red Rock, also led groups of Weeminuche people during this period. John Miller was recognized as tribal chief after Mariano's death, and Jack House succeeded Miller during the Bear Dance of 1935. Jack House was the last traditional chief of the Weeminuche (Ute Mountain Ute Tribe 1986a). He was born in 1886 and served the tribe for thirty-seven years, until his death in 1971. Chief Jack House, known as "Hand in the Sun," never formally attended school and spoke only the Ute language (Bowman, personal correspondence).

Chief House lived in three hogans within the Mancos River Canyon of Mesa Verde for much of his life, and into the 1950s. He raised cattle in the Mancos Canyon system that shelters spectacular Anasazi ruins, now included within Mesa Verde National Park and the Ute Mountain Tribal Park. The first Sun Dance performed by the Weeminuche band was arranged by the chief at a site in Mancos Canyon, and during the years between approximately 1900 and 1950, Chief House decorated the canyon walls with petroglyphs, rock paintings, and drawings in a distinctive style (Bowman, personal correspondence). Much of his rock art occurs at locations where Anasazi rock art is also exhibited.

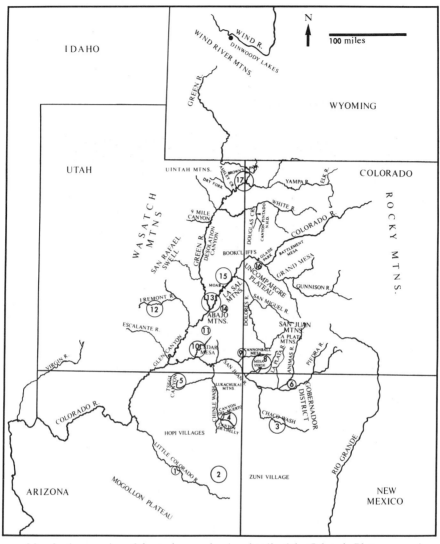

Map 1. *An overview of the study area showing details of the Colorado Plateau, associated mountain ranges, and the Four Corners region. Significant rock art areas are identified. Numbered locations are:*

1. Homol'ovi Ruins State Park
2. Petrified Forest National Park
3. Chaco Canyon National Park
4. Canyon de Chelly National Monument (Canyon del Muerto)
5. Navajo National Monument
6. Aztec Ruins National Monument
7. Ute Mountain Tribal Park (Mancos River Canyon, Mesa Verde)
8. Mesa Verde National Park
9. Hovenweep National Monument (McElmo Creek)
10. Grand Gulch Primitive Area
11. Natural Bridges National Monument
12. Capitol Reef National Park (Fremont River)
13. Canyonlands National Park (Needles District; Maze District)
14. Newspaper Rock State Park
15. Arches National Park
16. Colorado National Monument
17. Dinosaur National Monument

THE STUDY
OF ROCK ART

For the purposes of archaeological interpretation, it is necessary to put rock art and other remains in the context of time as well as place. Dating petroglyphs and rock paintings allows associations to be made between rock art and cultures that occupied a given area over time by comparing information from various sites. Proven techniques for directly dating rock art elements are not available, but research is ongoing to date petroglyphs by measuring the age of rock patina or varnish (Bard, Asaro, and Heizer 1978; Dorn and Whitley 1984; Dolzani 1988). Radiocarbon (Carbon 14 measurement) dating of organic binders in pigments has been attempted but has limited application because organic binders are not always present, and the process is destructive. At present, rock art is usually dated by relative techniques involving the direct dating of soils and architecture that bury or provide access to rock art. Other methods for the relative dating of rock art are estimates of the age of lichen growth and mineral deposits that cover rock art and adjacent rock surfaces, but these involve a number of variables that may be difficult to identify and measure (Beschel 1961; Dewdney 1970). Common methods for dating soils and architecture are by radiocarbon and dendrochronology, or tree-ring study (Cordell 1984). Based on the situation, rock art is thus shown to be earlier or more recent than the dated soils and architecture. Rock art depictions of dated subjects and events can also place rock art within relative periods of time, such as after the entry of Europeans into the Southwest in the 1500s. Examples are depictions of Euro-American subject matter, such as horses, guns, buildings, priests, and Christian symbols.

Repeated associations between rock art and dated sites are also useful for making temporal connections. An example is the correlation made by Guernsey and Kidder (1921:38, 113) between Basketmaker II period sites, handprints, and broad-shouldered anthropomorphic images in rock art of the Marsh Pass, Arizona, area.

Another method for establishing temporal links is the comparison between rock art subjects and dated materials, such as ceramics, wall murals, baskets, figurines, jewelry, tools, and weavings. For example, a number of associations have been made between materials of the San Juan Basketmakers and rock art imagery (Cole 1989b), and ceramic decorations of the Anasazi have clear similarities to rock art images through time (Hays 1988a, 1988b).

Less controlled methods for relative dating of rock art are those based on observations of rock art situations and conditions. These include observations as to differences in degrees of patination and lichen growth between rock art and background surfaces, and patination and weathering differences between various types and styles of rock art. Also, temporal distinctions can be made by observations as to geologic and soil changes that may have affected rock surfaces or the access to rock art locations. Superimposition of elements provides additional information on relative dates for rock art elements and styles.

Methods involving observation are most useful if observations are restricted to individual panels and situations within a specific environment and on a single geologic formation. The amount of petroglyph exposure to water and sunlight, the surrounding geological formations, and other conditions affect patination and lichen growth processes and can be significantly different from one situation to another, even within the same general location. Also, techniques of manufacture can affect appearances. For example, stipple-pecked, scratched, and abraded elements may not result in removal of as much rock surface and color as solid-pecked and incised elements. At some locations, the repatination process is rapid enough or slow enough that only those petroglyphs that are widely separated in time reflect patination differences. For example, petroglyphs made in basalt are relatively slow to show patina color change in comparison to petroglyphs in sandstone.

STYLE

Style categories (and types of elements within styles) are frequently used to organize rock art and other archaeological materials and designs for the purposes of description, comparison, and interpretation. Rock art styles have been assigned to Archaic hunters and gatherers, and to Anasazi, Fremont, and historic Indians of the Colorado Plateau and Rocky Mountains (Gebhard 1951, 1969; Turner 1963, 1971; Buckles 1971; Schaafsma 1971, 1980; Pilles 1975; Grant 1978;

McKern 1978; Noxon and Marcus 1985; Cole 1987). Styles are frequently named after type-sites or sites where the styles were first identified. In other instances, style names are descriptive of style characteristics or cultural and temporal affiliations.

The concept of style, or the particular manner in which something is done, is complex and includes techniques of manufacture, subject matter, formal attributes (structure), locations, and themes or relationships between elements. All of these traits provide criteria for the identification of styles in rock art. Individual variations within broad style categories are generally apparent.

Any one trait may crosscut individual style boundaries and those of time, space, and culture. In other words, an individual style component may be used in various styles, by different cultures, at the same or different times, and in different places. Examples are the use of pecking and incising techniques, the representation of simple stick-figure anthropomorphs (humanlike forms), and concentric circles, images that appear in rock art throughout the world (Grant 1967; Munn 1973; Wellmann 1979; Lewis-Williams 1981; Leakey 1983). Nevertheless, it is generally agreed that, taken as a whole, styles are specific to time and space and are related to functions and meanings established by the cultures and societies using them (Sackett 1977:370; Wobst 1976; Hodder 1982).

A single culture may use more than one art style at a given time depending upon the functions and meanings involved. Also, various media may have similar or quite dissimilar art styles based on the traditional uses of each medium and the physical restrictions involved with each. For example, types of images occurring in Mesa Verde ceramic decoration and rock art are alike, but the styles differ in a number of ways. One obvious difference is the emphasis in rock art on representational forms, such as anthropomorphs and quadrupeds, and the emphasis in ceramic decoration on geometric aspects.

Rock art style categories are often assigned to broad time periods, periods of more than one hundred years. However, examples of more precisely defined and dated rock art styles do occur, such as the Tsegi Painted Style (Schaafsma 1980) associated with Tsegi Phase cliff dwellings of the Kayenta Anasazi in northeast Arizona, dated between A.D. 1250 and 1300.

The concept of a style tradition is also used in rock art studies. "Styles that are similar in content and expression, and for which a temporal and cultural continuity can be demonstrated, constitute a tradition" (Schaafsma 1985:252–253). Style traditions have been identified in the Colorado Plateau and western Colorado areas (Turner 1963, 1971; Buckles 1971; Pilles 1975; Schaafsma 1980).

While styles are convenient tools of classification and have proven to be very useful in rock art study, it is important to point out the problems that often exist with regard to style identification and cultural associations. This situation has been clearly summarized by Castleton (1979:7) in his work with the rock art of Utah:

> For purposes of this discussion, I have described these styles as if they were discrete, easily separable entities, but this is, of course, an oversimplification. The styles share so many elements and figures; the panels often show evidence of having been executed during more than one time period and in more than one style. There are no absolute ways of tying a particular panel to a particular culture; even where a panel occurs near or directly above cultural material, there is no certain proof that the artist was one of those who lived or camped on the spot—hundreds, thousands of years may have intervened between the two appearances of man on this spot. For these and other reasons, these styles must be seen as convenient units of discussion, not as absolute, definitive subdivisions of Utah rock art.

In this volume, the term style is used to refer to specifically defined rock art, such as the Barrier Canyon Style, as well as to generalized categories of rock art with cultural and temporal associations. The generalized styles, such as those applied to Anasazi Basketmaker and to Fremont rock art, display consistencies with specific regional and local rock art styles associated with those groups.

INTERPRETATION

Rock art interpretation involves making associations between rock art and past cultures and attempting to explain how the rock art functioned and what meaning it might have had to past societies. Explanations of function and meaning are tentative because the rock art now exists out of its living cultural context. Archaeological records are fragmentary at best; the farther one goes back in time the possibility increases that records are incomplete.

Historic and ethnographic data can contribute significantly to prehistoric rock art interpretation if there are clear associations between sites and cultures of the past and historic present. For example, in the case of the Anasazi and historic Pueblos, clear archaeological associations exist. However, even these interpretations are tenuous (especially with regard to very early rock art) and are most meaningful on a systems or broadly defined level rather than on a specific level. Significant cultural and social changes have taken place and continue to take place among historic Indian groups.

For example, humpback and phallic flute-player images of the ancient Anasazi (Plate 52) cannot be equated to the historic Hopi katsina (also spelled katcina and kachina) known as Kokopelli despite certain parallels in symbolism and archaeological continuities between the Anasazi and Hopi; however, the roots of the katsina symbolism are certainly suggested by the image. Hopi katsinas are supernatural beings personated by masked performers, often wearing headdresses and elaborate clothing, for purposes of promoting rain, fertility, and general well-being. Katsinas are represented in historic Hopi rock art and wall paintings and by *tihu* or katsina dolls that are traditional gifts for Hopi children (Stephen 1969). Modern katsina dolls are popular forms of art. Kokopelli is particularly concerned with fertility and is personated with a large phallus and wears a backpack reportedly filled with fertile seeds; on occasion, Kokopelli Katsina carries a flute (Colton 1959).

In the case of historic Indian rock art, it is possible that relatively precise interpretations of rock art functions and meanings can be made by referring to historic records and ethnographic information if adequate documentation and informants exist. The identification of individual artists, such as Ute Chief Jack House, and the social context for the rock art is also possible.

Recent theories for the study of rock art and other archaeological materials have emphasized the roles played by context and symbolism. It has been proposed that symbols such as rock art images are most likely to be meaningful when examined within the contexts of time, place, culture, and society and with the knowledge that symbolism is part of information exchange, communication systems, and acts to express and reinforce group identities (Anderson 1971; Munn 1973; Vastokas and Vastokas 1973; Marshack 1977; Wobst 1976; Molyneaux 1977; Hodder 1982; Olsen 1985; Schaafsma 1985; Cole 1989a; Young 1985). Olsen (1985) interprets the locations and symbolism of Anasazi rock art in Hovenweep National Monument in the context of historic Pueblo clan organization, symbolic traditions, and agricultural systems. Young (1985) has demonstrated that ancient and modern rock art symbols have the power to evoke narrative traditions for the Zuni and to enhance the significance of places. Cole (1989a) has analyzed iconography and symbolism in prehistoric Little Colorado River rock art to demonstrate that a socially significant katsina cult, similar to that involving masked personators of the modern Hopi and Zuni, was present.

Rock art of hunters and gatherers and of the early Anasazi has been interpreted as being symbolic of shamanism, a religious system practiced by hunter-gatherers and agricultural societies throughout the world that is believed to be ancient (Eliade 1964; Furst 1977). Shamans are specialists in the sacred, able to call upon the powers of animal helpers, to see spirits, to go up into the sky or upper world and meet the gods, and to descend to the underworld to meet gods and fight demons, sickness, and death. Accordingly, shamans are identified with acts of transformation and rebirth. Essentially, the shaman is the ultimate specialist on fertility, health, sickness, and death and attempts to balance the universal forces for community well-being.

The very nature of sickness, death, and mythological personages and places is known to shamans and may be described to the living during or after trances in which spiritual journeys are taken. Scenes with these themes are exhibited on Huichol Indian yarn paintings (Furst 1977), and rock art may have been used by some cultures to record shamanistic experiences and mythological events (Munn 1973; Lewis-Williams 1981).

Grant (1978) has proposed that Basketmaker rock art in Canyon de Chelly National Monument has shamanistic content. He points out the presence of traditional shamanistic symbols such as horned head-dresses, masked faces, elaborate dress, "spirit guides" such as birds, deathlike or skeletal body forms, and possible scenes symbolic of spiritual transformation. Similar subject matter for Basketmaker and Archaic rock art in the western United States has been discussed by Grant, Baird, and Pringle (1968), Wellmann (1975, 1979), Schaafsma (1980), Hedges (1985), and Cole (1989b).

A particularly troublesome type of rock art for interpretation is geometric abstract art, composed of singular and complex groupings of lines, circles, frets, triangles, dots, and patterns that may symbolize concepts as well as nature forms in highly conventionalized ways. Similar abstract imagery is found in Southwest Indian basketry and ceramic designs. Abstract art out of its original cultural context is by its very nature even more subject to erroneous and incomplete interpretation than is representational imagery (that which depicts recognizable life forms).

Conventionalized symbols of a society obviously require a greater understanding of cultural processes than outsiders or the uninitiated can be expected to have, and such art is generally dependent on informants with traditional knowledge for precise identification. The identifications are obviously more meaningful in the case of late prehistoric and historic rock art where the passage of time has not been great.

Studies of abstract rock art imagery, prehistoric and historic, suggest that abstract imagery symbolizes things from nature, social groups, and concepts; is metaphorical; serves as mnemonic devices; and is used to join or relate things and concepts. Abstract images may be the result of practices that involve removing pieces of rock and for marking rock surfaces to indicate participation in some event and for accounting. Obviously, any or all of these functions and meanings can be combined in the making of abstract images. Studies of abstract rock art in a variety of locations emphasize the possibilities and limitations for the meaningful interpretation of rock art, be it abstract or representational. The following studies of abstract rock art symbolism illustrate this point.

Marshack (1977) has examined the use of meandering lines in paleolithic cave art of Europe and has determined that the meanders were renewed and reused as consistently as representational art, suggesting that the abstract lines were necessary for the recording or communicating of ideas by way of art. The use of the meanders to relate various images is viewed as indicative that "paleolithic imagery constituted a system that was not primarily representational, but was often abstract, sequential, cumulative, and interrelated at many levels" (Marshack 1977:316).

In an analysis of prehistoric Peterborough site petroglyphs in Ontario, Vastokas and Vastokas (1973) use the symbolic imagery of the historic Ojibwa for comparison. Abstract symbols of the Ojibwa were used for recording the visions of shamans and other sacred or spiritual symbols. As such, the imagery was only understood by individuals who had been properly instructed. The authors propose that abstract and representational petroglyphs at the Peterborough site functioned to emphasize the importance of a physical setting within the cosmology of the people and as a proper context for sacred images associated with shamanism.

Munn (1973) has made a study of the iconography of the Walbiri of central Australia. She observes that the pictorial elements are usually abstract and, to be understood, must be studied structurally and according to their function within society and the cosmology of the culture. A single Walbiri abstract element may be used to symbolize heterogeneous subjects, such as an ancestor, the path of an ancestor, emergence or descendence, or holes or waterholes; it may also symbolize places or serve as a journal of travel. While the meanings of some designs remain constant, others change meaning in accordance with the pictorial and physical contexts.

Munn interprets animal track or prints as part of abstract imagery used in stories to describe species of animals or animal movements as well as ancestors or the movements of ancestors symbolized by the tracks. In the latter case, a specific track design may "belong" to an ancestor and act to represent that ancestor.

Finally, Munn notes that Walbiri abstract art is used to denote a
sense of place, both mythic and natural, a concept also interpreted as
integral to Peterborough rock art discussed above. Munn illustrates the
concept in the following description: "Thus paintings on the cave wall
at Rugari, an important emu site west of Yuendumu, are the *guruwari*
(ancestor designs) of ancestral emus who came to the site and walked
around there. . . . At the same time, the prints provide narrative information on their direction of travel and indicate their presence at the
site" (Munn 1973:122-123).

As part of an interpretation of Anasazi rock art at Hovenweep
National Monument, Olsen (1985) describes iconography and symbolism of the Hopi and Zuni. A number of images identified by Olsen
(1985:19–23) are abstract to a modern student. In summary, the functions of various images are identified as "regulating ownership and
maintenance of land, identifying participation and validating hierarchi-
cal responsibilities of the priests and clan members, counting time,
documenting events, oral tradition and histories of clans and societies,
and commemorating portions of the cosmology" (Olsen 1985:32).
Physical context is seen as important for the interpretation of Hopi and
Zuni symbols, as it is for the Walbiri. In the use of symbols at shrines
and fields, often in rock art form, there is a sense of place inherent in
the symbolism that serves to reinforce cultural and spatial identity.

A similar relationship, specifically between rock art, physical setting, and Hopi culture and mythology can be seen at Tutuventiwngwu
(Willow Springs), Arizona (Weaver 1984). The site is probably a prehistoric shrine that the Hopi continued to visit into the historic period
(Titiev 1937; Michaelis 1981; Malotki and Lomatuway'ma 1987). The
shrine was a stopping place during visits to the inner gorge of the Little
Colorado River canyon near its confluence with the Colorado River in
the Grand Canyon. In that location, participants in a series of journeys
to collect salt and yellow paint have carved clan symbols on sandstone
boulders, resulting in rows of repetitive symbols representing some
twenty-seven clans (Weaver 1984:18). The expeditions are associated
with rites of the Hopi Soyal, a winter solstice katsina ceremony. The
trip involves physical danger to the participants and spiritual danger as
well, as the depths of the canyons are symbolic of the Underworld,
home of the dead (Malotki and Lomatuway'ma 1987).

The clan symbols are evidence of the significance of the place or
shrine and of the journeys to the Hopi. The symbols also evince
ancient relationships between clans and their representatives as well as
social relationships between the clans that participated in the journeys
and related ceremonies.

A number of clan symbols at Tutuventiwngwu are abstract in

appearance and others are highly stylized. Additional symbols realistically depict subjects for which the clans are named or that represent the clan names (e.g., bear tracks for the Bear clan). Recognition of the more abstract symbols through time is assumed to be dependent on instruction and the continuous repetition of symbols during clan activities that are central to historic Hopi social and ceremonial life.

Heizer and Baumhoff (1962) describe pecked pit and groove rock art that may have considerable antiquity in the Great Basin and is similar to rock art made by historic California Indian groups to promote or stop rain and to enhance fertility among women. A similar situation among the Zuni Indians is reported by Stevenson (1904:294; Pl. 12). Zuni women and men wishing to have a female child visit a shrine called "Mother Rock" where pregnant women remove grains of sandstone for an offering to be left at the site. An illustration of Mother Rock shows a surface that is densely pockmarked with abstract imagery, including small pits, larger holes or niches, and grooves. Vulvalike symbols have been formed by using pits and incised lines.

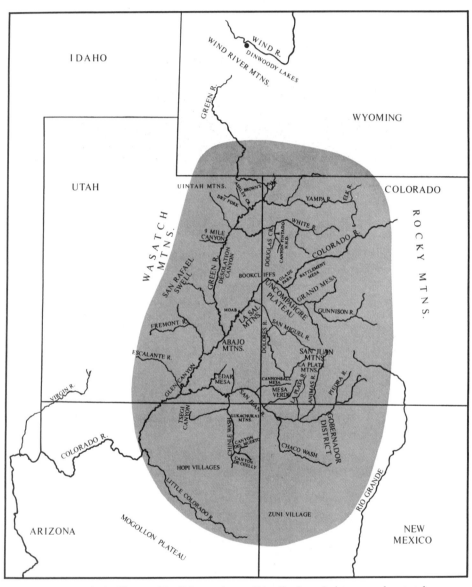

Map 2. *Archaic-Abstract Tradition rock art. Distribution of abstract rock art styles within the study area. The styles of petroglyphs and rock paintings are part of a widespread Archaic tradition also found in the Great Basin and Plains.*

ROCK ART OF HUNTERS AND GATHERERS

R ock art designs attributed to hunters and gatherers of the study area during the Archaic period encompass both abstract forms and representational life forms. Most rock art styles from all periods include both types of imagery, but generally one or the other is emphasized in the styles.

As discussed in the previous chapter, abstract rock art images are often vague and unidentifiable forms to modern viewers but are presumed to have been conventionalized symbols to the groups using them. The images may have been symbolic of life forms and concepts that are extremely difficult to identify outside the original cultural context. Predominantly abstract rock art styles on the Colorado Plateau have been identified and discussed as part of a Western Archaic tradition.

Archaic rock art of the Colorado Plateau that is predominantly representational of life forms has also been described. Much of this rock art is associated with distinctive anthropomorphic images that often characterize styles and mark the beginning of a long prehistoric anthropomorphic rock art tradition.

THE ABSTRACT ROCK ART TRADITION

?1000 B.C. to A.D. 1000

Abstract rock art with origins in the Archaic lifeway occurs as rock paintings and petroglyphs that have been assigned to a number of Colorado Plateau styles in the Great Basin, Southwest, and the Plains (Heizer and Baumhoff 1962; Schaafsma 1972, 1980; Sundstrom 1984; Buckles 1989). In the plains of southeast Colorado, Buckles (1989:129) has assigned a relative date of pre-A.D. 100 to a panel of abstract petroglyphs at Clay Creek. The date is based on a radiocarbon sample taken from soils covering the petroglyphs.

Two dated sites on the Uncompahgre Plateau in west central Colorado have abstract petroglyphs. One site, 5ME217, includes a rock shelter and pecked linear abstract petroglyphs. Deposits in the rock shelter have been excavated and reported by Lutz (1978), who assigns the site to an Archaic occupation dated between approximately 300 B.C. and A.D. 400 (Figure 1).

At a second site, the Harris Site (5MN2341; see Plates 12 and 13), examples of abstract groove petroglyphs are estimated to be more than 2,700 years old based on radiocarbon dating of soils covering the rock art (Tucker 1989). The proposed beginning date for abstract rock art in the study area is based on the above information and on correlations between western Colorado examples and rock art of the Great Basin and Plains. The late date for abstract art is based on the estimated ending date for Uncompahgre Style rock art that is believed to be related to abstract art in west central Colorado.

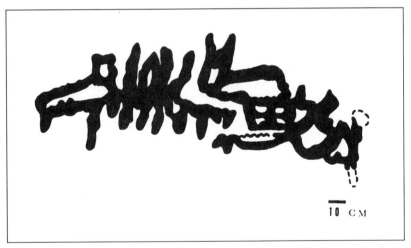

Figure 1. *Solid pecked abstract petroglyphs at site 5ME217, a rock shelter in the Gunnison River drainage, west central Colorado. Occupation of the site is proposed to date between 300 B.C. and A.D. 400 (Lutz 1978).*

An element inventory of abstract rock art in the western Colorado area includes curvilinear and rectilinear images that average between ten and sixty centimeters in length: circles; dots; concentric circles; chains of circles and diamonds; crosshatch images; gridirons; rayed circles or sunbursts; spirals; rake or fringe-like images; "one-pole ladders"; plantlike images; insectlike images; "bird tracks" or triads; straight, wavy, and zigzag lines; ovals and sectioned ovals; spoked "wheels"; "squiggle-mazes"; and long lines (some parallel) that extend over and around rock surfaces and follow the edges of boulders.

The abstract images may be divided into three general types: (1) closed elements, such as circles, dots, concentric circles, spirals, "wheels," and gridirons; (2) open element forms, such as lines (often parallel), "rakes," frets, crosshatches, "one-pole ladders," and "squiggle-mazes"; and (3) complexes, such as chains of circles; lines with attached circles, lines, gridirons, frets, and other elements; and rows of dots.

Representational elements do occur in limited numbers with abstract images and are part of abstract style expressions. Typical representational images are paw prints, possible bird tracks, zoomorphs (quadrupeds, snakes, and other animals), anthropomorphs, plantlike images, and insectlike images. Representations are clearly not dominant in abstract rock art styles, and they are generally simple forms. This clearly contrasts with rock art styles that feature representational forms.

In the study area, abstract rock art is best known from sites in west central and southwest Colorado and east central and northeast Utah. Based on archaeological records and published accounts, abstract petroglyphs are far more common than paintings throughout the study area.

Abstract Rock Paintings

Schaafsma (1980) describes the Chihuahuan Polychrome Abstract Style, named for type-sites in southwestern New Mexico, which is similar to painted rock art in Utah and western Colorado. The paintings are frequently in shallow caves or rock shelters located along canyon walls.

Examples of polychrome abstract paintings have been reported from south central Utah sites in the drainage of the Escalante River. The paintings occur in a variety of colors, including red, yellow, green, black, and white. At a site in the Escalante River drainage, paintings of zigzag lines, dots (finger prints), sunbursts, and "rakes" surround images of the Barrier Canyon Style, a representational rock art style discussed below (Plate 6). Associations between painted abstracts and the Barrier Canyon Style are also noted at other sites.

Noxon and Marcus (1985) have documented rock art at two sites in the Needles District of Canyonlands National Park that also exhibit polychrome abstract art. Three additional Utah polychrome abstract art sites are in Thompson Wash in the Book Cliffs, in Black Dragon Canyon in the San Rafael Swell area, and in a tributary canyon to Grand Gulch on Cedar Mesa.

At these sites, elaborate polychrome paintings of dots, short lines or finger prints, "rakes," zigzag lines, parallel lines, circles, plant and flowerlike images, insectlike images, tadpolelike images, paw prints,

Plate 6. *Overview of polychrome abstract and Barrier Canyon Style rock paintings at site 42GA2094, Escalante River drainage, south central Utah. The paintings include lines, dots, and "sunbursts" in green, yellow, red, black, and white.*

possible bird tracks, anthropomorphs, and a possible anthropomorph formed of dots and lines occur in colors of red, black, green, white, and cream.

Abstract rock paintings in Thompson Wash occur on the same panel with Barrier Canyon Style paintings and paintings that have traits of both the Barrier Canyon Style and Fremont style art. These images superimpose portions of the abstract art and appear much brighter and more recent than both the abstracts and the Barrier Canyon Style imagery (Plate 7). A variety of rock art, including historic Ute, occurs in the same general location.

Abstract art in Thompson Wash is composed of red and black dots and lines that appear in part to compose an anthropomorph holding a snakelike image or stemmed sunflowerlike image. The "anthropomorph" wears a headdress and is attached to several lines. Geometric abstract images also at the Thompson Wash site include a "rake," and a row of zigzag lines.

Black, red, and white abstract paintings in Black Dragon Canyon occur in a shallow rock shelter within a deep, narrow canyon and include dots or finger prints, lines, caterpillarlike images, representations of paw prints, and possible bird tracks. Barrier Canyon Style images occur nearby outside the rock shelter and along the same canyon wall (Plate 8).

Plate 7. *Polychrome abstract rock paintings in black and red (center) that appear to represent an anthropomorph holding a snake or sunflowerlike object and attached to various lines and dots. Anthropomorphs in the lower left of the picture are in the Barrier Canyon Style, and figures in the lower center resemble both Barrier Canyon and Fremont style forms.*

Plate 8. *Detail of polychrome abstract rock paintings at Black Dragon Canyon, San Rafael Swell area, east central Utah, showing fingerprint-like dots, plantlike forms, circles, lines, and paw prints in black, red, and white.*

At the Grand Gulch site, a large full-bodied anthropomorph with no arms and smaller figures that may represent anthropomorphs are depicted in cream color amidst more abstract forms in red, black, white, and green (Plate 9). The imagery includes tadpolelike forms, dots, "rakes," plantlike forms, insectlike forms, and rows of straight and zigzag lines. These occur on the upper rear wall and ceiling of a rock shelter, and a rock ledge that may have provided access to the rear wall has fallen. Anasazi Basketmaker rock art, probably dated prior to A.D. 600, is exhibited on a scar left when the ledge fell, indicating that the abstract rock art is older.

One site with painted abstract rock art, now quite faint and damaged by a spalling rock surface, is recorded in west central Colorado (Figure 2). The art occurs in a tributary canyon to the Colorado River near the Utah-Colorado line. A circle, parallel lines, and plantlike images are depicted in colors of red and black. It is remarkable that the paintings remain and are still visible as they are exhibited on a slightly overhanging cliff face that provides relatively little shelter from wind and rain. Presently, the paintings are located high above a meandering creek bed, and it appears that downcutting of the stream has removed soils that once provided access to the paintings. Historic Ute rock art

Plate 9. *Detail of polychrome abstract rock paintings in black, red, white, and cream showing plantlike forms, rakelike images, lines, dots, and insectlike forms. Possible stick-figure anthropomorphs, cream colored, with arms raised appear in the center of the photograph. Paintings occur at site 42SA3711, Cedar Mesa, southeast Utah.*

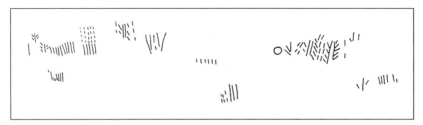

Figure 2. *Red and black abstract rock paintings at site 5ME1356, in west central Colorado near the Colorado River. Adapted from a field sketch by Glenn E. Stone.*

occurs at the same site, at eye level and below the abstract paintings. Barrier Canyon Style petroglyphs occur less than a mile downstream from the abstract paintings.

Abstract Petroglyphs

Several sites in western Colorado and eastern Utah have panels of abstract petroglyphs. In eastern Utah, panels of abstract petroglyphs occur in the Uinta Basin along the Green River, in the San Rafael Swell area, in Indian Creek, Salt Creek, and in Grand Gulch (Castleton 1978, 1979; Noxon and Marcus 1985) (Figure 3).

In western Colorado, abstract petroglyphs occur in a variety of environments, ranging from mountain valleys to canyon floors, in the drainages of the Green, Colorado, San Juan, Dolores, Little Dolores, Uncompahgre, and Gunnison (North Fork and main fork) rivers. The rock art is found on rock shelter walls, on canyon walls, and on boulders in open locations. The diverse locations suggest that abstract rock art was associated over time with a number of human activities.

The majority of abstract elements at the sites are linear rather than full forms and are both curvilinear and rectilinear. Closed element forms, such as circles, chains of circles, dots, spirals, gridirons, and wheel-like elements, occur but less often than the more open images, such as lines and line complexes, T-shape forms, "rakes," crosses, "bird tracks," plantlike forms, "centipedes," "one-pole ladders," and other crosshatch forms. Paw prints, quadrupeds, and simple anthropomorphic images also occur in combination with the geometric abstract forms. Repeated use of some sites is suggested by superimpositions and crowded elements. However, consistencies in patination levels and the weathering of rock surfaces at individual locations indicate that artists were not widely separated in time.

Abstract petroglyphs fall into two general categories based on techniques of manufacture: pecked (using solid and stipple pecking techniques) and ground and incised (composed of broad elliptical

grooves and more narrow incised grooves). Because of the differences
in techniques, abstract petroglyphs of each category appear quite different even though similar imagery is depicted. Groove art is generally
more simple than pecked, probably because the techniques involved do
not easily lend themselves to making curvilinear images, long lines, and
wide and highly detailed images. This is reinforced by the occurrence
of groove petroglyphs that repeatedly appear as relatively short lines,
"rakes," crosshatch images, "bird tracks" or triads, "centipedes," and
plantlike forms in contrast to more detailed abstract images that are
solid pecked, including "spoked wheels," chains of circles, spirals and
concentric circles, and gridirons.

Abstract style classifications often emphasize differences in techniques, although it is likely that a variety of techniques were used by
the same cultures over time. This is reinforced by the presence of various techniques (pecking, incising, drilled holes, ground surfaces, and
painting) in individual elements and panels associated with styles discussed below.

Pecked Abstracts

Sixteen west central Colorado sites, in rock shelters and along cliffs
and boulders, have panels with pecked examples of abstract rock art.
Petroglyphs at site 5ME217 in the Gunnison River drainage (proposed
to date between approximately 300 B.C. and A.D. 400) are a complex
of wavy and straight lines and a gridiron design (Figure 1). Pecked
abstract art at other sites in west central and northeast Colorado and
eastern Utah show similar linear art with straight and wavy lines, chains
of circles, "rakes," crosshatch lines, and spirals (Figures 3, 4, and 5). A
single west central site near the Gunnison River exhibits lines and elaborate "spoked wheels," bisected circles, and circles with radiating lines
(Figure 6).

A particularly large panel of pecked abstract art is on the North
Fork Gunnison River. These petroglyphs include wavy and zigzag
lines, crosshatch designs, rows of dots, and circles that have been
pecked around natural depressions in the rock face. Small simple
anthropomorphs and quadrupeds are also present. Panels of Uncompahgre Style rock art occur nearby at the same site (Plate 10).

Abstract Groove Art (Incised)

Panels at six west central Colorado sites in the drainages of the
Gunnison, Colorado, and lower Dolores rivers feature incised grooves.
Abstract groove art is reported by Wormington and Lister (1956),
Buckles (1971), Toll (1977), and Cole (1987; 1989c). In the upper

Figure 3. *Solid pecked abstract petroglyphs in the San Rafael Swell area of east central Utah.*

Figure 4. *Solid pecked abstract petroglyphs at site 5MN5, in the Uncompahgre River drainage, west central Colorado.*

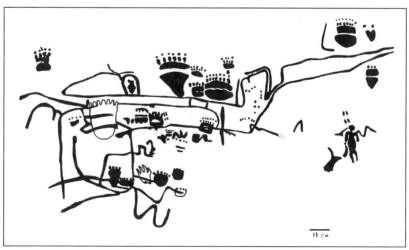

Figure 5. *Solid pecked lines, paw prints, and an anthropomorph at site 5ME1, in the Gunnison River drainage, west central Colorado.*

Plate 10. *Detail of pecked abstract rock art at site 5DT355, in the North Fork of the Gunnison River drainage, west central Colorado. Circle on the far left is pecked around a natural hole in the rock.*

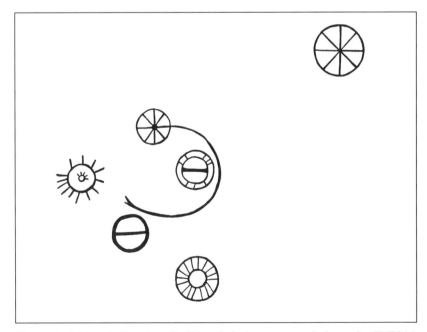

Figure 6. *Schematic drawing of solid pecked abstract petroglyphs at site 5ME164, near the Gunnison River, west central Colorado.*

Dolores River valley of southwest Colorado, Ives (1986) reports panels of groove art at fourteen sites. A few additional southwest Colorado examples are known to occur in the McElmo Creek drainage and on Mesa Verde to the south.

West central Colorado abstract groove art occurs in shallow rock shelters along cliffs and beneath boulders. Imagery includes rows of simple grooves, "bird tracks" or triads, "rakes," plantlike forms, "centipedes," and crosshatch forms. Pecked and stylized bear paw prints similar to those of the Uncompahgre Plateau also occur with groove art at some sites (Plates 11, 12, 13, and 14).

Abstract rock art formed of narrow and wide grooves, including rakelike images, parallel lines, "bird tracks," gridirons, plantlike forms, and crosshatch images, is exhibited in rock shelters in the upper Dolores River valley. Simple incised stick-figure anthropomorphs are also shown. At one site, a highly abstract pecked and incised flute-player may be depicted. Stylized pecked bear paw prints similar to those found on the Uncompahgre Plateau are shown at two of the sites (Figures 7, 8, and 9). In some instances, the groove art and pecked abstract imagery occur at sites with known Anasazi rock art styles and materials, such as pottery and architecture. Eight of the fourteen sites (57 percent) are associated with Anasazi ceramics dated between A.D. 600 and 1300 (Ives 1986).

Some groove petroglyphs of the upper Dolores River valley may have been made by Anasazi Basketmaker peoples as part of a pattern established during the Archaic period. The possibility that Basketmaker peoples made some of the upper Dolores River rock art is supported by the presence of similar art showing plantlike forms, wavy lines, and stylized paw prints incised in clay storage cist walls at North Shelter (Figure 10), a Basketmaker site in the La Plata Mountains area near Durango, Colorado (Morris and Burgh 1954: Fig. 77, 78).

Feyhl (1980:1–31) has experimented with replication of incised rock art forms and described techniques for the manufacture of broad and narrow grooves in sandstone. His experiments were approached from the perspective of the modification of tools. The sharp narrow incisions are viewed as being made by a hard sharpened tool, probably a stone (Figure 11). The broader grooves may have been formed by wet bone and antler-ends. Feyhl has proposed that the process of bone and antler-end modification is a likely reason for the existence of broad elliptical grooves. Bone awls are likely end products. Numerous such grooves at a site are seen as the result of using fresh abrasive surfaces to achieve desired tool shapes. Rows of parallel grooves and fanlike arrangements of grooves might result from the maker finding a comfortable position and suitable angle from which to grind.

Plate 11. *Incised abstract petro-*
glyphs on Monument Mesa, Un-
compahgre Plateau, west cen-
tral Colorado. Photograph by
Henry Schoch.

Plate 12

Plate 13

Plates 12 and 13. *Incised abstract petroglyphs at the Harris Site (5MN2341), west*
central Colorado. Plate 12 shows exposed panels designated as D and E. Plate 13
shows Panel G, which was buried and exposed during excavation. Based on radiocar-
bon dates from the site, Panel G is estimated to be more than 2,700 years old (Tucker
1989). Scale increments: 10 centimeters. Photographs by Bill Harris.

Figure 7. *Incised abstract petroglyphs and an anthropomorph at site 5MT2405, in the upper Dolores River Valley area, southwest Colorado. These may date from the Archaic and Basketmaker periods. Redrawn from Ives (1986:Fig. 8E.16).*

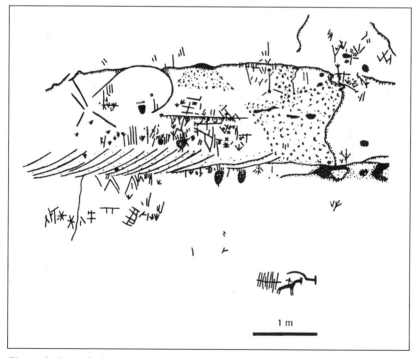

Figure 8. *Incised abstract petroglyphs and pecked paw prints at site 5MT2414, in the upper Dolores River Valley area, southwest Colorado. These may date from the Archaic and Basketmaker periods. Early Historic Ute Indian Style petroglyphs appear in the lower right of the panel. Redrawn from Ives (1986:Fig. 8E.24).*

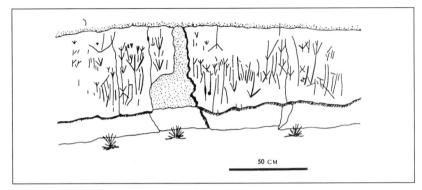

Figure 9. *Incised abstract petroglyphs showing bird-track-like images and other designs at site 5MT4726, in the upper Dolores River Valley area, southwest Colorado. These may date from the Archaic and Basketmaker periods. Redrawn from Ives (1986:Fig. 8E.59).*

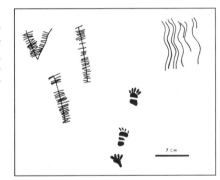

Figure 10. *Schematic drawing of impressed and incised images in plaster walls of Basketmaker storage cists at North Shelter, Durango Rock Shelters, La Plata Mountains, southwest Colorado. Drawn from photographs by Morris and Burgh (1954:Fig. 77).*

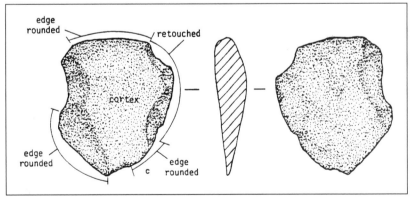

Figure 11. *Line drawing of an utilized flake of igneous material from site 5MN2341, west central Colorado. This flake (56.7 millimeters in length) has been smoothed and abraded and may have been used to incise abstract grooves that occur at the site. A similarly smoothed tool was found at the nearby Moore Rockshelter. Drawing courtesy of the Chipeta Chapter of the Colorado Archaeological Society.*

Feyhl acknowledges that narrow and broad indentations are some-times incorporated into recognizable (representational) rock art images, and he views this as a separate use for groove technology without exam-ining how tool modification may or may not enter into the process.

It is possible that the shaping of tools and making of rock art imagery may have been combined into single events. Also, grooves may have been a traditional way for artists to draw lines and more complex symbols on soft rock and may be equivalent to those that are pecked or painted. It is also possible that grooves indicate intentional removal of grains of rock at certain locations in a manner similar to that of the Zuni at "Mother Rock" discussed in a previous section. The creating of designs could be combined with the removal of grains of rock. The Harris Site (5MN2341), on the eastern slope of the Uncompahgre Plateau, is of particular interest because grooves at that site have an estimated radiocarbon date of more than 2,700 years ago, or prior to 950 B.C. (Tucker 1989; Cole 1989c). The buried petro-glyphs occur on a broken slab of sandstone buried in the fill of the rock shelter and are similar to those located elsewhere at the site and at other sites in west central and southwest Colorado (Plate 13).

Although a few repetitious lines and fanlike arrangements are pre-sent at the Harris Site, the use of grooves for making rock art imagery seems to be quite possible based on the overall nature of the imagery and the lack of bone and antler tools, such as awls, recovered during a test of the site (Tucker 1989; Cole 1989c). Images include geometric designs (crosshatched lines, "rakes," "one-pole ladders") and possible bird tracks and stick-figure anthropomorphs. A stone artifact found at the site (not in a datable context) shows evidence of having been ground until quite smooth, and it is of a size suitable for making nar-row incised grooves. A use for the artifact other than making petro-glyphs is not apparent (Figure 11).

Further support for the use of stones for making grooves is pro-vided by archaeological research at the Moore Shelter (Wormington and Lister 1956), located a few miles to the southwest of 5MN2341. Researchers observe that rock art grooves at that site (Plate 14) appear patterned, and a stone artifact uncovered during excavation had "one extraordinarily smooth edge," which was shown in replication experi-ments to make similar grooves. It is noted that bone artifacts were rare at the Moore Shelter, and only two awls were recovered.

It seems likely that abstract petroglyphs, pecked and grooved, in west central Colorado are associated with the Uncompahgre Complex. Buckles (1971) describes panels of predominantly abstract rock art at three Uncompahgre Complex sites; similar abstract art occurs at the Moore Shelter. The Moore Shelter is a type-site for the Uncompahgre

Plate 14. *Incised abstract petroglyphs and pecked and incised bear paw print forms at the Moore Rockshelter, west central Colorado. The site is associated with the Archaic Uncompahgre Complex (Wormington and Lister 1956).*

Complex, hunters and gatherers of west central Colorado (Wormington and Lister 1956:8–9). Solid pecked stylized bear paw prints occur with incised art at the Moore Shelter (Plate 14). Similar stylized paw prints are found with more representational rock art also associated with the Uncompahgre Complex and discussed below.

The relationship between abstract groove art and the Uncompahgre Complex is emphasized not only by its presence at sites and by associated materials but also by other forms of art. For example, an incised and notched pendant or stone ornament, possibly in the shape of a bird, was recovered from the Moore Shelter. Also, a fragment of deer bone from the Moore Shelter is marked on both sides by alternating rows of incised lines (Wormington and Lister 1956).

In a previous analysis, Cole (1987) includes incised abstract petroglyphs and representational images in a more broadly defined Uncompahgre Style but observed that the abstract groove art could be considered part of a separate abstract manifestation. That distinction is being made in this study.

REPRESENTATIONAL ROCK ART STYLES

A discussion of representational rock art in western Colorado and adjacent areas would be incomplete without a brief description of an anthropomorphic rock art tradition represented by styles that probably began on the Colorado Plateau during the Archaic period of pre-A.D. 1 and continued for two thousand years or more until the historic period. In these styles, anthropomorphs are featured subjects and fall within a pattern of shared forms and themes. In the western Colorado area, the tradition ends with the abandonment of the northern Colorado Plateau by Anasazi and Fremont peoples at approximately A.D. 1300–1500. Turner (1963) and Schaafsma (1980) have discussed the anthropomorphic rock art tradition. Turner (1963) describes and interprets rock art in the Glen Canyon region with such a tradition in mind.

> In Glen and San Juan canyons, the most common supposedly religious storytelling device is the headdressed human figure and other mixed zoomorphic and anthropomorphic variants. While they are not always portrayed at any specific activity, nevertheless, they seem to be part of a theme or recollection of the artisan as to how the figures were costumed, arranged, positioned, or ranked. Size of the petroglyphs may have had importance as well. . . . Head-geared anthropomorphs are perhaps the characterizing petroglyph of Glen and San Juan canyons (Turner 1963:29–30).

At another point, Turner (1963:41) describes the theme of the art as "anthropomorphic deification."

Through time, Archaic, Anasazi, Fremont, and Pueblo cultures on the Colorado Plateau have represented anthropomorphic images, frequently in rows or clusters, that appear supernatural and heroic, often life-size, with decorated bodies, decorated and masklike faces, and headdresses; they are shown holding or otherwise associated with a variety of forms, including animals, faces, head- and masklike images, shields, plants, and abstract geometric forms. Despite differences in styles, specific figure-types, and other details, these anthropomorphs fit a representational pattern expressed in Turner's concept of anthropomorphic deification.

Not all Colorado Plateau rock art styles include themes typical of the tradition described above. In particular, the Uncompahgre Style of west central Colorado is markedly different. Rock art styles of the San Juan River Anasazi generally do not show such themes after the early Pueblo II period, between approximately A.D. 1000 and 1300. However, the tradition continues north of the San Juan drainage in Pueblo II–III Anasazi and Fremont rock art styles. On the southern Colorado Plateau, in the drainage of the Little Colorado River, the tradition continued among Western Pueblo people into the historic period. Similarities and differences with the long-lived anthropomorphic tradition may be seen as evidence of cultural community and change and are helpful for archaeological interpretation.

The Glen Canyon Style 5

?1000 B.C. to A.D. 500

The Glen Canyon Style 5 is a petroglyph style that was identified by Turner (1963, 1971) from type-sites in the area of Glen Canyon on the Colorado River in Utah and Arizona. Glen Canyon Style 5 elements are made by solid and stipple pecking techniques. The style is associated with desert-based Archaic peoples and has proposed beginnings as early as 6,000 years ago. Turner notes similarities between the forms of Glen Canyon Style 5 petroglyphs, (Figure 12) and split-twig animal figurines (Plate 15) from the Grand Canyon (Turner 1971). Grand Canyon animal figurines are generally dated between 4,000 and 3,000 years ago (Jones and Euler 1979). Similar split-twig figurines from Utah have been dated between 3,000 and 1,500 years ago (Schroedl 1977). Likenesses also exist between the forms of certain Glen Canyon Style 5 anthropomorphs and wrapped vegetal fiber "figurines" from Hogup Cave, Utah (Plate 16), that are dated between 3,000 and 2,000 years ago (Aikens 1970; Jennings 1978: Fig. 63).

Figure 12. *Glen Canyon Style 5 petroglyphs showing quadrupeds and anthropomorphs (lower left and right) at site 42SV12 in the Green River drainage, east central Utah. Other figures are possibly Fremont in origin. All elements are solid pecked.*

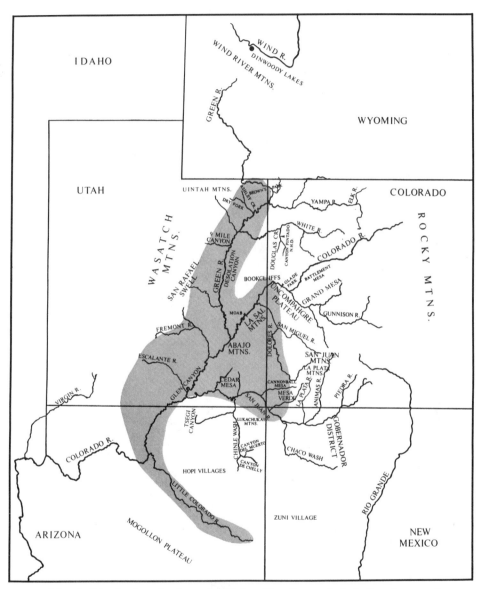

Map 3. *Distribution of rock art classified as Glen Canyon Style 5. Certain examples in the upper Green River drainage are probably more closely related to the Interior Line Style.*

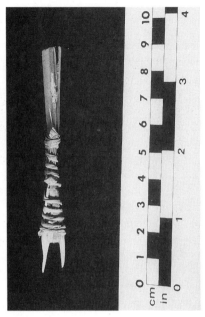

Plate 15   Plate 16

*Figurines associated with hunters and gatherers that resemble Glen Canyon Style 5
rock art forms and decorative details. Plate 15 shows a split-twig figurine of a
quadruped from the Grand Canyon, Arizona. Similar figurines have been dated between 4000 and 3000 years ago (Jones and Euler 1979). Plate 16 shows a possible anthropomorphic figurine of wrapped vegetal fiber from Hogup Cave (42BO36). This
and similar figurines are dated between 3000 and 2000 years ago (Aikens 1970:
120–121). Photographs courtesy of Utah Museum of Natural History, University
of Utah.*

Schaafsma has discussed the Glen Canyon Style 5 as the Glen
Canyon Linear Style and interprets the style to date approximately 700
B.C. to A.D. 100 (Schaafsma 1980:19). She observes that the style has
similarities to early Basketmaker rock art of the San Juan Anasazi, and
the two occur together at some locations on the San Juan River in
Utah. Style 5 art near the mouth of Butler Wash on the San Juan River
is superimposed by Basketmaker art, and generally appears older when-
ever the two occur together. The Style 5 may have directly influenced
San Juan Basketmaker rock art. Based on Turner's studies and similarities to Archaic styles discussed below, it is proposed that the Style 5
dates from 1000 B.C. or earlier to approximately A.D. 500.

Glen Canyon Style 5 petroglyphs are well represented in Glen and
San Juan River canyons and along the Little Colorado River farther to
the south (Turner 1963; Pilles 1975; Schaafsma 1980). Examples of

the style are located in the vicinity of Sand Island on the San Juan River in Utah and north of the Abajo Mountains in the Needles District of Canyonlands National Park. To the west in Utah, the style occurs along the Escalante River and to the north in the drainage of the Green River. Four sites with similar art are reported in west central Colorado. These sites are described by Toll (1977), and occur along the lower Dolores River (Plate 17; Figures 13, 14, 15, 16, and 17).

The Glen Canyon Style 5 is widely dispersed across the Colorado Plateau and appears to be most common along major rivers (Colorado, Dolores, Escalante, Green, and San Juan), indicating a relationship to Archaic populations that used these areas for such activities as gathering, hunting, fishing, ceremonies, and trade. The emphasis on river corridors where a variety of peoples and ideas were likely to interact over time perhaps explains similarities between Glen Canyon Style 5 petroglyphs and other rock art styles on the Colorado Plateau and outside. Examples of similar styles are the Barrier Canyon Style, the Coso Style of eastern California, and related art in Lincoln County, Nevada (Grant et al. 1968; Heizer and Hester 1978), and the Interior Line Style (Gebhard and Cahn 1950; Gebhard 1969) of western Wyoming, Utah, and Colo-

Plate 17. *Glen Canyon Style 5 petroglyphs at site 5SM10, lower Dolores River area, west central Colorado.*

Figure 13. *Glen Canyon Style 5 solid pecked petroglyphs of anthropomorphs at site 42SA5263, near the San Juan River, southeastern Utah.*

rado. The obvious nature of such relationships is illustrated by the fact that a single petroglyph site in the Dry Fork Valley of northeast Utah has been associated with two separate styles. Gebhard (1969:Pl. 68) observes that the petroglyphs are related to the Interior Line Style, while Schaafsma (1971:66-67) classifies them as Glen Canyon Style 5.

The Glen Canyon Style 5 is part of the Colorado Plateau anthropomorphic tradition and includes pecked representations of anthropomorphs; heads, masks, or faces; a variety of zoomorphs, including bighorn sheep, deer or elk, caninelike images, and snakes; wavy and zigzag lines; and spirals, "rakes," circles, and other abstract images commonly seen in the Abstract Tradition discussed above. Panels are often loosely composed but may feature precise rows of anthropomorphs and quadrupeds. These forms are generally less than a meter in length and most frequently appear in outline with abstract interior line and dot decorations. The images may also appear as outlined forms without interior decoration and as solid and stipple-pecked images. Anthropomorphic body shapes are generally elongated and rectangular in shape but may be seen as tapered or ovate; stick-figures also occur. A combination of outlining with solid pecking is common, and bodies may be outlined while faces are solid, or vice versa. Heads are rounded

Figure 14

Figures 14 and 15. *Details of Glen Canyon Style 5 solid pecked petroglyphs showing anthropomorph and faces at site 42SA3589, near the San Juan River, southeastern Utah. Dashed line indicates broken rock.*

Figure 15

Figure 16

Glen Canyon Style 5 solid pecked animals and anthropomorphs at site 42SA3589, near the San Juan River, southeastern Utah.

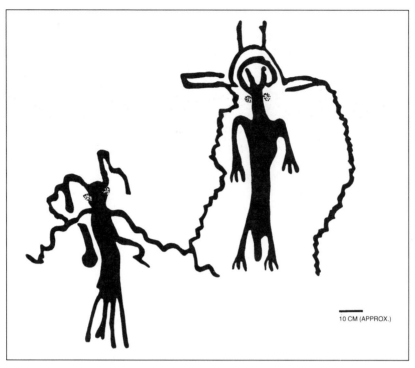

Figure 17. *Glen Canyon Style 5 solid pecked petroglyphs at site 5MN72, near the lower Dolores River, west central Colorado. Eyes of figures are more deeply pecked than surrounding portions.*

or tapered, and abstracted into a line with a "two-horn" or "rabbit ear" headdress; heads also appear as spirals. Extremities are rarely emphasized and may not be present, although phallic figures are shown.

Facial features, if present, consist of dot eyes and mouth; facial decorations (parallel lines) or masks are shown. Anthropomorphs are usually static but may be shown holding such items as "sticks" and "faces," or masklike objects. Generally, anthropomorphs have a ceremonial, even supernatural, appearance based on decorated and masklike faces, headdresses, and bodies with interior decorations (Figures 13, 14, 15, and 16).

Quadrupeds, usually bighorn sheep and deer or elk with antlers, have small heads and disproportionate large bodies that are rectangular or ovate. These bodies have similar design qualities to those of anthropomorphs. Quadrupeds may be shown as immobile or as if stiffly running.

Glen Canyon Style 5 rock art in western Colorado occurs in four locations along the lower Dolores River and includes anthropomorphs with two-horn headdresses and elongated solid pecked bodies and solid figures with outline faces; individual outline faces, scalps, or masks with "necks"; wavy lines; bighorn sheep and other animals; and tracks (Plate 17; Figure 17). Certain elements differ somewhat from Style 5 rock art in neighboring Utah. For example, interior line and dot decorations are not present on any anthropomorphs and quadrupeds at the Colorado sites. Also, arms, legs, hands, and feet exhibited on anthropomorphs at the Colorado sites are rare in Utah sites; anthropomorphs at the Colorado sites have exaggerated phalluses, also atypical of the style elsewhere. In general, body forms and exaggerated features give the Colorado figures more realistic appearances. Barrier Canyon Style rock art also occurs at one Dolores River site near Style 5 petroglyphs (Figure 18).

The Barrier Canyon Style

?1000 B.C. to A.D. 500

Barrier Canyon Style rock art was first described by Schaafsma (1971) from type-sites in Canyonlands National Park, Utah, and is part of the Colorado Plateau anthropomorphic rock art tradition (Plates 18 and 19). The style features anthropomorphic images that are often elaborately decorated and are ceremonial and supernatural in appearance. Presently, the Barrier Canyon Style is known to extend from the Grand Canyon in northern Arizona to the drainage of the White River in northwest Colorado (Plates 3 and 4), spanning much of eastern Utah and the northern Colorado Plateau. The Barrier Canyon Style has very limited representation in the San Juan River drainage of Colorado and Utah and in west central Colorado where it is likely that separate cultural developments took place.

Barrier Canyon Style rock art is represented at fifteen or more sites in northwest Colorado, and four sites have been documented in west central Colorado, near the Utah border. Northwest Colorado sites are located in the drainage of White River–Douglas Creek, and four west central sites are in the drainages of the Colorado and lower Dolores rivers. Several northwest Colorado sites are found within the Cañon Pintado National Historic District, along Douglas Creek south of the White River, and are described by Creasman (1982). Additional sites are found in the same general vicinity, north and south of the White River. In eastern Utah, Barrier Canyon Style sites are numerous and are concentrated in the Book Cliffs area, the San Rafael Swell area, near Moab, and in Canyonlands National Park. Utah sites have been described by Schaafsma (1971, 1980), Castleton (1978, 1979), Noxon and Marcus (1985), and Tipps and Hewitt (1989).

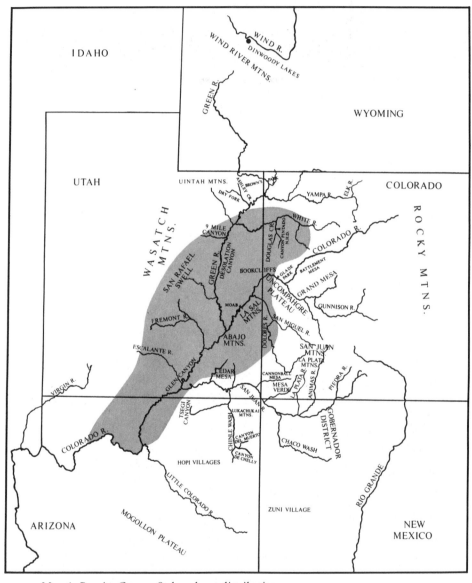

Map 4. *Barrier Canyon Style rock art distribution.*

Plate 18

Plate 19

Barrier Canyon Style red and white rock paintings at the Great Gallery, Maze District, Canyonlands National Park, Utah. Plate 19 is an enlarged continuation of the lower left portion of Plate 18. Note indentations that appear to be the result of sharp objects thrown or otherwise hit against the rock surface and the paintings. Larger figures in Plate 18 are approximately life-size.

Schaafsma (1980:70) proposes a chronology of the Barrier Canyon Style from approximately 500 B.C. to A.D. 500; however, it is possible that the style has beginning dates of 1000 B.C. or earlier. Early dates for the Barrier Canyon Style are supported by materials and radiocarbon dates from Utah sites. Unfired clay figurines from Cowboy and Walters caves, dated between approximately 8,800 and 6,600 years ago (Hull and White 1980), are very similar in form and details of decoration to Barrier Canyon Style paintings (Plate 20). Schroedl (1989:17) and Tipps and Hewitt (1989:125) report a radiocarbon date of 3,000 to 2,000 years ago from a hearth below a Barrier Canyon Style figure in the Needles District of Canyonlands National Park, but there is no definitive association between the two. Loendorf (1986:17) estimates that a possible Barrier Canyon Style figure from Rochester Creek, Utah, dates between 165 B.C. and A.D. 210, based on a radiocarbon date from stratified soils at the site. A late date of A.D. 500 proposed for the Barrier Canyon Style agrees with that of Schaafsma and is supported by similarities between the style and Anasazi Basketmaker rock art in the San Juan River drainage and in the Canyonlands area. The late date is also supported by examples of rock art that share characteristics of Barrier Canyon Style and Fremont rock art styles.

Plate 20. *Unfired clay figurine from Walters Cave (site 42WN42), east central Utah. This figurine and others from nearby Cowboy Cave are dated between approximately 8,800 and 6,600 years ago (Hull and White 1980) and resemble the form and decorative details of some Barrier Canyon Style anthropomorphs. Photograph courtesy Utah Museum of Natural History, University of Utah.*

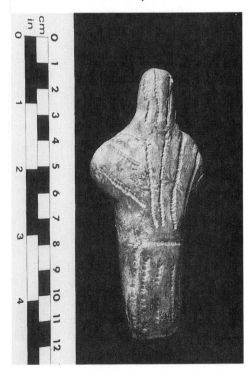

The Barrier Canyon Style includes both rock paintings and pecked petroglyphs (usually solid), but rock paintings are more common. In some instances, the style includes combination forms, paintings with details indicated by petroglyphs. This is particularly common in northwest Colorado sites where red-painted figures have petroglyph eyes and interior body decorations. A similar use of painting and petroglyphs is seen in Fremont style rock art of the same area. On occasion, background surfaces have been ground smooth prior to the painting and making of petroglyphs. Paintings are monochrome, usually red, and polychrome, including various shades of red, blue, blue-green, white, black, and yellow. Clay is also used as a pigment.

In general, examples of Barrier Canyon Style rock art in Colorado are not as elaborate as in Utah, although finely pecked and painted examples are present. Colorado sites exhibit a number of petroglyph sites with a variety of figures, and petroglyphs are relatively rare in Utah. Polychrome figures are relatively rare in Colorado, and Colorado sites usually exhibit fewer elements and do not show the wide range of sizes and variety of figure types seen at Utah sites. Combination painted and petroglyph figures appear to be more common at Colorado sites, particularly in the northwest.

The Barrier Canyon Style features immobile anthropomorphs with broad shoulders and long tapered bodies, ranging from rectangular to triangular; shoulders often appear to be hunched. Anthropomorphic figures range in height from a few centimeters to more than two meters and often appear in rows of two or more and crowded together, sometimes in separate groupings. Body extremities and facial features are not emphasized and may be missing. However, hands may be carefully depicted, and figures may be shown holding plantlike images and snakes. Large round and bulging eyes are commonly the only facial features, and faces often appear decorated and masklike. Heads may be small and round or bulging at the eyes, rectangular, abstracted into a line or lines, and with a two-horn headdress. Other headdress forms include "rabbit ears," plantlike images, crowns of dots, and arcs over the heads. Like those of the Glen Canyon Style 5, Barrier Canyon Style anthropomorphs also have a supernatural appearance.

Body forms are shown in outline, as stripes, and as solid forms. Outline and solid bodies may have a variety of interior decoration, including simple geometric designs formed by dots and lines and more complex textilelike designs; spirals and circles; small anthropomorphs; zoomorphs, including snakes and quadrupeds; and plantlike forms.

With regard to anthropomorphs, significant formal and thematic similarities exist between some anthropomorphic figures of the Barrier

Figure 18. *Barrier Canyon Style red and blue-green (stippled) rock paintings at site 5SM72, near the lower Dolores River, west central Colorado. Largest figure is approximately one meter in length.*

Figure 19. *Detail of Barrier Canyon Style red paintings in the Book Cliffs of east central Utah.*

Canyon Style and those of the Glen Canyon Style 5 (Plate 23), and it seems likely that the styles overlapped in time. This is particularly true of Glen Canyon Style 5 petroglyphs illustrated by Turner (1963). Unlike the Glen Canyon Style 5, however, which is generally restricted to river corridors of the Colorado Plateau, the Barrier Canyon Style is found away from rivers in dry canyons, in mountain valleys, and on foothills as well as along rivers. The Barrier Canyon Style may have also overlapped in time with early Basketmaker rock art in the San Juan River area as well as in the Canyonlands area to the north. Striking

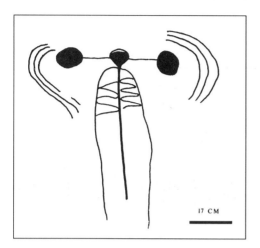

Figure 20. *Detail of Barrier Canyon Style red painting in the Book Cliffs of east central Utah.*

17 CM

Figure 21. *Detail of Barrier Canyon Style solid pecked petroglyphs in the White River drainage, northwestern Colorado.*

similarities exist between anthropomorphs of probable Basketmaker origin in the Canyonlands area and Barrier Canyon Style figures.

It is also likely that the Barrier Canyon Style overlapped in time with Fremont rock art styles. Evidence for this lies in anthropomorphic figures with characteristics of both styles and similarities in techniques of manufacture (Plates 7, 24, and 30). Relationships between Barrier Canyon and Fremont rock art styles in Utah have been discussed by Gunnerson (1969) and Schaafsma (1971).

In more complex panels of Barrier Canyon Style art, arcs, wavy lines, dots, circles, possible masks or faces, and plantlike images may surround

Plate 21. *Barrier Canyon Style red rock paintings, San Rafael Swell, east central Utah. Figures with bulging eyes are typical of the San Rafael Swell area. Note the small animals surrounding and "approaching" the large anthropomorphs. The figure on the right has indentations in the chest area.*

Plate 22. *Barrier Canyon Style red rock paintings from the Book Cliffs area of east central Utah. Barrier Canyon Style figures are superimposed by a Fremont or Anasazi style petroglyph on the far right and by early historic Ute petroglyphs in the center.*

Plate 23. *Barrier Canyon Style rock paintings, Maze District, Canyonlands National Park, Utah. Elements are painted with red and tan claylike pigments.*

Plate 24. *Red and white painted anthropomorphs with characteristics of both the Barrier Canyon Style and Fremont style rock art, Nine Mile Canyon area, northeastern Utah. Figures are approximately life-size.*

anthropomorphs. Handprints (solid and patterned) also occur. Smaller, and often realistic, anthropomorphs and, more often, zoomorphs, such as birds, canines, bighorn sheep, snakes, and rabbits, are frequently shown adjacent to larger more immobile and abstract anthropomorphs. Some smaller anthropomorphs appear active and hold various items, such as "spears," snakes, and plantlike forms. Tiny anthropomorphs and quadrupeds may be shown in vertical and horizontal rows. Unrealistic, possibly mythic animals, are also depicted. Smaller figures often appear to approach and hover around the larger figures, perch on their shoulders or hands, and stand nearby. These attributes and the grouping of anthropomorphs and other images lend a sense of narrative to the rock art (Plate 21, and 25; Figures 18 and 21).

The narrative sense is heightened by "compositions" that are symbolically related by repetition and juxtaposition of elements. Many rock art sites and panels within the sites appear to have been made over a period of time by the addition of figures and groups of figures, but some panels evince consistencies of theme and execution indicative of a single artist and possibly a single time period. One complex site in the San Rafael Swell area of southeast Utah has a series of panels; each appears to have a particular theme and is placed on a different section of a small rock shelter located high on the wall of a narrow canyon. All elements are carefully painted in red and white (Plates 26, 27, and 28).

Plate 25. *Barrier Canyon Style rock art in the Moab, Utah, area, showing an unusual panel of petroglyphs that includes several active anthropomorphs. Small figures lean forward and hold sticks and appear to approach larger, more static figures.*

One panel shows what appears to be a series of ceremonial events involving anthropomorphs, plants, and snakes, one of which has horns and emits a substance from the mouth. Anthropomorphs wear headdresses, and some have masklike faces. A bird is shown with long legs and humanlike feet. An anthropomorph has rootlike extensions from the feet and holds grasslike forms. A second panel shows an immobile anthropomorph with the lower portion surrounded by a "web" formed of fine lines. Within the "web" are relatively tiny images, including a flute-player, a "snake," and quadrupeds.

Hedges (1985) describes symbolism from the above-described San Rafael site that may illustrate supernatural transformations of shamans as well as spiritual guides and alternate forms represented by anthropomorphs, zoomorphs, and plants. Certainly, much imagery (birds, snakes, horn headdresses, masklike faces, decorated bodies, spirals, and circles) and themes of the Barrier Canyon Style are consistent with shamanism (Eliade 1964; Furst 1977). Schaafsma (1971:149) observes that, with regard to the Barrier Canyon Style,

> The concept of supernatural powers attributable to anthropomorphic form does seem to be implicit. Of course, one cannot be certain whether supernatural beings or men in ceremonial attire are portrayed, but in this case, the former seems more likely. The ghostly death image, specific to this style, cannot be ignored.

Plate 26

Plate 27

Plate 28

Barrier Canyon Style red and white rock paintings, San Rafael Swell area, east central Utah. Plate 26 is an overview of a panel of small images (anthropomorph on far right is 48 centimeters in length). Plates 27 and 28 are details of the left portion of Plate 26 and include a bird with anthropomorphic legs and feet attached to the "tail" and a snakelike form with arms, hands, and headdress that appears to have a substance dripping from the mouth. Note abraded lines across figures in Plate 27.

One may speculate that certain sites with religious significance were returned to again and again, and symbolism that had been previously illustrated was "renewed" by adding new art or by changing old art according to ceremonial dictates. This is not unlike the Hopi and Zuni, who have continuously placed repetitive and juxtaposed rock art symbols at shrines in Arizona and New Mexico (Stevenson 1904; Titiev 1937; Michaelis 1981; Young 1985). Schaafsma (1980) notes that certain Barrier Canyon Style sites have shrinelike qualities.

In some instances, however, it is obvious that the use of Barrier Canyon Style art has involved more than making new imagery that is symbolically related and changing earlier imagery. Obliterating images by removing paint and portions of the rock surface and by covering them with mud has also taken place.

Alteration of Barrier Canyon Style Rock Art

Alteration of Barrier Canyon Style rock art has widespread occurrence, but some forms appear to be limited to certain regions.

Scratched, incised, and abraded areas sometimes appear superimposed upon and around painted images in a complimentary manner. For example, scratches are parallel to painted lines, and painted areas are abraded and repainted. These changes are visible at northwestern Colorado sites. At one site, thin vertical lines have been incised on the bodies of painted anthropomorphs, and horizontal bands have been abraded across the chest of one. The abraded bands have been subsequently painted blue (Plates 3 and 4). At a Cañon Pintado site, abraded areas and pinkish paint outline a red-painted anthropomorph (Plate 29). These manifestations are distinguished from the relatively common occurrence of combining petroglyphs with paintings as part of what appear to be original compositions. In such cases, petroglyphs, usually pecked, may be used to represent facial features and details of dress on anthropomorphs. This is frequently seen in Barrier Canyon Style art of the White River-Douglas Creek area and is very common in Fremont style rock art of Colorado and in neighboring parts of Utah.

Another type of alteration that is visible at widely separated sites appears to have been caused by missiles thrown at the rock art. In some instances this has resulted in the removal of sizable portions of the rock face and art. For example, sites in northwest Colorado, in Canyonlands National Park, and in Capitol Reef National Park in east central Utah have rock art and background sandstone pockmarked with numerous indentations that were probably made by sharp stone missiles hurled with considerable force (Plates 3, 4, 18, 19, and 29).

Plate 29. *Barrier Canyon Style rock paintings in red, white, and pink at site 5RB372, White River drainage, northwest Colorado. Largest anthropomorph and adjacent images have been pecked and scratched. The large figure has also been outlined by abrasion and pinkish paint.*

Generally, the indentations are small, three centimeters or less in length; concentrations of marks suggest considerable control over the process. It is possible that individuals used thrust spears or atlatls with darts and stone projectile points to mark the rock art and background rock.* Some Colorado and Utah sites are significantly pockmarked with indentations as well as altered in other ways.

Large depressions appear in the bodies of figures at Utah sites such as the Bird Site (Harvest Scene) in the Maze District of Canyonlands National Park and at the Head of Sinbad on the San Rafael Swell (Plate 21).

A somewhat related form of change that also appears to have wide distribution is the removal of paint by pecking and abrading. In some cases, painted portions of anthropomorphs and zoomorphs have been pecked and abraded away. This is noticeable at type-sites in Canyonlands National Park, in the San Rafael Swell area, and at White River–Douglas Creek sites in northwestern Colorado. For example, tiny figures at the Great Gallery site have been precisely pecked, and abraded lines cross the bodies of figures shown in Plates 26 through 28. A Cañon Pintado site exhibits the partially pecked away head and hand of a red-painted anthropomorph and a snake shown above (Plate 29).

A well-preserved site in the White River–Douglas Creek area exhibits a near life-size Barrier Canyon Style anthropomorph painted in dark red that is superimposed by a red, yellow, and orange Fremont style figure. Another smaller Barrier Canyon Style figure painted bright red is on a facing rock face. The painted facial area and headdress of the larger Barrier Canyon Style figure and the face of the other have been removed by precise pecking. Pecked and incised lines appear in the body of the larger figure.

Some Barrier Canyon Style figures have been covered by mud. Examples of this type of alteration are found in the Book Cliffs of northwest Colorado and in neighboring Utah as far west as the San Rafael Swell. In some instances, individual painted elements have been mudded over; in other cases, entire panel surfaces appear to have been covered with mud. However, it is not always clear that Barrier Canyon Style art is covered. New images have been placed over mud in a few instances, and it is difficult to clearly distinguish the various layers and styles occurring on each. At least five White River–Douglas Creek sites with Barrier Canyon Style art have mudded-over rock art. At four sites, it is apparent that Barrier Canyon Style art has been mudded over.

At one site, a Barrier Canyon Style figure is mudded, and a Fremont style figure is on a surface that appears to have been mudded. Other examples of mudded rock art in nearby Utah show figures similar to Fremont and Barrier Canyon Style that have been mudded and painted on mudded surfaces (Plate 30).

Much work remains to be done to accurately document and analyze changes to Barrier Canyon Style rock art before functions and meanings can be meaningfully interpreted. A few explanations are possible, however. One is that Barrier Canyon Style art may have been symbolically renewed and ceremonially changed over time by the addition of pecked, scratched, abraded, and painted design elements. The throwing of missiles may also indicate ceremonial activities in which rock art symbolism was "attacked," perhaps to evoke sympathetic magic or dramatize events, real or mythological. The removal of parts of images may also have been ceremonial erasure or obliteration of symbolism. Mudding-over of designs may be related to concealment of symbolism. For example, esoteric kiva wall art of the Pueblos is covered with plaster at the end of ceremonies and painted anew as each ceremony requires (Smith 1952).

The possibility that some alterations to Barrier Canyon Style rock art may have been made by groups other than the original artists and even by people of a different culture cannot be overlooked. In northwest Colorado, where evidence indicates that the Fremont developed

Plate 30. *Mudded over Barrier Canyon Style red rock paintings and paintings that appear to have been painted over mudded rock surfaces. Panel occurs in the Book Cliffs area of east central Utah.*

directly from an Archaic base, symbols of the earlier culture may have been altered to meet the needs of the new.

Uncompahgre Style Rock Art

?1000 B.C. to A.D. 1000

Rock art, petroglyphs, and a few rock paintings associated with the Uncompahgre Complex of western Colorado have been described by Wormington and Lister (1956), Buckles (1971), and Cole (1987). Rock art sites are located in mountain valleys and in more arid canyons of the Uncompahgre Plateau, Grand Mesa, Battlement Mesa, and the La Sal Mountains. Sites occur in drainages of the Gunnison, Uncompahgre, Dolores, Little Dolores, and Colorado rivers in west central Colorado and east central Utah.

The limited geographic distribution of the rock art and site locations support the Black (1986) proposal that the Uncompahgre Complex was part of an Archaic Mountain Tradition that can be distinguished from neighboring Desert and Plains cultures. Additional support for this theory comes from the nature of the rock art itself, which is clearly different from representational rock art styles such as the Barrier Canyon Style and the Glen Canyon Style 5 and styles of the

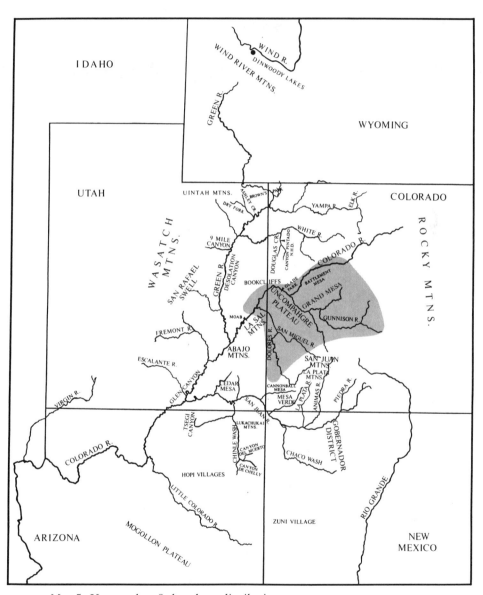

Map 5. *Uncompahgre Style rock art distribution.*

Anasazi and Fremont found in neighboring areas of the Colorado Plateau.

To date, Buckles (1971) has made the most detailed stylistic analysis of prehistoric Uncompahgre Complex rock art. Buckles limits his analysis to the formal attributes and thematic qualities of anthropomorphs and zoomorphs, although he notes the existence of other possible diagnostic imagery, including paw prints, other animal tracks, and "tool" grooves. (These grooves were discussed above as part of an abstract rock art tradition also associated with the Uncompahgre Complex.)

Buckles describes a relative chronology for the rock art by identifying three nonhistoric styles that he proposes represent a continuous graphic development consistent with the continuous cultural pattern of the Uncompahgre Complex.

Specifically, Uncompahgre Styles 3, 2, and 1 are viewed as a regional rock art tradition, representative of a visible continuum of forms, themes, and physical settings utilized by Archaic participants in the Uncompahgre Complex for more than a thousand years. The style sequence is viewed by Buckles as an evolution of formal attributes from realistic to linear and abstract. Themes of the styles are hunting, warfare, societal practices, and religion. An emphasis on individual rather than group activities is proposed for Style 1 (the latest) and, to some extent, for Style 2.

Style 3, the earliest, is proposed to date from the time of the early development of the Anasazi and Fremont (Buckles 1971:1118), approximately A.D. 1 to 700. Styles 2 and 1 are proposed to have directly followed Style 3 and to have continued until just before the historic period. Buckles observes that there is a correlation between linear forms of Style 1 and early historic Ute rock art. In fact, Style 1 may include imagery made by the Utes that does not show historically identifiable subject matter, such as horses and tipis.

Buckles considers Style 2 a transitional style between the more realistic Style 3 and the linear and abstracted Style 1. More overlaps are seen to exist between Style 2 and Style 1 than between Style 3 and Style 2.

Other researchers (Scott 1981; McKern 1978; Cole 1987) have also noted overlaps between the styles, including those between Style 3 and Style 2. Cole (1987) has studied Buckles's styles and concludes that overlaps between the three styles indicate greater contemporaneity and integration of rock art forms and themes than originally proposed and raise doubts as to the existence of a distinct style sequence, something that Buckles (1971) observes is possible. Rather than view the stylistic components of Uncompahgre Complex rock art as part of a tradition that moves from realism to abstraction over time, the various forms and themes may be seen as part of a long-lived graphic system comparable to the Barrier Canyon Style. Differences in rock art functions, cultural relationships, and population distributions over time,

Figure 22

Figure 23

Panels of Uncompahgre Style petroglyphs showing anthropomorphs and quadrupeds, including a bear with paw-print-like paws at site 5ME228, near the Gunnison River, west central Colorado. All elements are solid pecked.

rather than evolution of style, may account for variations. An inclusive rock art style, the Uncompahgre Style will be used in this study. This single category simplifies the rock art description and does not challenge the descriptive interpretations and variations offered by Buckles (1971) nor the proposal that Uncompahgre Complex rock art is generally indicative of cultural continuity. Dates proposed for the Uncompahgre Style range from approximately 1000 B.C. to A.D. 1000. Early dates for the style are based on early dates for the Uncompahgre Complex (Wormington and Lister 1956; Buckles 1971) and for incised or grooved abstract rock art associated with the Uncompahgre Complex (discussed previously). Late dates for the style are based on the presence of rock art traits associated with Fremont and Anasazi styles that are suggestive of interaction between the various groups prior to A.D. 1000.

Uncompahgre Style rock art may have endured longer than the Glen Canyon Style 5 and Barrier Canyon Style and may have coexisted with later Anasazi and Fremont styles of rock art. It is possible that abstract rock art continued to be made as long as the Uncompahgre Style rock art, because both are seemingly associated with the Uncompahgre Complex.

Historic Ute rock art, dated after A.D. 1600, and examined in this study, is distinct from the Uncompahgre Style. Protohistoric Ute rock art dated after A.D. 1150–1300, if present in the area, has not been distinguished from Uncompahgre Style rock art. However, Uncompahgre Style art is distinguished from what is thought to be historic Ute in origin (with and without historic subject matter).

Petroglyphs of the Uncompahgre Style are primarily pecked (solid and stipple), but drilled holes, cupules, and ground and incised forms also occur. The latter are sometimes incorporated into otherwise pecked images. Incised forms are similar to abstract groove art, discussed earlier, and may be used to indicate appendages such as fingers. As noted above, rock paintings are rare in the Uncompahgre Style. Sites examined for this study include twenty-six petroglyph sites and three painted sites. However, a number of rock paintings may have been lost as a result of weathering.

A distinctive characteristic of Uncompahgre Style rock art is the presence of images and entire panels that are technically complex. It is not known how much time or how many artists were involved in the making of the art, but patination levels and the nature of the subjects indicate that the various techniques are roughly contemporaneous. On a darkly patinated cliff in Glade Park on the northern end of the Uncompahgre Plateau, petroglyphs include solid pecked anthropomorphs with arms upraised that have incised (groove) fingers and toes.

Figure 24

*Details of Uncompahgre Style pet-
roglyphs showing anthropomorphs
and quadrupeds (one with tall
branching antlers) at site 5ME465,
in the Little Dolores and Colorado
River drainage, west central Colorado. Abstract petroglyphs and Fremont style anthropomorphs also occur. In Figure 24, elements are
solid pecked, stipple pecked, drilled,
and incised. Cupules are indicated
by circled crosses and drilled depressions by larger solid dots. In Figure
25, elements are solid pecked and
incised. Uncompahgre Style anthropomorph is shown in outline;
Fremont style anthropomorphs are
stippled. Solid abstract images
superimpose the Uncompahgre Style,
and Fremont style figures superimpose abstract forms.*

Figure 25

One figure stands before a quadruped, which is outlined by stipple-pecking and drilled and pecked holes, and has incisions in the body, solid pecked legs, and hooves formed by cupules. A smaller solid-pecked quadruped stands beneath the larger animal. Other pecked and incised elements surround these figures (Figures 24 and 25).

Petroglyphs at a rock shelter site in nearby Little Park show a bear paw print composed of a smooth ground surface with three horizontal grooves and four cupules indicating the toe imprints. Associated elements are solid pecked. At a second rock shelter location within a narrow canyon, petroglyphs include a combination of solid pecked, stipple-pecked, incised, and cupule forms with red ochre paint representing anthropomorphs, quadrupeds, snakes, and lines. Painted lines superimpose solid pecked forms (Figures 26 and 27).

Petroglyphs along the lower Dolores River show relatively large solid pecked bears with cupules indicating toe imprints. Nearby elements are solid pecked and incised and include a pecked "hummingbird" with incised wings (Figures 28 and 29).

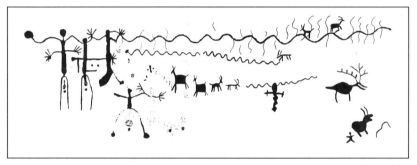

Figure 26

Figure 27

Left and right portions of a panel of Uncompahgre Style petroglyphs (solid and stipple pecked) and rock paintings at site 5ME4997, in the lower Gunnison River drainage, west central Colorado. Adapted from a field sketch by Glenn E. Stone.

Figure 28

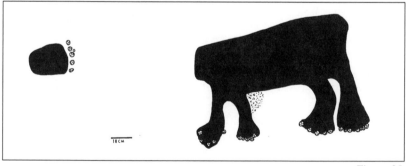

Figure 29

Details of Uncompahgre Style petroglyphs showing paw prints, a possible hummingbird, quadrupeds including probable bears, and anthropomorphs at site 5MN1186, near the lower Dolores River, west central Colorado. Anthropomorphs with side "hair-bobs" are atypical and probably reflect influences from the Anasazi or Fremont. Abstract petroglyphs also occur. Uncompahgre Style petroglyphs are solid pecked and incised with cupules indicated by crossed circles. Stippled areas are indistinct. Outlined forms are based on a sketch by Harley Armstrong.

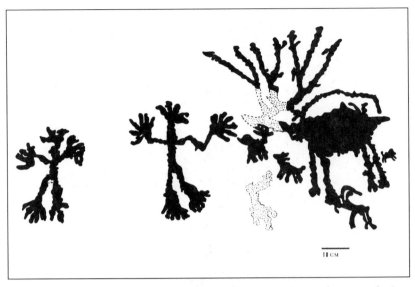

Figure 30. *Details of Uncompahgre Style petroglyphs showing anthropomorphs (two with headdresses and possible masks) and quadrupeds (one with tall branching antlers) at site 5DT355, near the north fork of the Gunnison River, west central Colorado. All elements are solid pecked; stippled areas are indistinct.*

    Subject matter and formal and thematic attributes of the Uncompahgre Style differ sharply from representational rock art styles examined above. The Uncompahgre Style is clearly not part of the anthropomorphic tradition prevalent in Colorado Plateau rock art during the Archaic and later Anasazi and Fremont periods. Anthropomorphs are not featured subjects of the Uncompahgre Style, and they are rarely heroic and supernatural in appearance. A few figures with headdresses and figures exhibited with animals, such as deer or elk and bears, appear to have heroic and supernatural qualities. Overall, the decorative details and emphasis placed on anthropomorphs in the Glen Canyon Style 5, Barrier Canyon Style, and later Colorado Plateau rock art styles are missing in the Uncompahgre Style.

    Anthropomorphs generally appear as sticklike figures and as somewhat more rectangular elongated forms. Heads are generally rounded, and arms often extend stiffly out to the sides or raised above the head. Large hands and feet with spread fingers and toes are shown. Some anthropomorphs are more realistic, and hold stick or spearlike items (Figure 32). Details such as headdresses, hair-bobs, and possible masks are exhibited on a few figures. Facial features and interior body decorations are generally not shown. Phallic figures are common in Uncompahgre Style art, and possible vulvas are indicated (Figures 23 and 26).

Plate 31. *Petroglyphs of the Uncompahgre Style showing paw prints, cloven hoof tracks, rows of quadrupeds with tall branching antlers, and abstract images. Small anthropomorph with headdress at the top is modern. Panel occurs at site 5MN27, Uncompahgre River drainage, west central Colorado, and is approximately 1.8 meters in length.*

Plate 32. *Uncompahgre Style petroglyphs with possible Ute and modern additions at site 5ME159, lower Gunnison River drainage, west central Colorado. Elements include paw prints, a bear and other quadrupeds, anthropomorphs, and abstract images. Bear image is approximately 40 centimeters in length.*

Figure 31. Uncompahgre Style solid pecked petroglyphs showing a tall anthropomorph with a ladderlike body with smaller quadrupeds and other elements at site 5ME5105, in the Gunnison River drainage, west central Colorado.

Figure 32. Uncompahgre Style solid pecked petroglyphs at site 5MN5, in the Uncompahgre River drainage, west central Colorado. The bighorn sheep figure is superimposed by the spearlike image.

Plate 33. *Detail of a panel of Uncompahgre Style petroglyphs at site 5ME167, lower Dolores River area, west central Colorado. Paw print on far right is approximately 25 centimeters in length.*

Figure 33. *Detail of Uncompahgre Style petroglyphs (pecked and incised) at site 5ME328, in the drainage of the Gunnison River, west central Colorado.*

A relatively few anthropomorphs exhibit broad shoulders and tapered lower bodies with arms hanging, as well as possible side hair bobs and earrings, traits that are more typical of neighboring Anasazi and Fremont rock art styles. These traits and the presence of stylized bear paw prints in Anasazi and Fremont rock art styles are indicative of possible relationships between the various cultural groups. Anthropomorphs are most often shown in association with zoomorphs and abstract elements. Zoomorphs, snakes, and quadrupeds such as deer, elk, bear, bighorn sheep, and canines are common in the Uncompahgre Style. The number of animals in a single panel may be as few as two or more than thirty. Quadrupeds range from rectangular full-bodied forms (sometimes bulbous) to elongated linear forms. Details such as antlers, ears, tails, and cloven hooves are represented. Deer and elk are commonly shown with elaborate and oversize antlers that are tall and branching. A number of aberrant animal forms occur in Uncompahgre Style rock art; these show misshapen quadrupeds, quadrupeds without heads, and quadrupeds with antlers projecting out of the foreheads (Plates 31 and 32; Figures 28, 29, and 30).

Deer or elk and other quadrupeds are often exhibited in groups and in rows, shown as if being driven or migrating and as if clustered together. Particularly clear examples of this are seen at sites on the eastern slope of the Uncompahgre Plateau and in the Colorado River drainage near Battlement Mesa.

Bear representations, some quite elaborate, occur at sites on the eastern slope of the Uncompahgre Plateau and along the lower Dolores River. Large "headless" bears occur at a lower Dolores River site (Figures 28 and 29). The paws of bears are occasionally signified by paw print images (Figures 23, 28, and 29; Plate 33). Individual bear paw print petroglyphs are also exhibited and are very common throughout west central Colorado (Plates 31, 32, and 33; Figure 29). These petroglyph images are probably the most distinctive in the area and have been described in detail by Huscher and Huscher (1940). Both front and rear bear paw prints appear to have been depicted and are shown as solid footlike forms and as banded stylized forms with rounded toes and elongated claws. Similar bear paw prints are also associated with abstract style rock art in west central Colorado, and indicate a link between the people who made the two art styles.

A variety of other prints or tracks are shown in the Uncompahgre Style. These include other paw prints, possible bird tracks, and ungulate hoof prints (possibly deer, elk, and bison) (Plate 31).

A few birds are depicted in Uncompahgre Style art and include representations of a wading bird shown at a site in the Gunnison River drainage and a carefully detailed "hummingbird" along the lower

Dolores River. The hummingbird "hovers" above an anthropomorph wearing a headdress and a large bearlike image. Additional anthropomorphs, a paw print, and various pecked lines and incised abstract images are nearby (Figure 28).

Hunting themes are present in Uncompahgre Style art and are suggested by anthropomorphs in juxtaposition with game animals. Some anthropomorphs hold and appear to be throwing sticklike objects, and doglike images appear with game animals in some panels. Sites with this imagery are found on the eastern slope of the Uncompahgre Plateau and in the Grand Mesa and Battlement Mesa areas.

Scenes of anthropomorphs with raised arms standing before and near quadrupeds, such as deer, elk, bear, and snakes, are common at sites throughout west central Colorado and may be symbolic of shamanism and hunting rituals. Some of these anthropomorphs have distinguishing characteristics, such as headdresses, and the subject matter suggests that they represent individuals with special powers, such as shamans. Within this context, the animals may represent animals of the hunt and spiritual helpers (Figures 22, 23, 24, 25, 26, 27, 30, and 31).

In one instance, a tall stick-figure with clawlike feet towers above a cluster of quadrupeds and other figures that are pecked on a tall boulder in a canyon on the Uncompahgre Plateau. The legs of the anthropomorph are superimposed by some quadrupeds and abstract linear images. Short horizontal lines cross the elongated body of the anthropomorph (Figure 31).

Smith and Long (1980) have interpreted a similarly marked anthropomorph at an east central Utah site as symbolic of the journey of a shaman's soul to the spirit world. The ladder or notched pillar image is closely aligned to the World Tree symbol in shamanistic ritual, and both are used to symbolize the supernatural power of a shaman to experience the various branches or levels of the cosmos (Eliade 1964).

Another Uncompahgre Plateau site shows three anthropomorphs standing before and linked with a two-headed snake that is more than eight meters in length. A second smaller snake is beneath the large one and "approaches" the anthropomorphs. An adjacent figure holds antlerlike devices and is "approached" by two quadrupeds (Figures 26 and 27).

At a Glade Park site discussed previously, an anthropomorph with upraised arms stands before three quadrupeds and a snake. One quadruped is a relatively large and technically complex deer or elk. A smaller animal between the legs of the deer or elk appears to be a canine or feline that emits something from the mouth (Figure 24).

Additional elements in Uncompahgre Style rock art are linear abstracts. In general, these take the forms of wavy and straight lines, "squiggle mazes," T-shape images, "one-pole ladders" and branchlike forms, "stars," "rainbows" or concentric arcs, and concentric circles. Lines are frequently attached to or superimpose one or more representational elements and other abstract elements, thereby relating various symbols on a panel. These "connecting" lines give a narrative quality to some rock art panels (Plates 31, 32, and 33; Figures 25 and 28).

Interior Line Style

Pre-A.D. 1 to 1000

The Interior Line Style was identified by Gebhard and Cahn (1950) and Gebhard (1969) based on studies of petroglyphs located in Dinwoody Canyon near upper Dinwoody Lake in the Wind River Mountains and elsewhere in western Wyoming (Plates 34, 35, and 36). Most of the rock art sites occur north and east of the study area, within the northwestern Plains cultural area (Jennings 1978). However, the style boundaries extend into Utah and Colorado, where they overlap with rock art styles of the Colorado Plateau. In the southern area, the style is found in the drainages of the Green, Yampa, and White rivers (Plates 37, 38, and 39; Figures 34, 35, 36, and 37).

Gebhard (1969) reports that sites with Interior Line style petroglyphs are located in the Wind River Mountains, the Boysen Basin,

Plate 34. *Detail of Interior Line Style petroglyphs at upper Dinwoody Lake, Wind River Mountains, western Wyoming. Elements are pecked in outline and as solid forms. This site features a number of birdlike forms. Anthropomorphs are approximately one meter in length.*

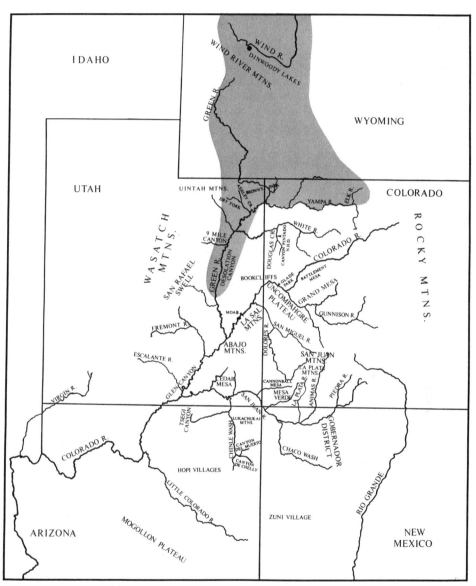

Map 6. *Interior Line Style rock art distribution within the study area. Examples in the upper Green River drainage of Utah share characteristics of the Glen Canyon Style 5.*

Plate 35   Plate 36

Details of Interior Line Style petroglyphs at Legend Rock (site 48HO4), Bighorn Basin, west central Wyoming. Smaller figures shown in Plate 36 are similar to those at Utah and Colorado sites. Radiocarbon dates from this site suggest that the style dates 1,900 to 2,000 years ago (Walker and Francis 1989). Larger anthropomorphs are approximately one meter in length. Photographs by Glenn E. Stone.

and the Big Horn Basin in western Wyoming. He identifies similar rock art in northwestern Utah and notes that the style may extend southward into Utah and Colorado. Gebhard (1969:22) proposes that the Interior Line Style dates prior to A.D. 1800, but may be no earlier than A.D. 1650, based on the appearance and the nature of the rock on which the petroglyphs are made. No historic subject matter, such as horses, is observed to be associated with the style. More recently, Gebhard (1972) gives a date of approximately A.D. 1500 for Interior Line Style petroglyphs. Relationships between the Interior Line Style and Fremont rock art are observed by Gebhard (1969:22), who argues that the style "grew out of the Fremont and later provided several important elements for late Plains art." Schaafsma (1971) also notes associations between the Interior Line Style and Fremont rock art, particularly with regard to the depiction of owl-like imagery.

This study proposes that the Interior Line Style dates from pre-A.D. 1 to 1000. This chronology differs substantially from that of Gebhard (1969, 1972) and is based on style comparisons, rock art appear-

Plate 37. *Interior Line Style petroglyphs at site 42DA14, in the Green River drainage, northeastern Utah. Elements are shown in outline and as solid forms. Small anthropomorph with headdress in the center is very similar to Barrier Canyon Style forms, and small figure in upper left resembles Fremont style forms.*

Plate 38. *Details of Interior Line Style outline and solid petroglyphs at Flat Canyon, Green River drainage, northeastern Utah. Quadrupeds with lines in the body resemble animal forms of the Glen Canyon Style 5. Larger anthropomorphs are approximately 50 centimeters in length.*

Plate 39. *Interior Line Style red painted anthropomorph, Douglas Creek–Cañon Pintado area, northwestern Colorado. The body of the figure is marked with vertical red lines that are barely visible in the photograph. Figure is approximately 65 centimeters in length.*

ances, and archaeological investigations in the Big Horn Basin of Wyoming. The Interior Line Style has obvious relationships with Archaic rock art styles of the Colorado Plateau, including the Glen Canyon Style 5 and the Barrier Canyon Style. It also has similarities to Fremont rock art. This information suggests that a chronology for the Interior Line Style generally corresponds to those of related styles. The early date proposed for the Interior Line Style, pre-A.D. 1, reflects those proposed for the Glen Canyon Style 5 and Barrier Canyon Style, and the late date, A.D. 1000, reflects the end of the major Fremont occupation of Dinosaur National Monument (Truesdale, personal correspondence) in northeast Utah and northwest Colorado.

Personal observations of Interior Line Style rock art at Wyoming, Utah, and Colorado sites do not agree with those of Gebhard (1969) with regard to the recent appearance of petroglyphs and fragility of rock surfaces. Extensive lichen growth was observed on petroglyphs, and some were darkly patinated; rock surfaces were generally well preserved. These factors probably indicate antiquity.

The beginning date of pre-A.D. 1 proposed for the Interior Line Style is supported by recent excavations at the Legend Rock petroglyph site (48H04) in the Big Horn Basin of Wyoming (Plates 35 and 36). A partially buried petroglyph of an anthropomorph in the Interior Line Style was uncovered, and levels of soil that buried the figure were dated. Three charcoal samples provided radiocarbon dates, and the investigators estimate that the petroglyph is between 1,900 and 2,000 years old (Walker and Francis 1989). Personal observations at the Legend Rock site suggest that the dated petroglyph is more recent than other elements at the site, and the style may have beginnings well before A.D. 1.

The Interior Line Style includes petroglyphs, pecked and incised, as well as red rock paintings. The original description by Gebhard and Cahn (1950) and Gebhard (1969) involved pecked petroglyphs. The Interior Line Style also includes anthropomorphs, zoomorphs, dot patterns, and straight and wavy lines; anthropomorphs are clearly featured. In a discussion of the style, Gebhard and Cahn (1950:225) observe that "the human figure has emerged as the center of attention."

In a manner typical of Colorado Plateau rock art styles, Interior Line Style panels frequently exhibit horizontal rows of static anthropomorphs that are elaborately decorated and supernatural in appearance. The figures range in size from approximately fifteen centimeters to two meters in length (Gebhard 1969). In some instances, anthropomorphs are shown lying horizontally, and upright figures may superimpose them. Superimpositions and crowding of figures within a panel are common. Gebhard (1969:14) views some superimpositions as design compositions and sees no chronological distinctions between various forms involved. This type of superimposition (composite forms) is discussed below.

Bodies are roughly rectangular in shape, and heads are relatively large, rounded, and rectangular in shape, and generally sit directly on the shoulders. Stick-figure bodies also occur. A majority of anthropomorphs appear in outline with interior body decorations. The remainder are solid forms. Interior body decorations commonly include geometric designs formed by lines, circles, and dots, and representational figures such as small anthropomorphs, footprints or paw prints, and possible bird tracks. On some figures, "breast plates" are indicated by chevrons and lines; and sashes, belts, pouches, and fringe may be shown. Generally, however, interior and exterior designs are abstract and are not recognizable as any particular type of dress or body decoration. Some figures are phallic, and circular breastlike designs are shown on some figures, perhaps indicative of females. Dots and lines (arcs) may surround heads and bodies of anthropomorphs, and lines extend from various parts of the figures. Dots and linear arcs also surround the heads of Glen Canyon Style 5 and Barrier Canyon Style figures. Interior line, dot, and representational decorations are also typical of these styles.

Facial features, eyes and mouths, are usually present; anthropomorphs may be shown with "bangs." Figures frequently have fringed "wings" and appear owl-like, especially those with large round eyes. Horned, fringed, and caplike headdresses are shown as well as headdresses (or auras) formed by radiating lines. Arms and legs are generally diminutive and may be missing. Arms are shown straight out to the side and raised at the elbow. Hands often appear with splayed fingers, and feet show splayed toes.

In some instances, Interior Line Style figures are quite complex, with parallel dots and lines surrounding and following the contours of bodies. These figures may be superimposed by or superimpose other elements. In addition, lines may attach anthropomorphs to other elements. Hendry (1983) discusses these complex images in Wyoming rock art as Composite Style composition, a technique used by artists to blend concepts by the ordering and placement of symbols. For example, a historic Kiowa painting of Peyote Woman uses similar symbolic construction. While this approach presumes that each composite design was made by a single artist, it is difficult to demonstrate that the work of a single artist or time period is involved. However, through time, one or more artists may have made use of rock art symbolism within a style context to express shared or divergent concepts resulting in the composite elements.

Zoomorphs are generally smaller than anthropomorphs and are most often shown in outline (some with interior decoration), although solid forms exist. Zoomorphs include quadrupeds, such as canines, deer, bear, and buffalo, as well as birds and insectlike images. Some quadrupeds are shown in outline with interior horizontal lines that are similar to quadrupeds of the Glen Canyon Style 5, although relatively small heads with large bodies typical of the Style 5 are not apparent. Animal imagery occurs near anthropomorphs and may be attached as well as shown above heads and arms, "approaching" the anthropomorphs in a manner typical of the Barrier Canyon Style. Smaller anthropomorphs, solid and outline forms, also appear attached to larger figures.

To the south of the main Interior Line Style area, petroglyphs are located at a southwest Wyoming site (Day and Dibble 1963) and at two northeastern Utah sites, one in the Dry Fork Valley north of Vernal (Gebhard 1969: Pl. 68) and one near Manila on the Green River (Plate 37). The Wyoming site exhibits solid-pecked realistic anthropomorphs with outline trapezoidal forms that have interior decorations (Figure 34). Utah sites show outline and solid figures with arms out to the side. At the Manila site, a relatively small anthropomorphic figure with a horned headdress is similar to figures of the Barrier Canyon Style. A Fremont-style figure also occurs and appears to be more recent.

Additional examples of Interior Line Style petroglyphs are located farther south in Utah, in Desolation Canyon of the Green River. These petroglyphs include outline and solid anthropomorphs with arms out

Figure 34. *Interior Line Style petroglyphs at site 48SW88, in the Green River drainage, southwestern Wyoming. Redrawn from Day and Dibble (1963:Fig. 3).*

to the side, outline and solid pecked quadrupeds, rows of dots, abstract geometric images, and paw prints (Plate 38). Some anthropomorphs have headdresses and dots and arcs around the heads. Two figures have masklike faces, and one figure wears a necklace. This site clearly blends traits of the Interior Line Style with those of various Colorado Plateau styles. This is most obvious in the presentation of anthropomorphs with small heads and long necks that wear headdresses or have arcs and dots around the heads and quadrupeds with interior body lines. Such figures are more typical of Colorado Plateau styles than of the Interior Line Style in Wyoming.

Three sites in northwestern Colorado have Interior Line Style rock art. An additional site in west central Colorado exhibits figures that are related to the Interior Line Style but are less typical than the northwest Colorado sites. Two northwestern sites are in the drainage of the Yampa River; one of these sites is located at the Sand Rocks near Craig, Colorado (Figures 35 and 36), and the second site is at Indian Rocks on the Elk River (Figure 37). A third site is in the White River drainage and is located along Douglas Creek in Cañon Pintado National Historic District (Plate 39). These sites are discussed below, followed by a discussion of possibly related rock art in west central Colorado.

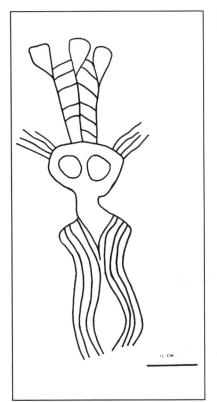

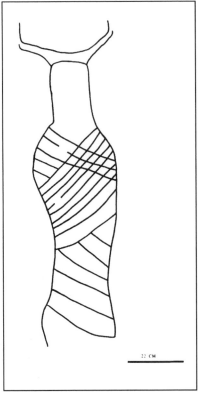

Figure 35   Figure 36

Interior Line Style incised petroglyphs at Sand Rocks site in the Yampa River drainage, northwestern Colorado.

The Sand Rocks sit above the Yampa River valley and form a prominent rock outcrop that exhibits a variety of prehistoric and historic rock art styles. Two incised Interior Line Style anthropomorphs are exhibited at the Sand Rocks (Figures 35 and 36). One figure has a bottle-shaped body and large round eyes, and wears an elaborate headdress formed of radiating lines and flowerlike images. A second figure is somewhat more abstract. No facial features are shown, although an earlike headdress is present. This figure is larger than the first and is also a bottle shape. Interior body decoration makes it appear as if the figure were "wrapped." Hendry (1983) shows a similarly "wrapped" incised figure from Wyoming.

At Indian Rocks, elements are painted on the ceiling and walls of a small rock shelter surrounded by groves of aspen and oak (Figure 37). The site is situated on a mountain ridge above the Elk River valley. The

Figure 37. *Red Interior Line Style rock paintings at Indian Rocks site, Routt County, northwestern Colorado. Stippled area is indistinct.*

largest figure is a red-painted anthropomorph with a rounded head, round eyes, and a tapered body. The arms are out to the side, and the figure has a "breast plate." The head and body of the figure are shown in outline with interior red vertical stripes. Another solid-red figure has a rectangular head and tapered body and also shows a "breast plate." This figure also has arms out to the side. A third figure is painted red and yellow and has broad shoulders and a tapered body. This figure (not pictured) resembles forms of the Barrier Canyon Style. Additional elements present at the site include a partial handprint and a Y-shape image that are painted red.

Interior Line Style red rock paintings in Cañon Pintado are similar to those at Indian Rocks and are located in a small rock shelter along Douglas Creek (Plate 39). One anthropomorph has a solid head, striped and outlined body, and "breast plate," and wears a "fringed ear" headdress. A second smaller figure (not pictured) is painted solid red and wears a two-horn headdress and has a striped "breast plate." Both figures have arms out to the side, and a quadruped is depicted adjacent to the smaller figure.

Two pecked anthropomorphs at a site in the Gunnison River drainage of west central Colorado resemble Interior Line Style figures (Figure 38). These figures occur at the head of a small narrow alcove in a sandstone cliff. The site was excavated and reported by Buckles (1971) and exhibits a number of panels of petroglyphs that are herein classified as part of the abstract petroglyph tradition and the Uncompahgre Style. The subject anthropomorphs are not consistent with either style expression. One figure is shown in outline with a rounded head, eyes, and a mouth. No legs are depicted, but short arms and hands with spread fingers are shown. The second figure is less realistic

Figure 38. *Detail of anthropomorphs, paw prints, and cloven hoof tracks at site 5ME1, Gunnison River drainage, west central Colorado. Anthropomorphs are similar to those of the Interior Line Style. Elements are solid and stipple pecked.*

and more than twice as large. This figure is also shown in outline with eyes and a possible mouth, but the figure appears as if wearing a shroud with no head and body definition.

In a discussion of Uncompahgre Style 2 rock art, Buckles (1971: 1110–1111) analyzes the two anthropomorphs and the site:

> Two figures . . . are different from the other rock art of the style by being predominantly outline figures and having facial features. . . . The site with which they occur appears to me to have been a rock art shrine with evidence of revisitation [indicated] by the repetitive bear tracks and other art forms. . . . The only cultural evidences were indeterminant stones used for pecking and incising, some bones, two calcite crystals, and a single very badly fractured human tooth. It was speculated that this atypical assemblage may have been related to rituals. The human figures and adjacent art in the apex of the cleft are probably fairly recent considering the lack of accumulation of fill after their manufacture.

Some differences between examples of Interior Line Style rock art in Wyoming and those in Utah and Colorado are noted. The more southern examples do not include the "winged," birdlike representations common at Wyoming sites. Also, the majority of anthropomorphs at Utah sites do not have large heads that sit directly on the shoulders. Rather, several figures have relatively small rounded heads and long necks; one figure has a spiral "head." Generally, the Utah figures appear more realistic and more clearly anthropomorphic. In Colorado, such distinctions are less obvious. At all locations, however, relationships with rock art styles of the Colorado Plateau, such as the Glen Canyon Style 5, Barrier Canyon Style, and Fremont styles, are obvious. This includes not only the sharing of anthropomorphic themes but the representation of specific figure types. This is indicative of relationships over time between cultures living in neighboring but diverse geographic regions characterized by deserts, mountains, and river valleys.

Relationships between Fremont rock art and the Interior Line Style proposed by Gebhard (1969), Schaafsma (1971), and others are based on both general and specific characteristics. Similar to Interior Line Style figures, Fremont style anthropomorphs are shown in outline and as solid forms, with facial features and horn headdresses, and often with heads directly on the shoulders. Fremont figures have "breast plates," belts, sashes, pouches, and interior and exterior dot and line decorations. The Fremont depicted realistic owls and owl-like personages in rock art. Such information suggests that the two styles overlapped in time, and that the Fremont interacted with hunting and gathering people living to the north.

Certain subject matter and themes of the Interior Line Style suggest that it, like the Glen Canyon Style 5 and Barrier Canyon Style, is symbolic of shamanistic practices. Wellmann (1979:134) notes that the part-human and part-birdlike figures in combination with headdresses and skeletonlike bodies fit the shamanic tradition. As noted previously, Shimkin (1986:325) reports that the historic Wind River Shoshoni interpret Dinwoody Lake art as representative of powerful Water Ghost Beings and Rock Ghost Beings. The location is viewed as sacred, and it and other rock art sites known as places of power (*poha*) have been used by shamans for power quests achieved through visions:

> A successful quest is expressed by a vision in which the *poha* appears, often transforming itself from one form to another, and bestows skills or protections, fetishes to call forth the power, a song, and individual taboos. The *poha* often resides within the shaman and may be coughed out, then transferred to another by blowing. Sometimes a person's *poha* departs, perhaps because of a breach of taboo. This is deadly; a shaman must come to track the *poha*, capture it, and then blow it back into the sufferer lest he die.

It is not clear that Wind River Shoshoni are associated with the creation of Dinwoody Lake petroglyphs. Interior Line Style art appears to predate the arrival of the Shoshoni in the Wind River mountains. Shoshoni informants have denied knowledge of the origins of Dinwoody rock art and have attributed it to Blackfoot people (Mallery 1893:130; Hebard 1930). Nevertheless, the Shoshoni interpret the rock art and obviously recognize power in certain of the images and in places where the art occurs. To that extent the style, despite its antiquity, retains viable symbolism that is incorporated into the traditions and ceremonies of historic peoples.

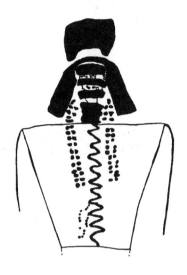

ANASAZI
ROCK ART

R ock art associated with the Anasazi cultural tradition occurs in two general locations within the study area. One is the San Juan River drainage of the Four Corners region, and the other is the Canyonlands area of east central Utah and west central Colorado, to the north. While both locations are included in the greater San Juan Anasazi culture area, significant distinctions exist between the two, and the rock art of each area will be discussed separately.

SAN JUAN RIVER ANASAZI

Anasazi culture and rock art of the San Juan River drainage have been extensively researched and described in the literature (Grant 1978, Schaafsma 1980, Cordell 1984, and others). The long continuous occupation of the region by the Anasazi (more than thirteen hundred years) has provided a considerable amount of cultural materials and information. This information has been used to date rock art styles and to interpret functions and meanings of Anasazi symbolism from the Basketmaker period to the late Pueblo III period when the study area was abandoned.

Basketmaker II and III

? 100 B.C. to A.D. 750

In the Colorado Plateau anthropomorphic tradition, distinctive rock art, petroglyphs and rock paintings, are attributed to Basketmaker II and III peoples living in the Four Corners region of Colorado, New Mexico, Utah, and Arizona. Basketmaker rock art is located throughout the San Juan River drainage and is found in the Glen Canyon and

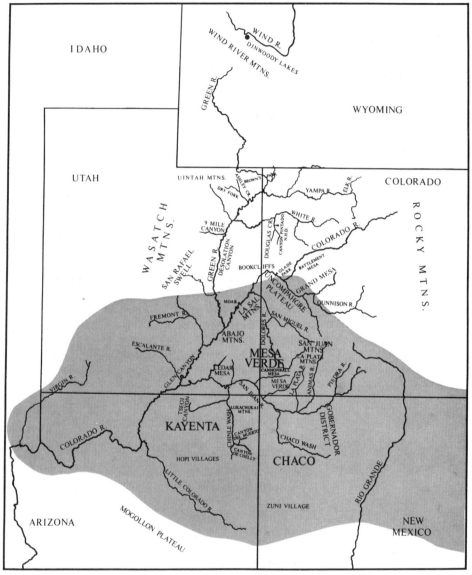

Map 7. *Anasazi culture area, north and south of the San Juan River, including regions occupied by late prehistoric and historic Pueblo people. General locations of three branches of the Anasazi (Mesa Verde, Kayenta, and Chaco) significant to the rock art study area are indicated. Styles of rock art are associated with Basketmaker II to Pueblo III and are dated pre-*A.D. *1 to approximately* A.D. *1300.*

Colorado River drainage to the west and in the upper Dolores River drainage to the north and east. Similar rock art also occurs in the Little Colorado River drainage to the south. While regional variations occur, the art has remarkable stylistic consistencies that may be attributed to the long duration of the Basketmaker lifeway and a broad sharing of materials, ideas, and ceremonial practices, some of which endure among the historic Pueblos. Basketmaker III rock art, like that of the following Pueblo I through III periods, is generally dated based on associations with materials such as ceramics. While the emphasis of Anasazi ceramic designs is abstract imagery, representational images including anthropomorphs are shown, and these provide comparative materials for relative dating of rock art (Figure 39).

Styles of Basketmaker rock art are often representational and show realistic details that give subjects a biographic quality. However, the art is rarely naturalistic, and the subject matter suggests that supernatural personages and mythic events may be symbolized as well as everyday occurrences.

Guernsey and Kidder (1921) have associated square-shouldered figures in rock art with Basketmaker II sites in northeastern Arizona. Grant (1978) has identified similar figures in Basketmaker and later Modified Basketmaker-Developmental Pueblo Style rock art in Canyon de Chelly and Canyon del Muerto, Arizona (Canyon de Chelly National Monument). Schaafsma (1980) has further defined Basketmaker and Pueblo I period art with similar anthropomorphs by the San Juan Anthropomorphic Style, the Rosa Representational Style, the Cave Valley Style, and the Chinle Representational Style from type-sites in Utah, New Mexico, and Arizona. Styles of the early Basketmakers feature broad-shouldered anthropomorphs, often elaborately appointed and supernatural in appearance. Bodies are rectangular, trapezoidal, and triangular in shape and range from approximately twenty centimeters to two meters in length. Anthropomorphs are often presented in horizontal rows and are shown in outline with interior and exterior body decorations and as solid forms. Body decorations include necklaces, arm bands, belts and sashes, aprons, diaperlike clothing (probably menstrual aprons), bandoleerlike designs, and lines and dots.

Heads are both rounded and rectangular, and faces frequently appear masklike and may be decorated. Facial features, if shown, are generally restricted to large eyes. Earrings and headdresses are common, and headdresses may be pointed and caplike, featherlike, or rectangular; they may be composed of rows of dots or crescents and lines. In some cases, abstract devices are shown protruding from ears. This is generally restricted to sites near Butler Wash on the San Juan River and

a

in Canyon de Chelly National Monument. A common hairstyle is two bobs, one hanging down on each side of the head. The hairstyle presumably represents hair bobs (two on each side and one in the rear) similar to those preserved in Basketmaker burials (Amsden 1949).

Arms, legs, hands, and feet (if shown) generally hang down; hands and feet may be large. Objects resembling bags, crooks, atlatls and feathered darts, and scalps are shown being held. Representations of bags and basketlike objects, crooks, atlatls and feathered darts, projectile points, and whole face and hair scalps also occur as independent elements, and similar artifacts have been found at Basketmaker sites (Kidder and Guernsey 1919; Guernsey and Kidder 1921). Phallic males and possible females with breasts and nipples are also shown.

Additional subject matter shown in early Basketmaker style rock art includes handprints (solid and patterned); circles, lines, and dots; yucca and other plantlike forms; wandlike devices; birds; snakes; paw prints; faces and masks; keyhole-shape images; and quadrupeds such as bighorn sheep. Birds shown appear to be turkeys, ducks, geese, and wading birds with long necks and legs. Painted handprints occur in great numbers in Basketmaker sites. Guernsey and Kidder (1921) note this for the Marsh Pass, Arizona, area; numerous rock shelters with handprints painted in a variety of colors also occur in the Cedar Mesa area of Utah. Some handprints are solid, and others have patterns of straight and zigzag lines that were presumably painted on the palms of the hands prior to being pressed against shelter walls. Petroglyphs showing hands are also exhibited but in fewer numbers (Plates 40, 41,

Figure 39. *Anthropomorphic pottery designs from the Anasazi area, Basketmaker III through Pueblo III periods (A.D. 575-1300). Similar anthropomorphic forms occur in Anasazi basketry (Morris and Burgh 1941), weavings (Guernsey and Kidder 1921), and in San Juan Anasazi rock art through time.*

a. *Detail from bowl, La Plata Black-on-White, A.D. 575-875. Drawn from a photograph by Lister and Lister (1978:Fig. 7).*

b. *Detail from bowl, La Plata Black-on-White, A.D. 575-875. Drawn from a photograph by Lister and Lister (1978:Fig. 9).*

c. *Detail from ladle, Kiatuthlanna Black-on-White, A.D. 825-910. Redrawn from Hays (1988a:Fig. 11).*

d. *Detail from bowl, Bluff Black-on-Red, A.D. 750-900. Redrawn from Olsen (Chappell Collection Data Base, Anasazi Heritage Center, Dolores, Colorado).*

e. *Detail from bowl, McElmo Black-on-White, A.D. 1075-1275. Redrawn from Olsen (Chappell Collection Data Base, Anasazi Heritage Center, Dolores, Colorado).*

f. *Detail from canteen, Mancos Black-on-White, A.D. 900-1150. Drawn from photograph (Olsen 1988:Fig. 34).*

g. *Detail from bowl, Mesa Verde Black-on-White, A.D. 1200-1300. Redrawn from Hays (1988a:Fig. 41).*

42, 43, 44, and 45; Figures 40, 41, 42, 43, 44, 45, and 47).

Later Basketmaker style rock art shows consistencies with the earlier art but is generally less decorative. Smaller anthropomorphs and a greater variety of subject matter and anthropomorphic types are shown. Figures are shown in active postures, and small thin figures as well as stick-figures appear. Linked and paired figures are quite common. Schaafsma (1980) identifies figures with sharply triangular bodies as part of the Rosa Representational Style, dated approximately A.D. 600–900 in northwestern New Mexico. Similar figures occur in Grand Gulch, Utah, and in the Mancos River canyon of Colorado (Plates 46 and 47).

Generally speaking, the stylistic uniformity of the earlier art is lacking in later Basketmaker art, particularly with regard to anthropomorphic representations. Distinctive imagery associated with later Basketmaker rock art includes turkey and ducklike birds, bird headdresses (ducks and turkeys), dot designs, linked figures (horizontal rows of attached and hand-holding anthropomorphs), paired figures, and flute-players (Plates 43, 46, and 47; Figures 44, 45, 46, and 47). Thin flute-players, without humpbacks, are often shown reclining as well as upright (Figure 41). Flutes and whistles have been recovered from Basketmaker III sites, and well-known examples are reported by Morris (1980) from the Lukachukai Mountains. Some or all of these subjects may have been repre-

Plate 40. *San Juan Anthropomorphic Style Basketmaker petroglyphs near the mouth of Butler Wash on the San Juan River, southeast Utah. Most of these elements probably date from the Basketmaker II period. Similar ear protrusions are seen in Basketmaker rock art at Canyon de Chelly National Monument, Arizona. The figure on the right appears to wear a large mask and is approximately life-size.*

Plate 41. *San Juan Basketmaker style red and white rock paintings at site 42SA3711, Cedar Mesa, southeastern Utah. Red figures on left precisely superimpose very faded white anthropomorphs with tall headdresses, suggesting renewal of earlier art. A possible birth scene appears at the right, and figures decorated with dots may represent females with emphasized breasts. Handprints are life-size.*

Plate 42. *Green, red, and white San Juan Basketmaker style rock paintings at a Basketmaker II occupied site in the Lukachukai Mountains, northeastern Arizona (Haury 1945). The largest anthropomorph is approximately one meter in length.*

sented during the Basketmaker II period, but it appears that they became more common during the Basketmaker III period.

A number of Basketmaker material objects can be associated with rock art and aid in its interpretation. In particular, Basketmaker II and III burials and storage cists have provided information on birds, wands, feathers, food, tools, clothing, menstrual aprons, jewelry, hairstyles, animal skin bags, decorated whole-hair scalps, figurines, and

Figure 40

Figure 41

Panels of San Juan Basketmaker style petroglyphs showing a masklike image, a stylized yucca plant with seed pods or flowers, a possible basket, crooks, anthropomorphs (including a possible copulating couple, a humpback and phallic figure holding a crook, two abstract "females" with possible necklaces and menstrual aprons, a reclining flute-player, and figures with headdresses), birds, paw prints, bags with handles, wandlike devices, keyhole-shape images, and spirals. Panels occur north of the San Juan River in southeast Utah. Yucca plant is approximately 80 centimeters in length; largest anthropomorph is approximately one meter in length.

Plate 43. *Early and late San Juan Basketmaker style red and white rock paintings in Canyon del Muerto, Canyon de Chelly National Monument, Arizona. Most anthropomorphs probably date from the Basketmaker II period, but the birds may date from a later period. The largest anthropomorph is approximately one meter in length.*

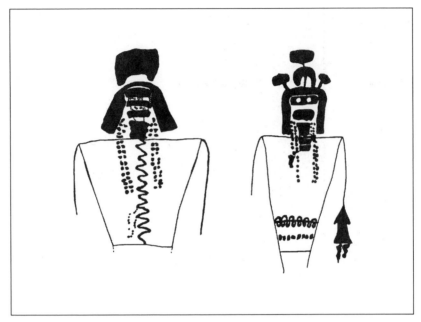

Figure 42. *Detail of San Juan Basketmaker style anthropomorphs showing faces decorated with horizontal bands at site 42SA17382, near the San Juan River, southeastern Utah. Figures are solid pecked and are one to one and a half meters in length.*

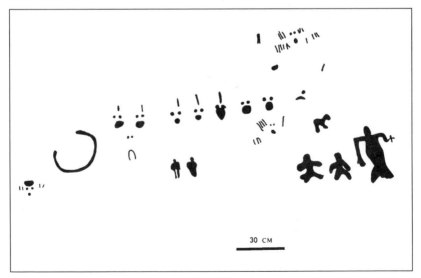

Figure 43. *Detail of a panel of San Juan Basketmaker style red-painted faces (masks?) and anthropomorphs at North Shelter, La Plata Mountains, southwestern Colorado.*

Plate 44. *A San Juan Basketmaker style rock painting in green, red, yellow, and white at site 42SA3711, Cedar Mesa, southeastern Utah. The rock surface on which the painting is placed was smoothed prior to painting. Mud balls probably dating from the late Pueblo II to Pueblo III period can be seen on the cliff below the painting. The painting probably represents a whole face and hair scalp decorated by bands of paint and a loop or handle above the head. A similarly decorated Basketmaker II scalp with hair worn in side and rear hair bobs with a leather thong attached to the top (see* Figure 48*) was excavated at Marsh Pass, northeastern Arizona (Kidder and Guernsey 1919).*

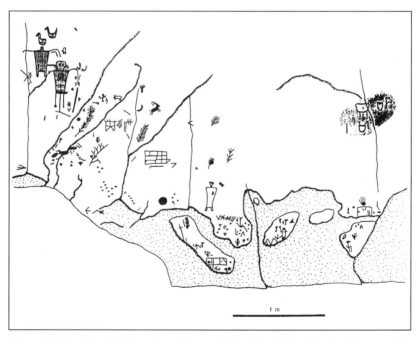

Figure 44. *San Juan Basketmaker style petroglyphs of broad-shouldered anthropomorphs, some wearing headdresses, and ducklike birds at site 5MT7491, in the upper Dolores River Valley area, southwest Colorado. Figures are pecked, and shaded areas indicate surfaces that have been smoothed by grinding. Abstract incised images may date from the Archaic and Basketmaker periods. Redrawn from Ives (1986:Fig. 8E.82).*

Figure 45. *San Juan Basketmaker style petroglyphs (solid and stipple pecked) showing anthropomorphs, birds, and other items at a Cedar Mesa, Utah, site. Figure at the top is beside atlatl and dartlike forms. Other representations include crooks and what may be digging sticks and snares. Large goose or ducklike bird is approximately 70 centimeters in length.*

Figure 46. *San Juan Basketmaker style gray, reddish brown, and white rock paintings from Keet Seel rock shelter, Tsegi Creek drainage, Arizona, showing anthropomorphs with birds on their heads.*

Plate 45. *Detail of San Juan Basket-maker style petroglyphs at site 42SA5263, near the San Juan River, southeastern Utah. Two probable representations of whole face and hair scalps with loops at the tops of the heads are exhibited in the upper center.*

Plate 46. *San Juan Basketmaker style petroglyphs at Ute Mountain Tribal Park, southwestern Colorado. Imagery includes figures with triangular bodies and reverse-V legs, quadrupeds, and dot patterns. The central figure wears a bird on the head and holds a crook. A horse petroglyph dating from the Ute reservation period appears in the lower portion of photograph. Scale increments: 10 centimeters.*

Plate 47. *San Juan Basketmaker style petroglyphs at site 5MT312, McElmo Creek-Cannonball Mesa area, southwestern Colorado. The figure on the far right wears a simple version of elaborate headdresses seen in earlier Basketmaker style rock art of the San Juan River area. The largest figure is approximately 40 centimeters in length.*

Figure 47. *San Juan Basketmaker style solid pecked petroglyphs at a Cedar Mesa, Utah, site showing an anthropomorph, birds, a spiral, and footprints or paw prints. Stippled areas indicate rock surface damage. Anthropomorph is approximately 35 centimeters in length.*

crooked sticks that are probably depicted in rock art (Plates 48 and 49; Figures 48, and 49) and symbolize related concepts (Kidder and Guernsey 1919; Guernsey and Kidder 1921; Morris 1951; Morris and Burgh 1954; Morris 1980; Cole 1989b).

As discussed previously, Basketmaker style rock art has been associated with shamanistic symbolism and practices by Grant (1978) and others. Specifically, Grant has pointed out the presence of birds as symbols of spiritual flight, skeletonlike forms, and a possible curing scene as evidence of shamanistic themes. Cole (1989b) has related various Basketmaker materials to rock art imagery to reinforce shamanistic associations. Among the materials discussed are a whole hair and face scalp decorated with paint, female figurines wearing aprons and menstrual pads, and crook "planting" sticks. These materials are viewed as symbols of death, fertility, and well-being based on archaeological context and historic Pueblo ceremonies. Ceremonies of the Basketmakers may have included similar themes and symbolism.

Type-sites of the San Juan Anthropomorphic Style attributed to the Basketmaker II by Schaafsma (1980) are located in the vicinity of Butler Wash on the San Juan River in Utah (Plate 40). Another important southeastern Utah area with Basketmaker style rock art is Cedar Mesa. Cedar Mesa is cut by deep sandstone canyons, such as White Canyon, Grand Gulch, and Comb Wash, that drain to the Colorado and San Juan rivers; it is in these canyons that Anasazi petroglyphs and rock paintings in a variety of colors (red, yellow, white, green) are exhibited (Plate 41). Basketmaker rock art is particularly abundant at Cedar Mesa sites and has been described by a number of researchers (Castleton 1979; Schaafsma and Young 1983; Cole 1984, 1985, 1989b). Among the many representations found at Grand Gulch sites are detailed paintings of whole hair and face scalps similar to one excavated with a burial by Kidder and Guernsey (1919:Pl. 87) (Figure 48). The scalp paintings show hair bobs, and some representations show loops or "handles" above the heads that probably correspond to a leather thong on the scalp artifact (Plate 44). Additional examples of scalplike imagery, painted and pecked, are found along the San Juan River at Sand Island, in Butler Wash, and to the south in Chinle Wash and Canyon del Muerto (Plate 45).

Basketmaker petroglyphs and rock paintings in northeastern Arizona, south of the San Juan River, also have contributed significantly to rock art studies. Basketmaker sites of this area described in the literature are those of Marsh Pass (Kidder and Guernsey 1919; Guernsey and Kidder 1921), the Lukachukai Mountains (Haury 1945; Morris 1980), and Canyon de Chelly National Monument (Grant 1978) (Plates 42 and 43). In northeastern New Mexico, Rosa Representa-

Plate 48. *San Juan Basketmaker style petroglyphs at site 42SA17382, near the San Juan River, southeastern Utah. The larger abstract figures probably represent females wearing waist belts and menstrual aprons. Two similar figures are shown in a nearby panel; one has "weeping eyes," an unusual trait on the Colorado Plateau south of the Fremont area. The details are similar to those shown on Basketmaker II and III clay figurines. Larger figures are approximately life-size.*

Plate 49. *A probable Basketmaker II unfired clay female figurine from southeastern Utah. This figurine is similar to representations in rock art and is shown wearing a necklace and diaperlike clothing that probably represents a menstrual apron. Photograph by A. J. Rota, courtesy Department of Library Services, American Museum of Natural History. Neg. No. 124089.*

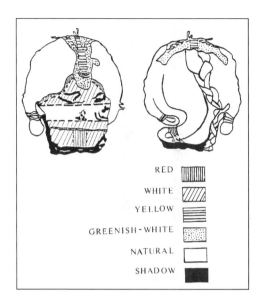

Figure 48. *Drawing of a Basketmaker II whole face and hair
scalp from Marsh Pass area,
northeastern Arizona. Scalp is
decorated by bands of paint and
has a leather thong attached to
the top. Drawn from Kidder
and Guernsey photograph
(1919:Pl. 87).*

RED

WHITE

YELLOW

GREENISH-WHITE

NATURAL

SHADOW

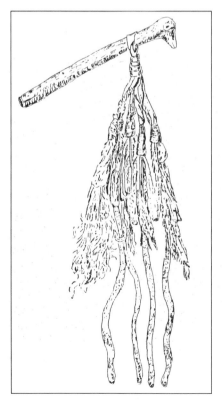

Figure 49. *Basketmaker II bird-
headed wand from Marsh Pass area,
northeastern Arizona. Redrawn from
Guernsey and Kidder (1921:Pl. 39).*

tional Style rock art is described for the Basketmaker III to Pueblo I period (Schaafsma 1980).

In western Colorado, San Juan Basketmaker style rock art is well known and has been documented at a number of locations including the upper Dolores River area, McElmo Creek–Cannonball Mesa–Hovenweep National Monument area, the La Plata Mountains, and Mesa Verde–Mancos River Canyon.

Ives (1986) illustrates early and late Basketmaker style anthropomorphs in a study of upper Dolores River rock art for the Dolores Archaeological Program (Figures 44, 50, and 51). Included are broad-shouldered anthropomorphs, petroglyphs and rock paintings, with rectangular-, trapezoidal-, and triangular-shaped bodies. Figures include simple forms, and those with hair bobs, necklaces, headdresses, and "fringed clothing." Several rectangular and trapezoidal-bodied figures are typical of San Juan Basketmaker II style rock art (Figure 44), and other forms are more typical of Basketmaker III style art. The latter group includes triangular-bodied figures that have raylike headdresses (Figure 51).

Other possible late Basketmaker figures from the upper Dolores River Area are painted. These figures have slender elongated bodies with arms downturned. The legs have a reverse-V shape and are very similar to figures from North Durango rock shelter discussed below. Other late Basketmaker imagery may include bighorn sheep, paw prints, a stick-figure flute-player, dot patterns, and abstract groove petroglyphs discussed earlier. Four rock art sites studied by the Dolores Archaeological Program include ceramics of the Basketmaker III period (Ives 1986:242). Ives' rock art study of sixteen sites demonstrated based on material associations that considerable diversity in rock art attributes and subject matter existed during the period between A.D. 600 and 950, when Basketmaker and Pueblo I populations occupied the upper Dolores River area.

McElmo Creek area art includes eroded white and green rock paintings of relatively small (approximately twenty to thirty centimeters in length) triangular-bodied anthropomorphs that may date from the Basketmaker III period. At one rock shelter location, green triangular figures are linked and form a horizontal row of figures.

Cannonball Mesa sites exhibit elaborate early and later Basketmaker style petroglyphs. These petroglyphs have been described by Trick (1982) and Olsen (1985) in studies of Hovenweep National Monument rock art. Early San Juan Basketmaker style petroglyphs in that area are very similar to those in the vicinity of Butler Wash, Utah, (Plate 40) and feature clusters of static solid-pecked anthropomorphs with elaborate headdresses, plantlike forms, paw prints, and abstract

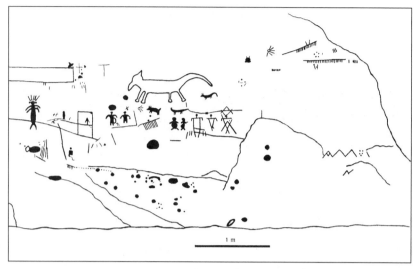

Figure 50. *Portion of a panel showing outline and solid pecked San Juan Basket-maker style anthropomorphs at site 5MT2216, in the upper Dolores River Valley area. Incised abstract petroglyphs are of possible Archaic and Basketmaker origin. Other pecked and painted representations may date from the Pueblo I period. Note similarity between hairstyle of anthropomorph on far left and that shown on Pueblo I period pottery (Figure 39d). Quadruped shown in outline is painted white. Redrawn from Ives (1986:Fig. 8E.1).*

Figure 51. *San Juan Basktmaker style petroglyphs at site 5MT4554, in the upper Do-lores River Valley area, southwestern Colorado. Redrawn from Ives (1986:Fig. 8E.43, 8E.47).*

linear designs. Some figures are a meter or more in length. Less elaborate anthropomorphs are also shown. Some of these are shown with
large hands and feet and with one upraised hand. These may date from
a later period (Plate 47).

Basketmaker rock art of the La Plata Mountains area is believed to
be among the earliest Anasazi rock art documented in Colorado and is
in association with sites occupied during the Basketmaker II and Basketmaker III periods. Falls Creek (Durango) rock shelters (North and
South) and nearby Talus Village sites were investigated by Morris and
Burgh (1954) and yielded significant information about the Basketmaker culture. Rock art at North and South Shelters is reported by
Daniels (1954, 1976).

The Falls Creek rock shelters feature rock paintings in a variety of
colors, including red, greenish blue, yellow, white, and black. The
paintings are distinctive insofar as most images are quite small in comparison with Basketmaker style rock art elsewhere. Otherwise, the
imagery is stylistically consistent and includes broad-shouldered
anthropomorphs (some with bird headdresses and some paired, linked,
and active), slender elongated figures with arms downturned and legs
with a reverse-V shape, bighorn sheep and other quadrupeds, masklike
faces with headdresses, flute-players, concentric circles, and birds (Figure 43).

Of particular interest at North Shelter are concentric circles
painted near the ceiling and approximately fifty red masklike faces on
slabs of rock. The majority of these are small (approximately ten to
twenty centimeters in length), but a few are approximately life-size.
The images are generally abstract and show eyes and mouth with cres-
cent-shape headdresses and pointed "caps" or single "feather" headdresses. It is possible that the faces represent masks or scalps such as
those shown in Basketmaker rock art on Cedar Mesa and elsewhere
(Plates 40, 44, and 45; Figure 40) but they are quite different.

The walls of clay storage cists at North Shelter are decorated with
incised plantlike forms and stylized paw prints, and parallel wavy line
impressions discussed previously (Figure 10). The forms and paw
prints resemble petroglyphs of the upper Dolores River valley to the
west and those of the lower Dolores River and Uncompahgre Plateau
to the north. These images suggest associations between Archaic
groups and Basketmakers of the La Plata Mountains. It is interesting
that all three rock art areas are mountainous in nature. The various cultural groups may have interacted; another possibility is that Archaic
cultures from these areas were ancestral to Basketmakers of the La
Plata Mountains, and the art style endured.

Mesa Verde–Mancos River Canyon Basketmaker rock art is located in the Ute Mountain Tribal Park, in the lower Mancos River Canyon. Most examples are pecked petroglyphs of late Basketmaker style, but a few early Basketmaker style rock paintings are exhibited (Plate 46). These are faded, and indicate that additional painted examples may not have survived. Mancos Canyon has a wide floor and permanent water and was continuously occupied by the Anasazi from the Basketmaker III to the late Pueblo III period, from approximately A.D. 550 to 1250 (Bowman, personal communication). A Basketmaker II occupation has not been determined, but rock art provides important evidence that Basketmaker II people used the canyon.

Early-style Basketmaker art in Mancos Canyon is executed in red and cream or white paint. The paintings are similar to Basketmaker art in Grand Gulch, Utah, and in Canyon de Chelly National Monument, Arizona (Plates 41 and 43). Two early-style anthropomorphic figures are approximately one meter in length and show large round eyes, headdresses, jewelry, and waist belts. These figures, a set of concentric circles, and certain handprints appear weathered and faded and are in association with brighter and less weathered elements that are painted red and white. These include smaller anthropomorphs (approximately twenty to thirty centimeters in length), handprints, zoomorphs, and a set of concentric circles.

The older-appearing anthropomorphs appear to have been originally painted with cream or white paint, with red paint representing possible collars, pendants or breast plates, eyes, and a headdress. Dark-red handprints superimpose the shoulder of one figure, and a larger bright-red handprint superimposes the breast of the other. The large handprint and a similar one nearby have been carefully pecked. At a subsequent period, it appears that one or both of the figures were outlined in red paint; a small white anthropomorph was superimposed on the outline of one figure. Outlined Basketmaker paintings are also present in Canyon de Chelly National Monument and at Cedar Mesa sites. A small red anthropomorph superimposes the small white figure. A white bighorn sheep superimposes the head of the other figure, and a red line superimposes it. Additional small anthropomorphs are placed between, above, and beside the older-style anthropomorphs. Such activities suggest that the rock art and location were important to various groups over time.

Most of the smaller anthropomorphs are slender elongated figures, and certain of these appear animated. One set of figures are linked. As described, some of these figures superimpose the larger, older-appearing anthropomorphs. In general, the smaller anthropomorphs are more similar to later San Juan Basketmaker style art, and superimpositions suggest that the smaller figures are, in fact, more recent.

Basketmaker III occupants of Mesa Verde are assigned to the La Plata Phase, dated between A.D. 500 and 700 (Hayes 1964). Schaafsma (1980:128–132) has proposed a style association between Mancos Canyon petroglyphs at Kiva Point and the Rosa Representational Style dated approximately A.D. 400 to 950. Kiva Point is a southern extension of Chapin Mesa, and petroglyphs at the site total approximately 228 elements (Fetterman 1976). Typical late Basketmaker style rock art at the site includes broad-shouldered and more slender anthropomorphs with a variety of body shapes (including triangular) and headdresses (one holds a crook and wears a bird headdress), rows of linked figures, paired figures, slender flute-players, elaborate dot patterns, bighorn sheep and other quadrupeds, birds, snakes, lines, paw prints, and possible bird tracks (Plate 46). Static as well as more animated anthropomorphs occur. Some anthropomorphs have legs with a reverse-V shape similar to figures in the upper Dolores River valley and at the Durango rock shelters.

Pueblo I

A.D. 700 to 900

Anasazi rock art style categories (Turner 1963; Grant 1978; Schaafsma 1980) generally include early Pueblo I rock art with that of

Plate 50. *Possible Pueblo I period petroglyphs at site MV2469, Battleship Rock, Mesa Verde National Park, Colorado. Two upper figures are approximately 60 centimeters in length.*

the Basketmaker III because of chronological and material culture overlaps between the two stages in various areas of the Southwest and the difficulty of associating broadly defined rock art styles with more narrowly defined culture stages and phases. Opportunities to identify examples of Pueblo I rock art with confidence are rare. However, in two southwestern Colorado areas, Mesa Verde and the upper Dolores River valley, the Pueblo I stage is well represented, and Pueblo I materials, ceramics, and architecture are found in association with rock art.

Accordingly, research at Mesa Verde National Park and in the Dolores Archaeological Program study area offer opportunities to examine rock art that is likely to be Pueblo I in origin. Not unexpectedly, the rock art at these sites is related to both San Juan Basketmaker and later Pueblo II–III style art, specifically with regard to anthropomorphic representations. On Mesa Verde, rock art at Battleship Rock (MV2469) probably has its beginnings during the Pueblo I period and has been interpreted as part of socioreligious systems that existed in nearby communities. In the upper Dolores River valley, six rock art sites in association with materials dated between A.D. 600 and 950 have rock art comparable to that at Battleship Rock.

Battleship Rock Petroglyphs

Battleship Rock petroglyphs (Figures 52 and 53; Plate 50) and nearby sites in Mesa Verde National Park are the subject of a study that attempts to interpret past community organization in the upper Soda Canyon (Wade 1979). Thus, the rock art is viewed within the context of neighboring archaeological sites and past social developments. This approach not only provides a chronology for the art but explains how the site may have functioned for people living in ancient communities.

The subject petroglyphs occur on an east-facing sandstone cliff near the top of Battleship Rock. Approximately sixty elements occur at the site (Fetterman 1976), and all are solid pecked. Elements range from fifteen centimeters to more than a meter in length. Anthropomorphs predominate at the site and have rectangular, rounded, and triangular heads. Anthropomorphs have horn or antennaelike headdresses, and one large horned figure wears what appear to be two sets of earrings. One anthropomorph has dots attached to the top of the head. Another figure had dots over the head. Additional elements at the site include deer or elk shown with antlers, other quadrupeds, lines, a handprint, a pair of "sandal tracks," and a paw print.

Body shapes for anthropomorphs are rectangular, tapered, and sticklike. One rectangular anthropomorph has a stick-figure attached to the head, and the two appear roughly contemporaneous (Figure 53;

Figure 52

Figure 53

Possible Pueblo I solid pecked petroglyphs at site MV2469, Battleship Rock, Mesa Verde National Park, Colorado. Rectangular heads appear in pottery decoration of the Pueblo I period (Figure 39d). *Thin "lizard man" anthropomorph on the lower right of* Figure 52 *may date from the Pueblo II-III period.*

Plate 50). Many of the anthropomorphs have arms raised or extended, and some show legs out to the side; a few figures have both. One figure has arms and legs hanging down, similar to Basketmaker figures. Hands and feet are exhibited on a few figures, and several are phallic.

The largest panel of petroglyphs is exposed to water running down the cliff from above, and the majority of elements are considerably eroded and have patination equal to the background rock. Superimpositions are present on this panel. The head and upraised arms of a rectangular figure are superimposed by an outline rectangular "box" that also contains a smaller anthropomorph with a rounded head and tapered body. Additional panels that have more protection from the weather show less erosion, and patination levels for these petroglyphs are somewhat lighter than background rock (Plate 50).

The beginnings of Battleship Rock petroglyphs are proposed for the Pueblo I period (Piedra Phase, A.D. 700–900), with continuing visitation and perhaps manufacture during the Pueblo II period (Ackmen Phase, A.D. 900–975; Mancos Phase, A.D. 975–1075). The final proposed period of use is Pueblo III (McElmo Phase A.D. 1075–1150; Mesa Verde Phase, A.D. 1150–1300). Seven sites with structures and ceramics from these periods are located in upper Soda Canyon below Battleship Rock (Wade 1979).

Stylistically, Battleship Rock petroglyphs are similar to Basketmaker rock art insofar as they feature rectangular and broad-shouldered anthropomorphs wearing earrings and headdresses. Other typical elements represented include quadrupeds and linear abstracts. However, style differences are apparent. In particular, some figures are shown with raised and extended arms and with legs out to the side. Ceramics indicate that anthropomorphs with similar arms and legs were represented during the Pueblo I period, between A.D. 750 and 910 (Figure 39). Small thin figures with rounded heads at Battleship Rock are very similar to "lizard men" and may have been made by later groups. Such figures suggest slender and stick-figure "lizard men" that dominate Pueblo II and III rock art and are shown on ceramics.

Wade (1979) estimates that a small community could have existed in the Battleship Rock area during the Piedra Phase when the petroglyphs were first made. The occupants of the area and original makers of the petroglyphs were probably members of nuclear families living in a dispersed settlement.

During the Ackmen Phase, larger populations with more complex social organization are proposed for the Battleship Rock area. Lineages replace the earlier extended families, and less dispersed community organization develops. Kivas associated with room blocks indicate the presence of a community-wide ceremonial system, and a detached great kiva built during this period is believed to have functioned as a specialized ceremonial center. A possible rock shrine near the great kiva and petroglyph site may also date from this period. A chronological continuum exists between sites of the Ackmen Phase and the following Mancos Phase, including use of the great kiva, rock shrine, and the petroglyphs.

During the Mancos Phase, the population again expands; two new kiva complexes were built. This suggests development of an elaborate ceremonial system operating on a community level (Wade 1979). In general, the Mancos Phase settlement pattern indicates a well-organized community.

A chronological continuum is also apparent in the Battleship Rock area between occupations and social practices of the Mancos Phase and the following McElmo Phase (Wade 1979). Construction and pottery techniques developed during the earlier period were refined during the later. During the McElmo Phase, population numbers remain stable, but a population shift from smaller to larger residences (aggregation) takes place. Also, there is movement away from a previously occupied area to an area near fertile soils for farming. Use of kiva complexes, the great kiva, and presumably the rock art continues.

During the final Mesa Verde Phase, the great kiva and perhaps the petroglyph site continue to be used but the two kiva complexes are no longer utilized nor are other features such as check dams (small structures of stone and earth that slow the run-off of water). The population is reduced, and previously occupied locations within the area are abandoned. Nevertheless, community-level social organization exists based on use of the great kiva and the complexity and location of habitation sites (Wade 1979).

It is argued that environmental and social factors are likely to have contributed to changes in the Battleship Rock area during the Mesa Verde Phase. Aggregation of populations into larger sites during the McElmo Phase may have led to a breakdown of local agricultural and social systems, resulting in movements of people from the area and abandonment of sites. Environmental factors, such as drought, and maintenance of the existing social order in the face of internal dissension are cited as reasons why people may have left the area.

Through time, Battleship Rock petroglyphs may have been part of religious ceremonies that honored agricultural deities. Historic Pueblo religious practices in combination with the presence of a great kiva and a possible rock shrine near the petroglyphs are viewed as supporting this interpretation (Wade 1979).

Interestingly, Wade observes that, in contrast to the two kiva complexes that were abandoned during the Mesa Verde Phase, the older great kiva may have retained significance and continued to be used because of its antiquity. This would presumably also be true of the ancient nearby petroglyph site and rock shrine. Wade does not further elaborate on this issue; however, a related interpretation is that the great kiva, shrine, and petroglyph site were controlled by certain social and religious organizations, possibly family- or lineage-based, that endured throughout the occupation of the area.

This approach is supported by ethnographic information from Hopi and Zuni villages, where control of kivas and shrines with rock art is held by certain clans, lineages, and allied ceremonial organizations (Fewkes 1901, 1906; Stevenson 1904; Titiev 1944; Stephen 1969). When various social groups and religious alliances break down, villages and kivas are abandoned, and local shrines may no longer be visited.

Upper Dolores Valley Rock Art

Rock art sites in the upper Dolores River valley exhibit general and specific style attributes noted for Battleship Rock petroglyphs. Ceramics associated with the sites are classified as Basketmaker III, Pueblo I, and Pueblo II (Ives 1986:242) and are generally dated between A.D. 600 and 950. The rock art occurs on cliffs and within rock shelters located near the Dolores River. Images are pecked, incised, and painted and include anthropomorphs, both full-bodied and sticklike, with rounded and rectangular heads. Some figures have arms and legs

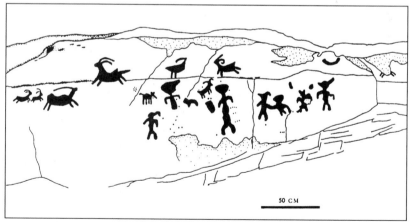

Figure 54. *Possible Pueblo I solid pecked petroglyphs at site 5MT4549, in the upper Dolores River Valley area, southwestern Colorado. Note similarity between headdresses on the right of the panel and those shown on Basketmaker III-Pueblo I pottery. Redrawn from Ives (1986:Fig. 8E.39, 8E.42).*

that are out to the side, similar to later "lizard men" forms, and others have arms and legs hanging down in the fashion of Basketmaker figures (Figure 54).

A possible Pueblo I petroglyph figure has a rectangular head with a two-horn headdress similar to figures at Battleship Rock. A short distance away on the same panel is a petroglyph showing an outlined equilinear cross. This image appears on Pueblo I pottery of the La Plata River district south and east of the upper Dolores Valley (Morris 1939). At a second location, a figure with a rounded head, arms raised, and legs extended down with feet turned to the side is quite similar to a figure at Battleship Rock. A rectangular figure at another site has one arm extended and the lower part appears to hang limply. This type of treatment of arms and hands is seen on two figures at Battleship Rock (Figures 52 and 53).

Pueblo II and Pueblo III

A.D. 850 to 1300

Pueblo II and Pueblo III style rock art is represented throughout the San Juan River drainage and has been described by a number of researchers. Turner (1963) describes Glen Canyon Style 4 rock art, dated A.D. 1050–1250, that includes Pueblo II to early III style rock art as well as rock art that is herein considered to be Basketmaker style. Grant (1978) has identified Great Pueblo Style rock art dated A.D. 1000–1250 in Canyon de Chelly National Monument, and Schaafsma (1980) identifies the Kayenta Representational Style dated A.D. 1200–1300 and Tsegi Painted Style rock art associated with Tsegi Phase occupations (A.D. 1250–1300) in the Tsegi Canyon-Navajo National Monument area of northeastern Arizona. Style conformity exists in rock art throughout the San Juan River area and certain representations, such as elaborate abstracts, "lizard men," and shield-figures, are shared with neighboring areas to the north and south during this period (Figures 55 and 56). This supports the material record indicating broad-based cultural interaction during the Pueblo II and III periods.

In the Four Corners area, Pueblo II–III style rock art is represented in the Cannonball Mesa-McElmo Creek region (Plate 51), the upper Dolores River region, and on Mesa Verde (Plates 52 and 53). The art is also well represented in neighboring areas of Arizona, Utah, and New Mexico. Rock art on Cedar Mesa in Utah is comparable to art in the Mesa Verde area as well as to rock art in the Tsegi Canyon drainage of Arizona. Farwell and Wening (1985) describe rock art from Pictured Cliffs along the San Juan River in New Mexico that is very similar to that found in the nearby Mesa Verde area. Of particular

Figure 55. *Detail of Pueblo II-III style solid pecked petroglyphs in the Little Colorado River drainage, near Homol'ovi II Ruin, Homol'ovi Ruins State Park, northeastern Arizona. Dashed lines indicate broken rock.*

Figure 56. *Detail of Pueblo II-III style solid pecked petroglyphs in the Puerco River-Little Colorado River drainage, near Puerco Ruin, Petrified Forest National Park, northeastern Arizona. Dashed lines indicate broken rock.*

Plate 51. *Pueblo II-Pueblo III style petroglyphs in the San Juan River area, showing spirals, lines, insectlike forms, and possible bird tracks with quadrupeds at site 5MT309, McElmo Creek-Cannonball Mesa area, southwest Colorado.*

Plate 52. *Pueblo II-Pueblo III style hump backed flute-player petroglyph in Mancos Canyon, Ute Mountain Tribal Park, Colorado. Figure is approximately 30 centimeters in length.*

Plate 53. *Detail of typical Pueblo II-Pueblo III style rock art in the San Juan River area at site MV1001, Petroglyph Point, Mesa Verde National Park. The panel shows "lizard man" anthropomorphs, quadrupeds, handprints, birds, and abstract linear images. A possible katsina mask representation is in the lower right.*

interest at Pictured Cliff is a detailed and phallic "lizard man" with face shown in outline (Figure 57). Facial features include eyes, nose, and mouth. Outline faces such as this are unusual in the San Juan River drainage, but are represented in rock art of the Little Colorado River area before and after A.D. 1300 (Figures 56 and 62).

Pueblo II–III style rock art occurs in association with ruins and in more isolated locations. Pueblo II–III style rock art in the upper Dolores River region is sparsely represented but is exhibited at petroglyph sites reported by Ives (1986). Nine rock art sites from the Dolores Archaeological Program research area have Pueblo II–III period ceramics and architecture in association (Ives 1986:242). These and other sites with no material associations and with earlier ceramics in association show a variety of images that are stylistically related to Pueblo II–III rock art throughout the San Juan culture area (Figure 58). Some of this rock art occurs at sites with earlier styles of rock art, including Archaic, Basketmaker, and Pueblo I styles discussed above.

At Mesa Verde National Park, rock art is in association with cliff dwellings and at remote locations. Petroglyph Point at Mesa Verde exhibits a complex panel that includes many of the attributes associated with Pueblo II–III style rock art in the San Juan River area (Plate 53).

Figure 57. *Detail of Pueblo II-III style solid pecked petroglyphs at Pictured Cliffs site, San Juan River drainage, northwestern New Mexico. Drawn from a photograph by Farwell and Wening (1985:Fig. 15).*

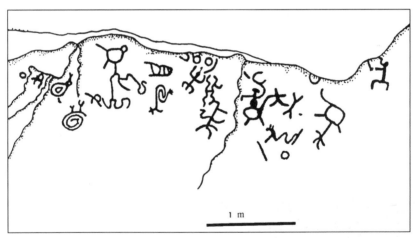

Figure 58. *Pueblo II-III style solid pecked petroglyphs at site 5MT4491, in the upper Dolores River valley, southwestern Colorado. Redrawn from Ives (1986:Fig. 8E.29, 8E.31).*

An inventory of sites in the park indicates that approximately twenty-five ruins of the Pueblo II–III period have petroglyphs and rock paintings that are typical of the style period. Some of this art is found on rock shelter walls enclosed within cliff dwelling rooms. Mesa Verde ruins also exhibit painted and incised designs on stone and plastered walls (Copeland and Ives n.d.), and similar architectural art is found elsewhere in the San Juan area. W. Smith (1952) discusses painted kivas of the San Juan area, and H. Smith (1980) describes an example from Salmon Ruin.

In some instances, decorative art occurs on natural rock shelter walls enclosed within cliff dwelling rooms as well as on the masonry walls. However, art on natural walls may be related to previous occupations. This is most obvious in situations where Pueblo II and III masonry walls cover Basketmaker style art.

Architectural art of the Pueblo II–III period includes representations of bighorn sheep and other quadrupeds, snakes, handprints, birds and "bird tracks," shieldlike images and shield-figures (anthropomorphs with shields in front of the bodies), humpback and other figures (some with horned headdresses), orbs and crescents (possible moon phases), "spider webs," rows of dots, connected triangles on a base line, geometric step patterns and others that resemble sandals, sashes, and blankets. Particularly elaborate red and white wall paintings from New Fire House at Mesa Verde have been reported by Fewkes (1916) and Schaafsma (1980). Images at that site occur on natural and masonry walls and include depictions of vertical snakes, quadrupeds, a "horned" snake with "mounds" on the back, a flute-player, and figures with bows and arrows wearing headdresses that resemble the horns of bighorn sheep.

Copeland and Ives (n.d.) describe various painted and incised images in rooms of Cliff Palace ruin. These include painted geometric abstract designs, incised birds, a "spiderweb," and shield-figures (Figure 59).

Of interest in the Mesa Verde area are wall decorations that combine solid bands of paint, horizontal rows of "cones" or triangles on base lines, and rows of dots. Clear examples occur at Painted Kiva and Cliff Palace ruins at Mesa Verde National Park (Plate 54) and Eagle House in the Ute Mountain Tribal Park. Variations on this combination are found at other Mesa Verde sites, at a Cedar Mesa, Utah, site (Plate 55), and at Salmon Ruins, New Mexico. Morris (1939:Pl. 309) illustrates triangles and dots that are part of an encircling pattern on Pueblo III pottery from the Mancos River. Morris interprets this sherd design as an example of early (Basketmaker III to Pueblo II) or aberrant Mesa Verde encircling-band patterns. Other distinctive decorations that resemble textiles are painted inside the tower at Cliff Palace ruin and on a wall at Spruce Tree House (Plate 54).

During the Pueblo II–III period, San Juan Anasazi rock art undergoes significant stylistic changes from preceding periods. Imagery and themes of earlier styles, such as broad-shouldered anthropomorphs with elaborate headdresses and body decorations, keyhole symbols,

Plate 54

Plate 55

Wall decorations of the late Pueblo II-Pueblo III period. Plate 54 *shows a tower at Cliff Palace, Mesa Verde National Park, Colorado. Visible are red paintings of textilelike designs, vertical lines with tic marks, and a solid band of red topped with triangular projections and dots.* Plate 55 *shows a white painted variation on the solid band, triangles, and dots at a Cedar Mesa cliff dwelling, southeast Utah.*

Figure 59. *Pueblo III shield-figures incised in wall plaster of Kiva K, Cliff Palace ruin, Mesa Verde National Park, Colorado. Heads are not shown. Redrawn from Copeland and Ives (n.d.).*

bags, and crooks, are not evident in the later art. Scalplike images are also absent, but a few masklike images are present. Anthropomorphs are represented during the Pueblo II–III period, but the anthropomorphic tradition as previously described for the San Juan area is no longer apparent.

Anthropomorphic figures of Pueblo II–III style rock art are generally smaller and less elaborate than those of earlier periods and are frequently "lizard men," shown with arms and legs out to the side and raised or lowered at the elbows and knees. As noted above, this pose may have developed during the Pueblo I period and may be symbolic of lizards and possibly frogs, creatures that also appear in rock art and jewelry of the Pueblo II–III period.

"Lizard men" are frequently phallic or have "tails;" hands and feet are not emphasized and may be missing. Bodies are generally sticklike or are slender elongated rectangles; heads are generally rounded. Facial features are usually not shown and body decorations are rare. Figures may wear horn headdresses and exhibit side hair bundles or "whorls" (similar to those worn by unmarried Hopi girls) and earrings (Plate 53). Other anthropomorphic types are more realistic and often have animated poses, which include sitting and standing flute-players with humped backs (Plates 52 and 53).

Pueblo II–III period ceramic designs show anthropomorphs that are similar to those in the rock art of the same period. For example, "lizard-men" and more realistic and animated anthropomorphs are depicted on San Juan Anasazi ceramics dated between A.D. 850 and 1300 (Figure 39e, f, g).

Anthropomorphs share rock art panels with a variety of images that have been represented in the past and some achieve greater emphasis and elaboration during the Pueblo II–III period. Imagery includes handprints (petroglyph hands and negative-painted handprints made by blowing or otherwise placing pigment around a hand held against a rock face); concentric circles; spirals (round, rectangular, and triangular); wavy, zigzag, and straight lines; paw prints; "bird tracks;" "sandal tracks"; "squiggle-mazes"; snakes (often wavy and zigzag); and bighorn sheep. Concentric circles with dots in the center and a variety of spiral designs, round and rectangular, are exceedingly common. The concentric circles may be related to shieldlike elements that make an appearance during this period and are discussed in more detail below. Numerous examples of concentric circles and spirals are found on Mesa Verde, Cedar Mesa, and in the Cannonball Mesa-McElmo Creek area. A particularly complex and striking example of the use of spirals is seen in a "kneeling figure" petroglyph from the San Juan River in Utah. This figure depicted above ruins of a cliff dwelling has a spiral head, and its body is formed of lines extending from the spiral (Figure 60).

Bighorn sheep and other quadrupeds, however, continue to be represented in significant numbers. On occasion, these quadrupeds are shown with distorted bodies and open mouths, traits that may have begun during the previous period. In some cases, sheep have claw or birdlike feet (Grant 1978). Examples of human bodies with bighorn sheep heads may date from this period.

Certain other subjects represented in the past continue to be represented but have diminished roles, such as handprints and dot patterns. Birds continue to be represented but are not as common as during the Basketmaker period. Birds include turkeys, parrots or macaws, and eagles or other raptorlike birds. Parrots or macaws are shown in profile with open beaks and long tails. Two probable parrot or macaw

Figure 60. *Pueblo II-III style solid pecked petroglyphs near the San Juan River, southeastern Utah. "Kneeling" figure is approximately 60 centimeters in length.*

petroglyphs are shown at Petroglyph Point in Mesa Verde National Park (Plate 53, left). This type of imagery may have appeared first during this period, as do distinctive eaglelike images with spread wings shown from a frontal view and heads shown in profile. This type of image is represented as a petroglyph near a Mesa Verde cliff dwelling (MV990). Parrot or macaw representations are found on ceramics of the same period (Hays 1988a, 1988b). Scorpion and centipedelike images are depicted at San Juan River sites (Figure 60).

Geometric patterns, such as rows of connected triangles, dots, diamonds, spirals, and step and terrace designs, are seen in petroglyphs and rock paintings, often in association with ruins (Plate 51). Wavy and zigzag snakes, handprints, and "lizard man" figures also occur near ruins. Often elaborate and large abstract geometric designs are found in association with "lizard man" forms near ruins in the Cedar Mesa area and south in the Tsegi Creek drainage of Arizona. Complex petroglyph panels showing round and rectangular spirals, parallel lines, rows of bighorn sheep, and other images are found in the Cannonball Mesa area (Plate 51) and elsewhere in the Four Corners.

Circular and oval designs that resemble shields make an appearance in late Pueblo II–III style rock art (post A.D. 1000). In some instances, the shieldlike images occur as individual elements, often with interior decoration, such as an anthropomorph, and various geometric designs (Plates 56 and 57). Shield-figures are also shown (Figure 61). This type of image is also seen in Fremont rock art to the north and is common in historic rock art of the Great Plains. Schaafsma (1971) has sug-

Plate 56. *Painted shieldlike images in association with cliff dwellings of the late Pueblo II-Pueblo III period in the San Juan River area. Such highly visible images may have symbolized family, religious, and social organizations that were present at the sites. Green and white painted shieldlike images shown here are located above Jailhouse Ruin on Cedar Mesa, southeastern Utah.*

Figure 61. *Pueblo II-III style white painted shield-figure and handprint from Chinle Wash, near the San Juan River, southeastern Utah. The figure is approximately one meter in length and occurs near a cliff dwelling.*

gested that shieldlike imagery may have been passed to the Pueblos from the Fremont.

Shieldlike imagery (including shield-figures) is presented at a variety of locations in the study area. As noted above, it is incised on plastered walls at Cliff Palace on Mesa Verde. The imagery is frequently exhibited on cliff walls above or below cliff dwellings where it is highly visible. Numerous examples of painted "shields" are associated with cliff dwellings and storage structures on Cedar Mesa. As many as eight with different interior designs are found at one Slickhorn Canyon site. Other "shields" occur at Jailhouse Ruin in the Grand Gulch area of

Utah (Plate 56), at Betatakin and Bat Woman House ruins in the Tsegi Creek area of Arizona in Navajo National Monument (Plate 57), and at various sites in Butler Wash and elsewhere along the San Juan River in Utah (Figure 61). At one San Juan River cliff dwelling location, a white-painted San Juan Basketmaker anthropomorph has been changed into a shield-figure by the addition of a red and white shield covering the torso.

Pueblo III basketry shields reported by Morris (1924) and Morris and Burgh (1941) were found at Mesa Verde, Aztec Ruins National Monument, New Mexico, and in Canyon de Chelly National Monument, Arizona. The round Mesa Verde shield is undecorated, but the slightly oval (36 inches long, and 31 inches wide) Aztec shield is elaborately decorated with concentric bands of red and greenish blue stain and an overlay of pitch and selenite. This shield was found in the "Warrior's Grave" in the Aztec Ruin Annex dated to the Mesa Verde occupation of that site. The design is similar to concentric circle and dot rock art imagery in the Mesa Verde area. A round Pueblo III basketry shield with a painted decoration from Mummy Cave Ruin in Canyon del Muerto is similar to a white and negative shieldlike rock art image at Betatakin Ruin in the Tsegi Canyon area to the northwest. Both circular "shields" have "lizard man" forms in the interior (Plate 57).

In a study of Pueblo III ruins in the Tsegi Creek drainage, Anderson (1971) proposes that shield images may have had heraldic symbolism for various social groups occupying cliff dwellings. In such situations, shields may have symbolized lineages or clans and associated societies similar to those at historic Hopi and Zuni villages (Stevenson 1904; Fewkes 1892; Stephen 1969). Shields at Hopi villages serve as fetishes of warrior societies and represent the masks of deities and katsinas that are associated with various clans. Sun (Tawa) shields are worn by dancers and are featured in *paho* (prayer feather)-making ceremonies. Shield and shield-figure petroglyphs from the vicinity of Hopi villages are identified as being symbolic of the Apache and Ute as well as the ancient village of Sikyatki (Stephen 1969).

Rock shelters associated with late Pueblo II–III cliff dwellings are often marked by mud balls that have been hurled toward bare walls and ceilings. Examples of this practice are found north and south of the San Juan River, most noticeably in the Tsegi Creek area of northeast Arizona and at Cedar Mesa, Utah, sites. In some instances, rock art has been hit by the mud balls, and it appears that the rock art was a target. However, it is not always apparent that mud balls were intended to actually hit the art but were probably aimed at adjacent areas. This is indicated by rock art that would not have been difficult

Plate 57. *Basketry shield from Canyon del Muerto, Canyon de Chelly National Monument, Arizona, showing a design similar to that of a white rock painting at Betatakin Ruin, Navajo National Monument. Catalog no. 231776, Department of Anthropology, Smithsonian Institution.*

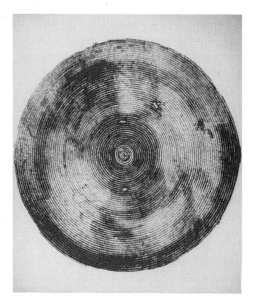

to hit and is surrounded by mud balls. A good example of this is found at a site on Cedar Mesa, Utah, where mud balls partially surround a polychrome painting of a scalp that dates from the Basketmaker period (Plate 44).

Throwing mud balls may have been associated with making mortar used to construct masonry walls, and the widespread nature of the practice suggests that it was a late Pueblo tradition. What function the mud balls may have served beyond the level of amusement is not clear, but it does appear that, on occasion, mud balls were intentionally placed in association with rock art.

Masklike images of Pueblo II–III style rock art are different from San Juan Basketmaker examples, resembling instead masklike images in rock art of the Little Colorado River and Rio Grande drainages to the south and east. These representations are generally associated with rock art styles dating after A.D. 1200–1300, the time of abandonment of the San Juan River drainage and the northern Colorado Plateau by the Anasazi. Turner (1963) identifies two masks as Glen Canyon Style 4, dated between A.D. 1050 and 1250, and others as Style 3 or Style 2 masks that were possibly made by Hopi Indians visiting the area after A.D. 1200–1300. The earlier Style 4 masks are decorated with abstract symbols similar to those seen on pottery of the same period and differ stylistically from the later Style 3 and Style 2 masks that clearly correspond to historic katsina mask symbolism. Similarities exist between

Katsina mask representations and the earlier Glen Canyon masks that may represent protokatsina masks.

In the Little Colorado and Rio Grande areas, katsina mask representations are numerous (Figure 62) and often are in association with ruins dated from approximately A.D. 1250 into the historic period (Schaafsma and Schaafsma 1974; Pilles 1975; Schaafsma 1980; Cole 1989a). Ceramics of the Little Colorado River area dated post-A.D. 1250 to 1450 show similar masks (Ferg 1982; Hays 1988a, 1988b). Kiva murals at the ancient Hopi villages of Awatovi and Kawaika-a also exhibit similar masks. The murals are dated between the late 1300s and early 1600s (Smith 1952).

The masks are symbolic of the katsina cult (also spelled *katcina*, *kachina*, and *katchina*), a religious organization that integrates various aspects of Pueblo society and serves to reinforce village mythology and

Figure 62. *Details of late thirteenth to fourteenth century katsina mask petroglyphs near Homol'ovi II Ruin, Homol'ovi Ruins State Park, Little Colorado River drainage, northeastern Arizona. Elements are solid and stipple pecked.*

leadership. Supernatural beings known as katsinas are personated by masked members of the cult during elaborate ceremonies for rain and general well-being. The katsina cult and related activities and symbols have been extensively described by Southwest ethnographers and historians, and the majority of the information comes from the villages of the Hopi and Zuni (Fewkes 1901; Stevenson 1904; Bunzel 1932; Titiev 1944; Stephen 1969; Dockstader 1985). Symbolism of the Hopi katsina, Kokopelli, is briefly discussed in Chapter III.

In western Colorado, a possible katsina mask petroglyph is exhibited at Petroglyph Point in Mesa Verde National Park (Plate 53). The image is pecked on the lower-right portion of a petroglyph panel that contains approximately 109 elements (Fetterman 1976). The representation appears to be generally contemporaneous with adjacent Pueblo II–III style rock art based on the appearance and weathering of all elements. The possible mask is abstract in appearance and is superimposed over a zigzag pecked line. It is structurally composed of a circular outline marked with nine equally spaced triangles and dots. A rectangular outline "mouth" with beardlike lines extends below the mask outline, and three "eyes" are indicated by a short line and dot on one side and a dot on the other.

In 1952, Hopi informants identified various images at Petroglyph Point site according to their oral and artistic traditions. The masklike image was described as a symbol of the Katsina Clan (Mesa Verde Museum document n.d.).

Some historic Hopi representations of the Tawa katsina mask are circular with equally spaced triangles (Fewkes 1897), and petroglyph masks at Homol'ovi on the Little Colorado River are also circular with equally spaced triangles. Two possibly bearded masks and masks with three "eyes" are also shown at Homol'ovi (Cole 1989a). These katsina mask petroglyphs are believed to date approximately A.D. 1250–1400 and may have overlapped in time with the Petroglyph Point example.

Apparently, masking has a long tradition on the Colorado Plateau and among the Anasazi, as evinced by rock art of the Archaic, Basketmaker, and Pueblo periods. The best evidence indicates that katsina mask depictions are generally restricted to the Little Colorado River region and the Rio Grande area, where they are believed to date after A.D. 1250–1300. The Glen Canyon Style 4 masks discussed above may precede katsina cult symbolism or be part of a separate but possibly related iconography. The possible katsina mask at Mesa Verde may date after A.D. 1250–1300 and represent contacts with the Little Colorado River region. The mask may have been made by Anasazi occupying the area just prior to abandonment or by Pueblo visiting the area following abandonment.

THE CANYONLANDS ANASAZI

Rock art associated with Anasazi groups that occupied the Canyonlands area of eastern Utah and western Colorado is much less well known than that of the San Juan River drainage. This lack of information is probably due not only to more limited archaeological data but also to the cultural complexity of the area. The following description of Canyonlands rock art is generally divided into style categories thought to be associated with earlier and later stages of Anasazi development. These categories are compared to better-known rock art of the San Juan River area.

Basketmaker II, III, and Pueblo I

Pre-A.D. 1 to 900

Rock art associated with early Anasazi of the Canyonlands area is exhibited at sites located in the vicinity of the La Sal Mountains of Colorado and Utah, in canyons on the north slope of the Abajo Mountains in Utah, and on the Uncompahgre Plateau in Colorado. Most of the known sites occur in Utah. Overall, Anasazi rock art and other archaeological remains are not well understood north of the San Juan drainage; as noted earlier, the Canyonlands area is one of cultural complexity. Anasazi, Fremont, and hunting and gathering cultures with both desert and mountain associations are all likely to have used the area over time and, as neighbors, are likely to have continually influenced each other.

Dating of early Anasazi rock art in the Canyonlands area is based on stylistic qualities and comparisons with better-known rock art styles of the San Juan region.

In Utah, the best known early sites are located in Indian Creek Canyon and the Needles District of Canyonlands National Park north of the Abajo Mountains, and in canyons draining out of the La Sal Mountains near Moab, Utah. The sites generally lie within the Colorado River drainage. In western Colorado, early rock art occurs within the San Miguel and Dolores River drainages in the eastern La Sal Mountains, and in the lower Gunnison River drainage on the eastern slope of the Uncompahgre Plateau.

Early Canyonlands rock art is most commonly petroglyphs, but some rock paintings are known. These include anthropomorphs, abstract designs, quadrupeds, and numerous handprints (patterned and plain). Anthropomorphs are featured subjects of the early style art and continue to be featured during later cultural periods. Generally speaking, the rock art can be divided into two categories. One category has strong stylistic associations with Basketmaker rock art of the San Juan and upper Dolores River Anasazi areas. The second is art that combines traits of various rock art styles (Barrier Canyon Style, San Juan Basketmaker styles, Fremont styles) of the Colorado Plateau into a distinctive regional expression herein referred to as the Abajo-La Sal Style.

Art more typical of the San Juan area may have been made by groups from or closely allied with that area, while the Abajo-La Sal Style is viewed as a local development that reflects the cultural complexity of the region north of the San Juan River.

A panel of near life-size anthropomorphic petroglyphs typical of San Juan Basketmaker art occurs in Indian Creek Canyon, Utah. One figure has a face decorated by horizontal bars in the manner of figures and scalps represented at Butler Wash and Cedar Mesa sites in Utah. Painted figures at sites in the Needles District of Canyonlands National Park are also similar to San Juan Basketmaker figures. Two broad-shouldered figures wearing elaborate painted headdresses similar to *tablitas* (decorated thin wooden boards used by modern Pueblo people) are exhibited at a site in the Needles District (Plate 58). These

Plate 58. *Detail of red and white rock paintings at site 42SA1452, Needles District, Canyonlands National Park, Utah. Based on comparisons with San Juan Anasazi styles, the broad-shouldered anthropomorphs with large headdresses and the patterned handprints probably date from the Basketmaker-Pueblo I period; active anthropomorphs, the quadruped, and related elements probably date from the Pueblo II-Pueblo III period. Anthropomorph in center is approximately 50 centimeters in length.*

headdresses are not unlike Basketmaker headdresses of the San Juan River area. Large numbers of painted handprints in the Needles District are also typical of the San Juan area. At the Cave of 200 Hands site, more than three hundred handprints painted in red, brown, and pink are present (Noxon and Marcus 1985:136).

Other figures similar to San Juan Basketmaker style art are found at sites along the lower Dolores River and in the San Miguel River drainage of Colorado. One Dolores River site has panels of petroglyphs on large boulders. One panel shows broad-shouldered anthropomorphs, some with reverse-V shape legs, arms hanging from the shoulders, headdresses, and interior body decorations. Quadrupeds, a large bird, abstract images, and stylized paw prints are also exhibited at the site with two keyhole-shaped designs similar to those seen in the San Juan River area (Figure 63). Similar Basketmaker-like petroglyphs are found near Moab, Utah (Plates 59 and 60).

A petroglyph site in the San Miguel River drainage exhibits a remarkable anthropomorph that is approximately a meter and a half tall with a carefully sculptured face showing eyes, "nose," and mouth. The chest is decorated by horizontal bars. The figure is phallic and has feet turned to one side. One arm hangs limply from the shoulder. This figure occurs near site 5MN868, Tabeguache Cave I, a Basketmaker II site excavated by Hurst (1940–1942) and tree-ring dated between

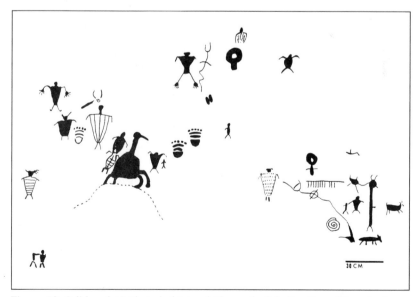

Figure 63. *Solid and stipple pecked petroglyphs north of the San Juan River drainage, at site 5MN439, in the lower Dolores River drainage, west central Colorado.*

Plate 59

Plate 60

Details of Anasazi petroglyphs north of the San Juan River drainage near Moab, east central Utah. The darkest, more patinated figures shown in Plate 59 probably date from the Basketmaker period; the largest anthropomorph is similar to San Juan River Basketmaker stlye rock art. These figures contrast with more lightly patinated figures shown in Plate 60 that probably date from the Pueblo II-Pueblo III period. Largest anthropomorph is approximately 40 centimeters in length; "backpackers" are approximately 10 to 20 centimeters in length.

approximately 10 B.C. and A.D. 300 (Gooding, personal communication). The large figure is situated above fourteen smaller anthropomorphs that are less detailed (Figures 64 and 65).

A rock shelter (site 5MN2777) along the lower Dolores River exhibits a row of broad-shouldered anthropomorphs painted white and brownish red. The figures have hair bobs like those of San Juan Basketmaker style figures, and one has interior body decoration. Another rock shelter site in the San Miguel River drainage shows rows of linked broad-shouldered figures in a faded red paint (Figure 66). These are quite similar to figures seen in the San Juan drainage.

At a site, in the lower Gunnison River drainage, petroglyphs similar to San Juan Basketmaker style art show anthropomorphs with quadrupeds. One anthropomorph appears to hold a crook (Figure 67). A notable difference between anthropomorphs in the Canyonlands area and those of the San Juan area is the placement of feet. While those in the San Juan area generally hang down, Canyonlands figures often have feet turned to the side. Also, Canyonlands figures are generally less ornate than images in the San Juan River area, particularly those attributed to early Basketmakers.

Figure 64   Figure 65

Solid pecked and ground petroglyphs north of the San Juan River drainage. Elements occur near site 5MN868 (Tabeguache Cave I), a Basketmaker site in the drainage of the San Miguel River, west central Colorado. Figures shown in Figure 65 are grouped as shown, but groups are schematically arranged. Elements are approximately 10 to 40 centimeters in length.

Figure 66. *Detail of red paintings north of the San Juan River drainage. The six linked anthropomorphs are exhibited with others on the rear wall of a rock shelter, site 5MN388, in the San Miguel River drainage, west central Colorado.*

Figure 67. *Detail of solid and stipple pecked petroglyphs north of the San Juan River drainage, at site 5ME159, in the lower Gunnison River drainage, west central Colorado.*

Abajo-La Sal Style

Abajo-La Sal Style rock art is less obviously related to San Juan River Basketmaker style art and shares characteristics of both Barrier Canyon Style and Fremont style rock art (Plate 61; Figures 70, 71, and 72). Examples of this style are found in the Abajo Mountains area, in Indian Creek Canyon, in Mill Creek Canyon, and other canyons near Moab, Utah, and in La Sal Creek Canyon and along the lower Dolores River in Colorado. A good example of Abajo-La Sal Style art is shown at a large La Sal Creek Canyon, Colorado, petroglyph site that exhibits panels with broad-shouldered anthropomorphs with arms out to the side and curved "winglike" arms, slender flute-players, broad-shouldered figures (with fringed headdresses typically seen in Fremont rock art to the north and east), and a variety of quadrupeds (Figures 68 and 69).

In addition to anthropomorphs, lines, dots, paw prints, foot prints, spirals and circles, snakes, and quadrupeds (bighorn sheep, deer or elk, canines, and bears) are exhibited. Anthropomorphs are most often static, but some active figures are shown. These are generally smaller figures. Anthropomorphic figures are commonly triangular and trapezoidal in shape. Other body forms are rectangular, sticklike, and tapered, while others are roughly ovate. Figures are often phallic. Arms are frequently shown straight out to the side, hanging down, and some figures have curved, winglike arms. Hands and feet are not always shown, and fingers and toes may be spread when shown.

Heads take a variety of forms, and earrings are shown infrequently. Facial features are also rare, but side hair bobs are common. Heads are represented by lines and circles; small rounded heads sit on long necks, and rounded and rectangular heads sit directly on the shoulders or on short necks. Two-horn headdresses, single "feather" headdresses, as well as antennaelike headdresses, are often shown on figures (Plate 61). Utah and Colorado sites exhibit relatively small anthropomorphs with floppy earlike headdresses and hair bobs with elevated crowns (Figures 68, 70, and 72). Flat headdresses similar to cap brims are also exhibited at Colorado sites. Arcs and wavy and zigzag lines are shown over heads and attached to the heads of large figures. This attribute is found at La Sal Creek and Indian Creek sites (Figures 68, 69, and 70).

Interior body decorations, such as lines, dots, waist bands, "breasts" and "breast plates," are occasionally depicted but are not common (Plate 62; Figure 70). "Hem fringe" is shown on figures in Indian Creek Canyon (Figure 70). At Moab sites, anthropomorphs are in association with what appear to be atlatls or darts similar to those shown in Basketmaker style rock art in the San Juan River area. Baglike devices are also shown being held.

Figure 68

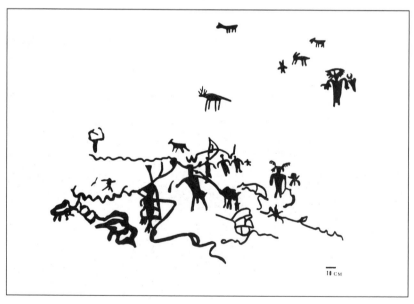

Figure 69

*Details of solid and stipple pecked Abajo-La Sal Style petroglyphs in the eastern La Sal
Mountains area, west central Colorado. Fringed headdresses shown in* Figure 69 *are
similar to those seen in Fremont style rock art.*

Plate 61. *Details of Abajo-La Sal Style petroglyphs near Moab, Utah. Similarities clearly exist between this style and the Barrier Canyon Style, San Juan River Basket-maker styles, and Fremont styles. Note the addition of a stylized paw print to the tail of a quadruped. Smaller elements are approximately 20 centimeters in length.*

Plate 62. *Abajo-La Sal Style at a site near Moab, Utah. Solid figure on upper left may depict a birth; adjacent figure shown in outline appears to have a dart, or large arrow through the body. Later, more lightly patinated forms include "sandal tracks" with textilelike designs and smaller tracks. Scale increments: 10 centimeters.*

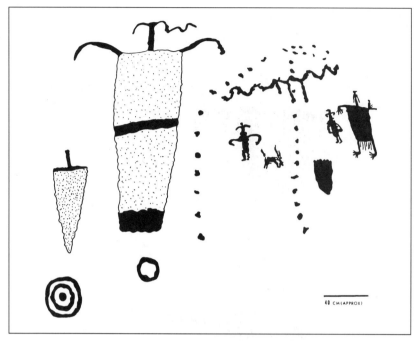

Figure 70

Abajo-La Sal Style solid and stipple pecked petroglyphs, Indian Creek drainage, north slope of Abajo Mountains, east central Utah.

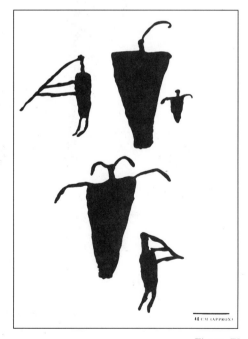

Figure 71

Figure 72. *Abajo-La Sal Style solid pecked petroglyphs in the western La Sal Mountains area near Moab, east central Utah.*

Figure 73

Figures 73, 74, and 75. *Details of Abajo-La Sal Style solid and stipple pecked petro-glyphs in the western La Sal Mountains area near Moab, east central Utah. Dashed lines indicate broken rock.*

Figure 74

Figure 75

Rows of linked or hand-holding figures are shown in Abajo-La Sal Style art. Twenty or more linked figures are depicted at a lower Dolores River site in Colorado, and linked figures are also prominent at Mill Creek, Utah, sites (Figures 69, 72, 76, and 77). Linked figures are generally smaller than solitary figures shown in the same panels. Pairs of figures are also represented in the Canyonlands area in a fashion similar to those in the San Juan River area but are apparently more rare.

Flute-players are present at a number of Utah and Colorado sites and are shown standing upright and as active. The flute-players do not have obvious humps on their backs but appear slightly hunched. Generally, the figures resemble slender flute-players of San Juan River Basketmaker style rock art. Flute-players at sites in Indian Creek and Mill Creek canyons in Utah, and in La Sal Creek Canyon, Colorado, are very similar. These flute-players hold the flutes against their heads with both hands and may wear headdresses formed of a single line extending behind the head. A common scene in the Abajo-La Sal Style shows static broad-shouldered anthropomorphs juxtaposed with flute-players (Figures 68 and 71).

Pueblo II and Pueblo III

A.D. 900 to 1300

In contrast to rock art in the San Juan River area, late Anasazi rock art in the Canyonlands has a continued emphasis on anthropomorphs and shows new types of figures in this tradition. Most examples of Pueblo II–III rock art are known from the Needles District of Canyonlands National Park, Indian Creek Canyon, and from canyons surrounding Moab, Utah. It is possible that Anasazi-related groups abandoned west central Colorado by A.D. 1150 (Gleichman et al. 1982:452). If so, that may explain why less art is known for Colorado sites. Rock art imagery from this period includes anthropomorphs, handprints (particularly white painted negative handprints), quadrupeds, snakes, bears, bear paw prints, ungulate tracks, "sandal" tracks, scorpion and centipedelike images, lines, "squiggle-mazes," spirals and circles, geometric designs similar to those on pottery (rows of connected triangles, "sunbursts," lines, rows of dots), bow and arrows, shield-figures and shieldlike images. Bighorn sheep and a variety of other quadrupeds are frequently depicted with open mouths and distorted body shapes. This type of image as well as geometric abstract designs, negative handprints, shieldlike images, and shield-figures are also shown in the San Juan River area during the same time period.

Late Canyonlands anthropomorphs include broad-shouldered,

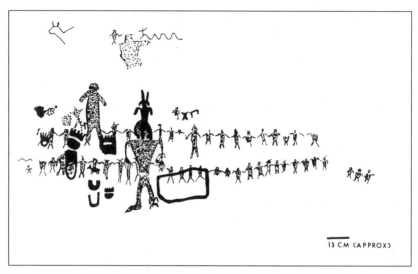

Figure 76

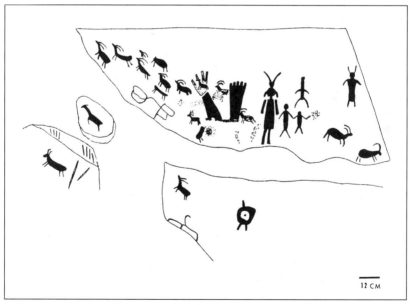

Figure 77

Details of solid and stipple pecked Abajo-La Sal Style petroglyphs at site 5MN443, in the lower Dolores River drainage, west central Colorado. All elements in Figure 76 except those in upper left are solid pecked. Elements shown in Figure 77 occur on slabs of rock, and include possible shield-figures. Adapted from Toll (1977:Fig. 25, 26, 29, 30).

ovate, sticklike, and rectangular figures as well as figures with upraised arms, humpback flute-players, and shield-figures. Shield-figures often wear ear, horn, and antennaelike headdresses. Some broad-shouldered figures are relatively large and have a supernatural appearance, while others are relatively small, more realistic figures in active poses. Examples are humpback figures, possibly representative of people wearing burden basket packs, that appear in rows. Such figures are frequently phallic and appear to be walking and running. Good examples of red-painted "backpackers" are exhibited at the Cave of 200 Hands site in the Needles District of Canyonlands National Park (Noxon and Marcus 1985), and petroglyph examples are exhibited at a site near Moab, Utah (Plate 60).

This continued emphasis on anthropomorphs in late Canyonlands Anasazi rock art clearly differs from the situation in the San Juan River drainage, where anthropomorphic images appear to be less important after A.D. 900. The "lizard-man" image that is so prevalent in the San Juan River area after that period is virtually unknown in the Canyonlands area.

Interaction with Fremont peoples who represented elaborate anthropomorphs in rock art and clay figurines may explain the emphasis on anthropomorphs in the northern area. Certain representations, particularly the Faces Motif discussed below, bear a striking resemblance to certain San Rafael Fremont figurines in shape and details of decoration (Plates 63, 64, 65, 66, 70, and 71) and, to a lesser degree, Fremont style rock art figures. Fremont symbolism apparently had a strong influence on late Canyonlands Anasazi art. It also appears to have somewhat influenced groups in the northern San Juan River area during the late Pueblo II–III period, indicated by the depiction of anthropomorphs on a structure wall at Kachina Bridge Ruin in Natural Bridges National Monument on Cedar Mesa (Plate 67) and possibly by the representation of shields and shield-figures at various Pueblo II–III locations in Utah, Colorado, and Arizona. In addition, a clay figurine resembling those of the Fremont in form and detail was recovered from a late Pueblo II–III structure (site 42SA4355) on Cedar Mesa.

Distinctive Pueblo II–III anthropomorphs of the Canyonlands are broad-shouldered and tapered figures, commonly with facial features and often with details of jewelry, clothing, and headdresses. These figures are frequently torsos without appendages, and are pecked and painted or both. More elaborate and distinctive examples are painted in one or more colors and occur in the Needles District of Canyonlands National Park (Plates 63, 64, 65, and 66).

Noxon and Marcus (1985) refer to this type of figure as the Faces Motif and include it (along with shield-figures, geometric designs,

Plate 63. *Pueblo II-III style petroglyphs at site 42SA13797, Indian Creek Canyon, east central Utah. Note anthropomorphs that are similar in form to Fremont style rock art and figurines, and the presence of a shieldlike image in the upper right.*

handprints, and small active figures) in the Canyonlands Anasazi Style associated with the late Pueblo II–III occupation of the Needles District (approximately A.D. 1000–1050 to 1300). Tipps and Hewitt (1989) identify the Faces Motif as a separate Faces Motif Anthropomorphic Style. They question the validity of the inclusive Canyonlands Anasazi Style and observe that element types present in the area are frequently associated with rock art styles outside the area.

It is observed that Faces Motif anthropomorphs are characterized by a smoothing of the background rock prior to painting, especially in the facial area. Also, many of the figures have been overpainted, suggesting periodic renewal of imagery. Faces Motif figures are found in rock shelters (often in association with Anasazi structures), ceramics, grinding areas, and possible prehistoric farmlands (Noxon and Marcus 1985).

Faces Motif figures occur as single representations and also in groups and horizontal rows. Eyes are frequently dashed lines and ovals; one figure at the Four Faces site has a cross indicating the left eye and a dash indicating the right. The same site exhibits a single rectangular masklike face with only eyes shown. Mouths, when present, are lines curved upward and straight. Chin areas are frequently decorated by dots or solid areas. Dots also outline the cheeks on some figures. Overall, these faces have a decidedly masklike appearance.

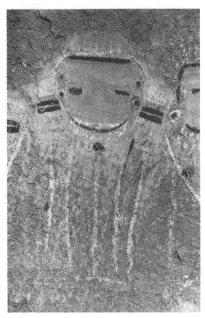

Plate 64   Plate 65

Details of Faces Motif rock paintings associated with Pueblo II-III style rock art in the Canyonlands area of east central Utah. Plate 64 *shows a detail of a combination rock painting and petroglyph at site 42SA1638, Needles District, Canyonlands National Park. This example of the Faces Motif is painted red and blue-green and is approximately one meter in length.* Plates 65 *and* 66 *show details of the Faces Motif at site 42SA7736, Needles District, Canyonlands National Park. Figures are painted red and white, and faces were ground before painting. Forms and decorative details of these images are remarkably similar to those of the Fremont Pillings figurines (see* Plates 70 *and* 71*) believed to date after* A.D. 1000. *Figures are approximately 1.75 meters in length.*

Plate 66

Plate 67. *Cream-colored paintings on the plastered wall of a late Pueblo II-Pueblo III period circular room at Kachina Bridge Ruin, Natural Bridges National Monument, Utah. These anthropomorphic forms are not typical of Pueblo II-III style rock art elsewhere in the San Juan River area, but are similar to Pueblo II-III Anasazi rock art in the Canyonlands area to the north.*

Heads are shown as both flat and rounded on top and sit directly on the shoulders. Hair (or possibly shoulder decorations) appears as side bundles in the shape of an hourglass or bow. The latter are also found on Fremont clay figurines, as are slit "coffee bean eyes" made of clay appliqué. Several painted examples closely resemble the Pillings (Plates 70 and 71) and Old Woman site figurines of the San Rafael Fremont (Morss 1954). Fremont figurines are classified as female and male but the rock art does not have obvious gender symbolism. However, hairstyles and clothing may have indicated gender.

Earplugs or earrings are indicated on several figures, and head-dresses are indicated by vertical lines and arcs. Possible collars, breast plates, pendants, waist belts, and kilts are shown on several figures. Interior body decorations include parallel lines and other geometric patterns. Handprints occur beside and beneath some figures, and individual masklike faces are depicted at some sites.

Interestingly, Faces Motif figures share formal traits of katsina representations in rock art of the Little Colorado River and Rio Grande areas dated after A.D. 1250–1300, particularly with regard to the masklike faces. It is possible that the Faces Motif influenced the develop-

Plate 68

Plate 69

Shield-figures in the Canyonlands area of east central Utah, that probably date from the Pueblo II-III period. Plate 68 shows a shield-figure petroglyph at an Indian Creek Canyon site. Lighter patinated quadrupeds at the bottom of the picture were probably made by historic Ute Indians. The shield-figure occurs near a late Pueblo II-III cliff dwelling and resembles a rock painting at Bat Woman Ruin in Navajo National Monument, Arizona. Plate 69 shows a red, white, and blue rock painting of a shield-figure in association with a late Pueblo II-Pueblo III masonry structure at site 42SA1614, Needles District, Canyonlands National Park. The figure, known as the All American Man, has been chalked, and details visible on the face and neck may have been changed from the original. Figure is approximately 1.75 meters in length.

ment of katsina iconography to the south following the abandonment of the Canyonlands area after A.D. 1250–1300.

Shieldlike representations are common in the Canyonlands area but are not as consistently associated with cliff dwellings as in the San Juan area. Cliff dwellings are relatively rare in the Canyonlands area outside of Indian Creek and the Needles District of Canyonlands National Park. A shield-figure petroglyph is depicted below a small cliff dwelling in Indian Creek Canyon (Plate 68), and the famous red-, white-, and blue-painted "All American Man" shield-figure appears with handprints on the wall of an alcove adjacent to a masonry structure in the Needles District (Plate 69). The Indian Creek petroglyph shows a shield-bearing figure that wears upright "ears" on the head. This is similar to a white painted shield-figure at Bat Woman House, a Pueblo III cliff dwelling in Tsegi Creek drainage, Arizona, south of the San Juan River.

Other painted and pecked shieldlike images and shield-figures are found scattered throughout the Canyonlands area on canyon walls and rock outcrops, some near springs and passes over ridges (Plate 63). White shield-figures in Salt Creek Canyon superimpose faded Barrier Canyon Style figures; at a Courthouse Wash site in Arches National Park, shieldlike images are painted on a panel of Barrier Canyon Style art. The "shields" superimpose some of the earlier figures, and one "shield" is shown as if being held by a Barrier Canyon Style anthropomorph.

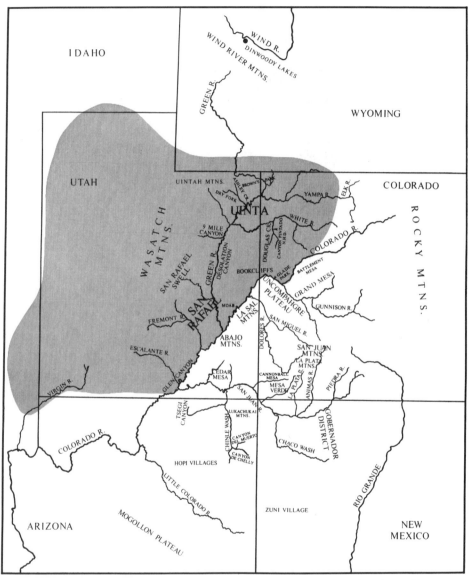

Map 8. *Fremont culture area and general locations of two regional variants (San Rafael and Uinta) significant to the rock art study area. Associated styles of rock art date between approximately A.D. 400 and 1500.*

FREMONT ROCK ART

Styles associated with regional divisions of the Fremont culture are described by Schaafsma (1971) in a study of Utah rock art. Stylistically similar art is found in west central and northwest Colorado (Cole 1987) and southwestern Wyoming (Day and Dibble 1963). Major Fremont rock art areas in Colorado are Dinosaur National Monument, the Brown's Park area, and the White River-Douglas Creek (Cañon Pintado) area of northwest Colorado; Glade Park on the northern Uncompahgre Plateau (Little Dolores River drainage); and along the Colorado River in west central Colorado.

The easternmost examples of Fremont style rock art appear to be in the upper White River drainage of Colorado. Dating of Fremont rock art in the study area follows the estimated range of dates for the culture, approximately A.D. 400 to 1500.

Of particular importance in the study area are the Classic Vernal Style, associated with the Uinta Basin Fremont, and the Northern and Southern San Rafael styles associated with the San Rafael Fremont. Type-sites for the Classic Vernal Style are located in Dinosaur National Monument and Ashley and Dry Fork valleys of Utah (Plates 72, 78, 79, 80, 81, 83, 84, and 87). Type-sites for the Northern and Southern San Rafael styles are in the Nine Mile Canyon, Utah, area (Plates 85 and 86) and the Fremont River area in Capitol Reef National Park, (Figure 78), respectively. Classic Sieber Canyon Style rock art in the Glade Park, Colorado, area has been described by Conner and Ott (1978). This style is consistent with the Classic Vernal Style (Plate 75; Figures 81, 82, 87, and 88).

Recent radiocarbon and tree-ring dating of archaeological sites in Dinosaur National Monument (Truesdale, personal correspondence) make it possible to estimate the age of Classic Vernal Style rock art

Figure 78. *Detail of Southern San Rafael Style Fremont petroglyphs at Capitol Reef National Park, Utah. Elements are solid and stipple pecked. Solid anthropomorph is approximately one meter in length.*

with some assurance. For example, Wagon Run site (site 42UN49) and Wholeplace Village (site 42UN57) in the Cub Creek drainage (representative of the Cub Creek Phase) date approximately A.D. 610 and A.D. 640, respectively. These sites are in association with several panels of Classic Vernal Style petroglyphs, and other prehistoric styles are not obvious. Deluge Shelter (site 42UN178) to the east is decorated with panels of red paintings and dates approximately A.D. 735 and 920. As discussed earlier, it is estimated that the Fremont had abandoned much of the Dinosaur National Monument area by A.D. 1000. If so, the Classic Vernal Style in that location is likely to date from prior to that period.

Styles of Fremont rock art are within the anthropomorphic tradition discussed previously. Fremont elements generally have geometric qualities and show sharply angular anthropomorphs that can be distinguished from similar representations in Archaic and Anasazi rock art, although in some cases, style overlaps are striking. This is particularly true with regard to Barrier Canyon Style and San Juan Basketmaker style figures.

Characteristics of San Rafael Fremont style rock art are shared with Barrier Canyon Style art that occurs in the same geographic area, and characteristics of Uinta Fremont style art are markedly similar to San Juan River Basketmaker style art (Schaafsma 1971; Cole 1987). Such information supports archaeological data that indicates the development of the Fremont from indigenous Archaic peoples and cultural interaction between the Fremont and Anasazi over time. In Cañon Pintado of northwest Colorado, this transition is likely to have taken place after A.D. 450, when it is estimated that the Fremont developed from local Archaic groups (Creasman 1981, 1982).

Fremont style rock art includes well-made petroglyphs, rock paintings (monochrome and polychrome), and combination petroglyph-rock paintings that feature heroic and supernatural-appearing anthropomorphs, often near life-size. Some have detailed facial features, headdresses, masklike faces, clothing, and elaborate body decorations. Others are relatively simple solid pecked and painted figures. Anthropomorphs and other elements are shown in outline and as solid forms.

Fremont anthropomorphs are predominantly broad shouldered and roughly trapezoidal in shape; they may wear elaborate headdresses, jewelry, and clothing, and have abstract interior body decorations, such as dots, circles, spirals, and lines. The forms and details of anthropomorphs generally resemble Fremont unfired clay and stone figurines described by Morss (1954), Breternitz (1970), and others (Plates 70 and 71). Some figures have long tapered bodies similar to those of the Barrier Canyon Style, while others have hourglass, rectangular, and bottle-shape bodies. Phallic males are shown. More realistic figure forms are also shown. Anthropomorphs are frequently depicted in horizontal rows in a manner similar to that of Archaic and Anasazi rock art styles previously discussed in this volume. Anthropomorphs that have characteristics of both Fremont and Barrier Canyon Style rock art occur in the study area. Examples are found in the Book Cliffs of east central Utah, in the Nine Mile Canyon area, and in the Douglas Creek-White River area of Colorado (Plates 24 and 30).

Heads shown in rock art are rectangular, helmet-shaped, and rounded and frequently sit directly on the shoulders. Side hair bobs similar to those seen on Anasazi Basketmaker figures are frequently exhibited at northeastern Utah and western Colorado sites. Facial features (usually eyes and mouth) are common on Fremont anthropomorphs, but are not always shown. Solid pecked and painted figures generally do not show facial features, and these are probably the most commonly represented types, especially in northeastern Utah and western Colorado. Stylized dot and solid line "tear streaks" (known as the "weeping eye" motif) are frequently shown, as are other facial decorations that suggest masks (Plate 89). "Tear streaks" are shown on anthropomorphs and possible scalp representations. "Tear streaks" also occur in San Juan Basketmaker rock art at a Butler Wash, Utah, site and appear in historic art of the Great Plains.

Headdresses include fringed "sticks," horns, antlers, "ears," antennaelike forms, rectangular "tablitas" (thin wooden boards with decora-

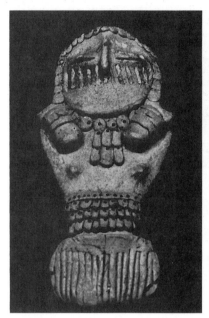

Plate 70   Plate 71

Two unfired and painted Fremont style clay figurines, probably female and male, from the Pillings collection. These are elaborate examples of Fremont clay figurines dated approximately A.D. 900-1000. Paint colors are red, black, and buff. Figurine shown in Plate 70 is 13.5 centimeters in length; figurine in Plate 71 is 10.4 centimeters in length (Morss 1954:Fig. 6, 7). Photographs and figurines in collection of Prehistoric Museum of the College of Eastern Utah, Price, Utah. Pearl Oliver, photographer.

tion), "feathers," and elevated caplike devices. The last are frequently described as reverse-bucket shaped heads (Plates 74 and 75; Figures 81, 82, 87, and 88). A similar headdress is found in San Juan Basketmaker rock art (Plate 42). Elaborate Fremont headdresses give a decidedly ceremonial appearance to many anthropomorphs. "Feather" headdresses shown on figures at a Dinosaur National Monument and Dry Fork sites (Plates 72 and 81) resemble an elaborate flicker feather headdress from another site in the monument (Plate 73).

Distinctive headdresses of western Colorado and northeastern Utah are "fringed sticks" (Plates 74, 75, and 81; Figures 79, 87, and 88). These are also common in the Glade Park area and are seen at Capitol Reef National Park, Uinta Basin, and Nine Mile Canyon, Utah, sites (Castleton 1978). The "fringed sticks" are worn singly and as a pair with the fringe turned up as well as down. "Fringed sticks" are also shown as independent items (Plate 76) and being held. The representations possibly signify or share symbolism of split and fringed plant fiber artifacts described by Morss (1931) from the Fremont River area

Plate 72. *Fremont style red rock paintings from site 42UN178, Dinosaur National Monument, Utah. Anthropomorphs wear headdresses that are similar in form to an elaborate flicker feather and ermine headdress from Mantle's Cave, a Fremont site in nearby Castle Park, Colorado (see Plate 73).*

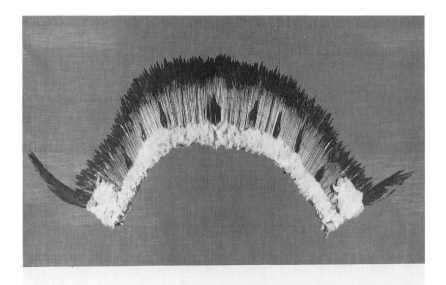

Plate 73. *Headdress made of red-shafted and yellow-shafted flicker feathers bound to a fur strip of ermine pelts from Cache No. 1, Mantle's Cave, Dinosaur National Monument, Colorado (Burgh and Scoggin 1948). The form and details of the headdress resemble those shown in Fremont rock paintings.*

Plate 74. *Detail of Fremont style petroglyphs at site 5MF492, Brown's Park area, northwestern Colorado. Shown are bison and other quadrupeds as well as a variety of anthropomorphs. The small headless figures may represent "backpackers" or people wearing burden baskets. The large figure shown in outline is apparently the most recent figure on the panel and wears a fringed headdress. This panel occurs above a narrow ledge on a canyon wall.*

Plate 75. *Fremont style petroglyphs showing figures wearing fringed headdresses at site 5ME458, Glade Park area, west central Colorado. Damage to larger figure is by gunfire; figure is approximately one meter in length.*

Plate 76. *Fremont style red and white rock paintings at a site in the Cañon Pin-tado–Douglas Creek area, northwestern Colorado. The petroglyphs at the ground level are Barrier Canyon Style. The Fremont art shows anthropomorphs, an elaborate spiral, horned masklike forms, and a "fringed stick" similar to those carried and on headdresses.*

10 CM

Figure 79. *Solid pecked Classic Vernal Style petroglyphs at 5MF353, Brown's Park area, northwestern Colorado. Adapted from a field sketch by Lynn Bloomfield.*

in Utah. Similar artifacts are reported by Hewitt (1980) from Cowboy Cave in Utah (Plate 77) and from Basketmaker sites in west central Colorado (Hurst 1944, 1947, 1948).

Large necklaces and pendants are shown, as are earrings, kiltlike clothing (some with fringe), sashes, and waist belts. Some figures are shown with possible breast plates, while others have abstract line and dot patterns in the interior of the body (Plates 78, 79, 80, and 81). One painted and pecked figure in the White River-Douglas Creek area has small figurinelike anthropomorphs painted in the chest area (Plate 89).

Round and trapezoidal stone and bone artifacts probably representing parts of pendants, necklaces, and breast plates have been excavated from Cub Creek sites in Dinosaur National Monument (Breternitz 1970). In particular, thin flat shaped stones (Plate 82) are similar to certain rock art renditions in Dinosaur National Monument and elsewhere in the Uinta Basin (Plates 74, 78, and 79).

Feet and hands are often enlarged, and arms and hands may hang down or be raised. Feet rarely hang down and are more commonly turned to one or both sides. Extremely large feet are shown at sites in the Dry Fork Valley, Utah. Realistic muscular definition is shown in the arms and legs of some figures, while appendages on other figures are sticklike. Still other figures have no arms or legs. Left feet are deliber-

Plate 77. Split rod or splint of squawbush wrapped and split to create a fringe along one edge. These examples are from Cowboy Cave, site 42WN420, east central Utah (Hewitt 1980:72-74). This type of artifact is generally associated with late Archaic, Basketmaker, and Fremont occupations on the Colorado Plateau and is unidentified as to function. Photograph courtesy of the Utah Museum of Natural History, University of Utah.

Details of Fremont style petroglyphs from a site in Dinosaur National Monument, Utah. Plate 78 shows probable male and female figures holding hands. These are typical Classic Vernal Style figures shown in outline. The figures are situated above a narrow ledge near the top of a cliff. Plate 79 shows adjacent figures that probably represent males. Larger figures are life-size.

Plate 78

Plate 79

Plate 80

Plate 81

Fremont style petroglyphs and combination petroglyphs and rock paintings in Dry Fork Valley, northeast Utah. Colors are red and black. These Classic Vernal Style representations include figures holding head and scalplike images and shields, and figures with "weeping eyes." Larger anthropomorphs are near life-size.

Plate 82. *Shaped stones from site 42UN178, Dinosaur National Monument. These stones resemble chest decorations seen in Fremont rock art, but it is not apparent how they may have been worn. Scale is in centimeters.*

ately omitted from figures at two Colorado sites, near Brown's Park and in Glade Park (Figures 80 and 81).

Fremont figures frequently hold items that resemble wands or staffs, spears, bows and arrows, knives, shields, bags, masks, heads, and scalps. In some instances, knifelike images are large and may represent "Fremont blades," or large shouldered blades or projectile points (Plates 75 and 83). Particularly large blades, from ten to thirty centimeters in length, are reported. Examples from Dinosaur National Monument are described by Breternitz (1970).

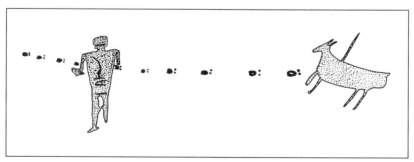

Figure 80. *Detail of solid pecked Fremont style petroglyphs at site 5MF492, Brown's Park area, northwestern Colorado. These elements occur high above the floor of a narrow canyon. All elements are solid pecked. Anthropomorph is approximately life-size.*

Figure 81. *Solid pecked Fremont style petroglyphs at site 5ME465, Glade Park area, west central Colorado. Possible bird-headed staff held by upper and lower figures are similar to a Basketmaker II cermonial wand from northeastern Arizona (*Figure 49*) and may represent wands used by the Fremont.*

At a Glade Park, Colorado, petroglyph site, two anthropomorphs hold large blades and what appear to be bird-head staffs that are fringed or notched along the length (Figure 81). A "fringed" triangular "bundle" is suspended from the neck of one. Guernsey and Kidder (1921:Pl. 39) report a remarkably similar carved wooden bird-head wand from which is suspended a triangular bundle composed of feathers, shell, and rawhide. The neck of the wand has a series of incised lines (Figure 49). The artifact is from a Basketmaker II site in the Marsh Pass, Arizona, area. Comparable wands or staffs may have also been used by the Fremont.

In a study of petroglyphs at Dinosaur National Monument, Burton (1971) concludes that solid elements are earlier than those shown in outline, and the most recent elements are highly abstracted anthropomorphs without body forms, represented only by such details as headdresses, facial features, jewelry, and waistbands.

Burton sees Fremont art as becoming more abstract over time. It is possible, however that many of the more abstract anthropomorphs were combination petroglyph-rock painting forms, and the paint has weathered away, leaving only the petroglyph details visible. Use of the combination technique and the presence of paint remnants with petroglyphs at locations in Dry Fork Canyon and Little Brush Creek, Utah, suggest that at least some of the more abstract petroglyph figures are not in original forms. If this is accurate, abstraction may not have been intended by Fremont artists; in fact, details of body decoration may have been emphasized during the later period.

More heroic and decorative figures, including shield-figures, are generally static forms. More active flute-players, "hunting," "walking," "copulating," and linked figures are generally more realistic. In the Classic Vernal Style, smaller, active, and realistic figures occasionally occur in association with larger static figures, and the larger figures appear dominant. San Rafael Fremont rock art styles show a greater number of more active, realistic figures in association with a variety of animals and geometric abstract images. Hunting scenes are common in San Rafael Fremont rock art styles.

Additional elements seen in Fremont rock art include faces, possible scalps, masks, and heads; concentric circles, spirals, lines, and other geometric designs; quadrupeds such as bighorn sheep, pronghorn, deer or elk, bison, and canines; scorpion and centipedelike images and other possible insects; lizards; snakes; shieldlike images; owls, wading birds; and sandal or moccasin tracks, footprints, paw prints, and ungulate tracks.

Examples of Fremont rock art occur high on cliff walls and in locations that have difficult access and often precarious footing for modern viewers and presumably for artists of the past. Falling from cliff ledges would have been a very real possibility, and artists appear to have worked very close to their subjects with limited visibility and perspective. The high settings emphasize the heroic and ceremonial nature of the subject matter and emphasize the skill and physical balance of artists. The ceremonial nature of some sites is attested to by the amount and workmanship of the rock art, the height and inaccessibility of the art, and by the subject matter. High and exposed rock art settings occur in the Dry Fork Valley, Utah, in Dinosaur National Monument, in the Brown's Park area, and in Glade Park, Colorado (Plates 74, 78, and 79; Figures 80 and 82).

Possible themes of Fremont rock art are shamanism, mythology, warfare, fertility, and hunting. Shamans and mythological personages

Figure 82. *Solid pecked Fremont style petroglyphs from site 5ME724, Glade Park area, west central Colorado. Dashed line indicates broken rock. Largest anthropomorph is approximately one and a half meters in length.*

are suggested by heroic, masked, and supernatural-appearing anthropomorphs (Plates 83, 84, 85, 86, and 88; Figure 84). Birdlike figures are also suggestive of mythology (Plate 92). Warriors are possibly signified by shield-figures and by figures holding shields, large blades, spears, bows and arrows, and possible scalps or heads. Wormington (1955) notes that a high level of lithic production and the presence of a human mandible at the Turner-Look site suggest an emphasis on warfare (and hunting) for the Fremont. It is also possible that war imagery is symbolic of mythological warfare and has ritual significance. Such imagery may have illustrated mythic heroes such as those of the Pueblos and Navajo that are invoked during warrior society ceremonies, and during curing ceremonies.

Fertility themes are suggested a number of ways in Fremont style rock art. Sites at Dinosaur National Monument and elsewhere show realistic and stylized phallic imagery. One site shows a couple, probably a phallic male and a female, holding hands. These figures share a panel with a row of similarly phallic males (Plates 78 and 79).

A Brown's Park panel shows male and female symbolism and a possible birth or copulation scene (Figure 83). Other, less detailed scenes that may show copulation occur elsewhere in the Brown's Park area (Cole 1987).

In the White River drainage, Fremont style anthropomorphs have been painted around natural holes in the rock suggesting female (vulva) symbolism. Less obvious female symbolism may be expressed by the depiction of fringed kiltlike or apronlike clothing. Fremont figurines (Plate 70) that are obviously female with protruding breasts have similar clothing (Morss 1954).

Plate 83

Plate 84

Fremont petroglyphs from Dinosaur National Monument, Utah, showing figures with masklike faces, a shield-figure, a large bladelike device, and possible shields and bags. Bison are shown in Plate 83 and appear elsewhere in Fremont style art. Scale increments: 10 centimeters.

Hunting themes are expressed by hunt scenes and representations of carefully depicted game animals and canines. This subject may also be related to shamanistic activities to bring hunting success based on the frequent association between game animal representations and anthropomorphs with headdresses, some of which are shown holding bows and arrows. Good examples of these scenes occur in the Nine Mile Canyon area of Utah (Plates 85 and 86) and in the Brown's Park and Glade Park areas of Colorado.

A Brown's Park panel shows a carefully pecked near life-size anthropomorph holding an unidentified device. A series of cloven hoof tracks cross the body of the anthropomorph and end just in front of a large quadruped, possibly a pronghorn, that is some meters away on the same level. The quadruped has a line (possibly a spear or dart shaft) protruding from the back (Figure 80). A second Brown's Park site shows a row of anthropomorphs above a row of quadrupeds (Plate 91).

A distinctive characteristic of Fremont style rock art is the organization of subject matter that is frequently visible at sites. Some panels have discrete groupings (or feature a single element) within; at some sites, entire panels appear to be composed of intentionally grouped and thematically related elements. Some panels have strong narrative qualities, particularly those with hunting and fertility themes. Good examples of this situation are found in the Nine Mile Canyon area, in

Plate 85. *Northern San Rafael Style Fremont petroglyphs from Nine Mile Canyon area, northeastern Utah. This crowded panel with hunting themes is typical. Note the small shield-figure in the center of the panel. Scale increments: 10 centimeters.*

Plate 86. *Fremont style white rock paintings in Nine Mile Canyon, Utah. Paintings show an anthropomorph with a headdress and a quadruped with an ovate body. This imagery is frequently seen in Fremont rock art.*

Plate 87. *Detail of typical Fremont style shield-figures from the Dry Fork Valley, northeastern Utah. The figures are combination red rock paintings and petroglyphs. The shield of the leftmost figure on the facing wall is masklike. Shield-figures are approximately one meter in length.*

Plate 88. *Detail of a probable Fremont shield-figure from the Book Cliffs area of east central Utah. This faded red painted and scratched shield-figure is obviously older than dark red elements to the left and above that are probably of historic Ute origin. Scratches may have also been made by the Ute. The shield-figure resembles one at site 5RT698, in northwestern Colorado, and is approximately 1.3 meters in length.*

Figure 83. *Solid and stipple pecked Fremont style petroglyphs at site 5MF354, Brown's Park area, northwestern Colorado. The panel has male and female symbolism, and upper images may depict copulation or a birth.*

Figure 84. *Fremont style rock paintings at site 5ME529, near the Colorado River, west central Colorado. Outlined areas indicate white pigment; stippled areas indicate claylike pigment, and the solid figure is painted red.*

Dinosaur National Monument, and in the Brown's Park area, where individual elements as well as groups of anthropomorphs and quadrupeds, often tightly clustered and superimposed, have been pecked and painted on discrete cliff areas, boulders, and rock faces.

Possible scalps are shown in Uinta Fremont rock art and are "carried" by anthropomorphs. A number of these subjects are exhibited in Dry Fork Valley, Utah (Plates 80 and 81). While they are stylistically different from scalps shown in San Juan Basketmaker style rock art, they do show straps or "handles" at the top of the head, hair bobs, and necks and thus are similar to Basketmaker examples.

Two whole hair scalp artifacts in association with a Fremont site in Nine Mile Canyon, Utah, are described as "two scalps of the whole hair part of the head, the inside of the scalps being faced and the two placed face to face" (Reagan 1931a:128). In addition to the scalps, Reagan (1933a:58) reports a "mummy-skeleton" from the same site that may have been scalped.

Other possible rock art examples of scalps are more abstract and less detailed, and some or all may represent faces and masks. A painted red-and-white example with a flattened head is shown at a Douglas Creek-Cañon Pintado site. A decidedly masklike image at the same site is painted white and has a headdress of long curved horns (Plate 76).

Two animal-like, possibly bear, masks are shown at a site in Dinosaur National Monument. One masked figure is a shield-figure (the shield is less carefully pecked and was possibly added later) and is superimposed by a bison representation. The other masked figure holds a large bladelike device that is also held by an adjacent figure. Heads are solid pecked and have eyes and bearlike ear headdresses (Plate 83). Earlike headdresses are seen elsewhere on Fremont figures (Plate 81). Warner (1984) has analyzed headdresses, ear, and hairstyles in Fremont rock art and notes the presence of possible bear symbolism as well as the possibility that caps and animal skins were being worn.

A white-painted "bear," standing upright, is exhibited at a site near the Colorado River in west central Colorado. The figure appears to wear an armband and may represent a human in ceremonial dress, although the body is not typically broad-shouldered. Nearby images are broad-shouldered anthropomorphs (a white one wearing a head-dress and a red one with a small rounded head), and a white horned "snake" (Figure 84).

Shield-figures and shieldlike images are frequently exhibited in the Uinta Basin of Utah. The shields are decorated with various pecked line and dot designs. Some have painted designs, and others may have once been painted. A number of "shields" and shield-figures are shown in the Dry Fork Valley and in Dinosaur National Monument, Utah (Plates 81, 83, 84, 87, 88, and 89). Dry Fork Valley examples have masklike decorations. To the south, painted shield-figures are exhibited at Diamond and Westwater canyons in the Book Cliffs of Utah (Plate 88) and in Nine Mile Canyon (Plate 85).

Fremont shield imagery is relatively rare in Colorado. In west central Colorado, two mud-painted shield-figures and a "shield" of possible Fremont origin are exhibited at a site in the Gunnison River drainage on the eastern slope of the Uncompahgre Plateau (Figure 85). One shield-figure has a rounded head shown in outline and wears

Plate 89. *Shield-figure shown is painted two shades of red and white. The darker red appears to have been rubbed over the lighter painted surface, perhaps by later artists. The figure occurs upstream from the Turner-Look Fremont site (Wormington 1955) and is approximately 40 centimeters in length.*

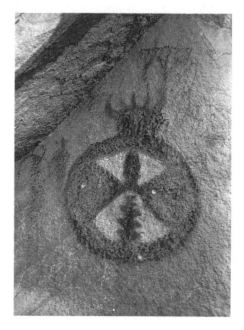

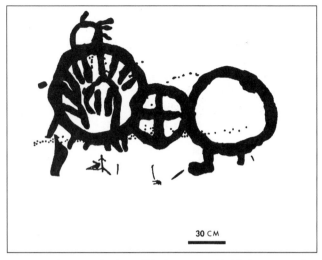

30 CM

Figure 85. *Detail of possible Fremont shield-figures and a "shield" from site 5DT1, near the lower Gunnison River, west central Colorado. Figures are painted with a claylike pigment and are shown with small incised elements of possible historic Ute origin. Adapted from a drawing by Buckles (1971: Fig. 146).*

a "feathered" headdress. This figure has no legs or feet. The interior of the shield is decorated with raylike lines around a semicircle with two vertical lines inside, and fringelike lines hang below the shield. This figure is linked to a "shield" that is, in turn, attached to a second shield-figure that has legs and a foot but no head.

A typical Fremont style petroglyph shield-figure is exhibited at a site near the Colorado River at the northern end of the Uncompahgre Plateau (Figure 86). The figure has a rectangular head shown in outline. The legs and feet are realistic in shape, and the large shield is solid and stipple pecked. The interior decoration is a complex pattern of six triangular and two comma-shaped forms, and four dots. From the left side of the shield, ten raylike lines formed of pecked dots protrude. This shield-figure occurs on a slab of sandstone near the top of a shallow canyon and is tilted upward. At this angle, the figure faces the rim of the opposite canyon wall and the eastern horizon. The location facing the dawn sky as well as the roundness of the shield and the "rays" seem symbolic of the sun. The Fremont shield-figure motif is discussed by Wormington (1955:160), and relationships with rock art of the northwestern Plains are noted:

In Pictograph Cave, near Billings, are found paintings which are remarkably like the shield-bearing anthropomorphic pic-

tographs of the Fremont Culture. The similarities as regards
methods of presentation and design motifs on shields are so
close that they must certainly be more than coincidental.

Keyser (1975) has proposed that the shield-bearing-warrior motif
of northwestern Great Plains rock art has its origin with Shoshonean
peoples who entered the area after A.D. 800–1000. Keyser observes
that it is possible that contact with the Fremont influenced the Shoshonean motif. Shields and shield-figures are depicted in association
with Cub Creek Phase sites in Dinosaur National Monument, where
they may have been made as early as the A.D. 600s.

Paired figures and rows of linked and hand-holding anthropomorphs are exhibited in Utah and Colorado. These types of figures are
well represented in Dinosaur National Monument, Dry Fork Valley,
and the Brown's Park area (Plates 78, 80, and 91). Rows of relatively
small humpback figures, possibly wearing burden baskets, are depicted
in Nine Mile Canyon, Utah, and in the Brown's Park area (Plate 74).
The "backpackers" often appear to be walking and are similar to those
seen in the Canyonlands Anasazi area. Certain "backpackers" are quite
abstract and appear as triangular forms.

Flute-players are not as common in the Fremont area as in the
Anasazi area, but a number of petroglyphs of flute-players are found in
the study area in Dry Fork Valley, Utah, in Dinosaur National Monument (Schaafsma 1971; Castleton 1978), and in the Brown's Park
area. The flute-players are shown reclining and walking; still others
appear to be falling backward. The reclining flute-players resemble
those of San Juan River Basketmaker style rock art.

Figure 86. *Fremont style solid and
stipple pecked shield-figure at site
5ME677, near the Colorado River,
west central Colorado. Figure is approximately one meter in length.*

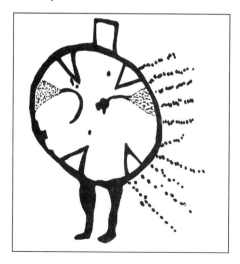

Spirals and concentric circles are frequently displayed. Large numbers are present at Dinosaur National Monument sites and elsewhere in the Uinta Basin, in the White River drainage, and at Glade Park sites (Plates 75, 76, 81, 83, 84; Figure 81). At one site, a figure holds a shieldlike device formed of a spiral (Plate 84). At a Glade Park site, an anthropomorph "carries" or is attached to a spiral (Figure 81); at nearby sites, six similar anthropomorphs are shown with spirals on their chests, and concentric circles surround a starlike design on the chest of a figure. This figure is the largest of a panel of several anthropomorphs described by Wormington and Lister (1956). The figure wears a double-fringed stick headdress, hair bobs, and an elevated "cap," and holds a bow in one hand and a bladelike device in the other (Plate 75).

Birds are shown at a number of sites, and some have anthropomorphic qualities. A large owl (more than a meter in height), painted red, pink, and cream (Plate 90), is reported from the vicinity of the Turner-Look Fremont village site (Wormington 1955). Three abstract owl-like petroglyphs occur at a Glade Park, Colorado, site and are in association with anthropomorphs wearing headdresses. One "owl" wears a necklace, another is attached to the foot of an anthropomorph (Figure 88), and another appears to be dancing beneath a large snake poised above it (Plate 92).

A stylized red bird, representing a heron or other wading bird with a long beak and elongated body, is depicted near the Colorado River in western Colorado. This bird has a dot-and-line pattern in the interior of the body. A possible turtle, a "sunburst," and other images surround the bird.

It may be intentional that some bird images have characteristics of both birds and humans. In a discussion of Fremont figurine heads from the Fremont River, Utah, Morss (1931:47) notes:

> The nose in profile is in many instances markedly convex, and terminates sharply, approaching a parrot or owl-beaked form, an effect which is heightened by the fact that the mouth is never represented. In some cases, however, the face is much more human in appearance, and it is impossible to state definitely whether an anthropomorphic, or perhaps zoomorphic, cast of countenance is intended.

Other distinctive animal and insect forms shown in Fremont style rock art in the western Colorado area include carefully pecked lizards (Plate 93) at Dinosaur National Monument sites and possible centipede, scorpion, and beetle forms at Glade Park and Brown's Park sites.

In west central Colorado, Fremont rock art shows carefully pecked

Figure 87

Details of solid and stipple pecked petroglyphs at site 5ME458, Glade Park area, west central Colorado. Dashed outline areas in Figure 87 indicate rock damage by gunfire. Note abstract owl-like figure to the right of the anthropomorph in Figure 88. The bottom of the "owl" is attached to the left foot of the anthropomorph. Elements at the site range between 30 centimeters and one and a half meters in length.

Figure 88

Plate 90. *Polychrome painted owl from the Book Cliffs area of east central Utah, a few miles upstream from the Turner-Look Fremont site (Wormington 1955). This very elaborate painting is in red, pink, and cream and is approximately 1.5 meters in length. Note that the eyes are of different colors.*

Plate 91. *Fremont style petroglyphs from site 5MF2691, Brown's Park area, northwestern Colorado. Largest anthropomorph is approximately 60 centimeters in length.*

stylized bear paw prints and what appear to be human footprints. Particularly elaborate bearlike tracks occur at Glade Park sites. They are similar to those found in Uncompahgre Style rock art in west central Colorado. A series of realistic footprints on the top of a flat boulder at a Glade Park rock shelter site. Seven footprints occur, and all are oriented in a single direction. Two are attached by a pecked line that joins the heels of each (Cole 1987).

An additional series of six footprints also oriented in a single direction occurs on the tops of rock slabs in a rock shelter along the Colorado River. These footprints are not as consistent in appearance and technique as the other seven. At both sites, however, the footprints are in similar settings; both sets are situated below Fremont style anthropomorphic rock art.

Plate 92. *Detail of Fremont style petroglyphs at site 5ME458, Glade Park area, west central Colorado. The photograph shows an owl-like figure that appears to dance with a large snake poised above. The snake is approximately one meter in length.*

Plate 93. *Fremont style anthropomorphs and lizards from Dinosaur National Monument, Utah.*

LATE FREMONT STYLE ROCK ART

Rock paintings located in a narrow mountain valley in the Beaver Flattop Mountains of northwestern Colorado may represent art of Fremont people remaining in the area after A.D. 1250-1300. If the art is not Fremont in origin, the makers were clearly influenced by Fremont style symbolism (Figure 89).

In the recent past two panels of rock paintings were located on the rear wall of a small rock shelter. A creek runs through the rock shelter, and lower paintings are just above the streambed. During flood situations, the water probably washes over the paintings.

The rock paintings were photographed in 1976, and only part of one panel remained in 1986. An examination of remaining art revealed that, while the paint was relatively bright, the sandstone surface on which the paintings appeared had exfoliated, probably as a result of moisture and stream action. Because of this situation, it is felt that the paintings could not have survived more than a few centuries.

Fremont subject matter and themes are exhibited, but some style differences are apparent. Elements in the largest panel include charcoal or black-painted torsos and heads of three anthropomorphs wearing "fringed stick" headdresses. All three have facial features; one appears to wear a necklace, while another holds a sticklike device. One figure has an elongated face with a possible nose representation, and both are uncharacteristic of Fremont style rock art. Also, the head and body forms of the three figures are not as sharply angular as typical Fremont style figures.

Additional subjects are a stick-figure bowman that appears to be shooting an arrow toward two simple quadrupeds with antlers or ears, a possible bear, a masklike face with a "fringed stick" headdress, a snake, two "sunbursts," and three elements that resemble arrow points. While hunting scenes are common in Fremont rock art, the stick-figure bowman and very simple quadrupeds are not typical. The "mask" is somewhat elongated and has facial features, including a nose.

Two of the three anthropomorphs with headdresses occur side by side, and the remaining one is at the same level but separated. The "mask," snake, and a complex "sunburst" design are tightly grouped on a small rock face. The hunting scene is separated from other elements. The bearlike image is on the same level as the hunting scene but is separate. The three "arrow points" and a "sunburst" are grouped together. Overall, it appears that panel imagery has been spatially organized into discrete sections of presumably related symbolism similar to that noted for Fremont rock art elsewhere.

The second panel at the Beaver Flattop site shows what appear to be a faded reddish shield-figure and a separate small black "arrow point" image. The shield-figure does not have a visible head or legs, but curved horns protrude from the top. The shield is decorated by being divided into as many as six solid and negative outline segments. The shield-figure is similar to a more detailed and realistic form in the Book Cliffs of Utah (Plate 88).

Individual subject matter shown in the two panels generally fits within variations of Fremont style rock art, particularly that in the Uinta Basin and Brown's Park north and west of the Beaver Flattops. However, atypical characteristics, such as less angular figures, nose representations, a stick-figure bowman with simple quadrupeds, as well as the unusual "arrows," suggest a period of change for Fremont rock art that may be related to cultural events taking place prior to the demise of the Fremont culture by A.D. 1500 (Creasman and Scott 1987). By that time in northwest Colorado, it is possible that Fremont people were interacting with Numic-speaking Eastern Shoshoni and Utes who represented shield-figures in rock art of the Rocky Mountains and Plains, a motif that was possibly borrowed from the Fremont.

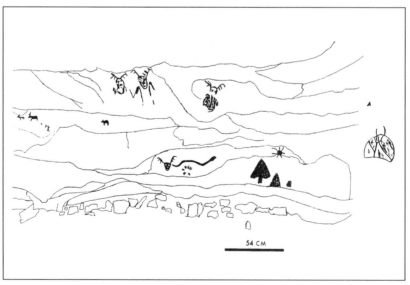

Figure 89. *Possible late (post-A.D. 1250–1300) Fremont rock paintings at site 5RT698, in the upper White River drainage, northwestern Colorado. Elements occur on the rear wall of a small rock shelter just above a creek. Shield-figure on the right is pale red, and other elements are black and gray. The drawing is based on photographs taken in 1976; portions of only seven elements were visible in 1986. Photographs on file at the Bureau of Land Management Little Snake Resource Area Office.*

NAVAJO ROCK ART

Rock art of the Gobernador Phase (A.D. 1696–1775) has been described by Schaafsma (1963, 1972, 1980) from examples in the Gobernador District, along the upper San Juan River in northwestern New Mexico and southwestern Colorado. Related rock art also occurs in Canyon de Chelly and Canyon del Muerto, Arizona (Grant 1978), and in the areas of Chaco Canyon and Gallup, New Mexico. These places were homelands of the Navajo following their migration from the Great Plains to the Southwest, and are featured in their narrative traditions. Additional examples are known from extreme southwestern Colorado and adjacent areas in New Mexico. Some of this rock art may have been made following the Gobernador Phase, but it is stylistically consistent.

The Gobernador Representational Style includes rock paintings and petroglyphs as well as incised and painted forms. Schaafsma (1980) interprets paintings as being more standardized in form and as occurring at the most sacred sites. Following the Pueblo revolt of 1680–1692 and the subsequent reoccupation of the Rio Grande area by the Spanish, Pueblo refugees lived with the Navajo in the upper San Juan River area. This resulted in acculturation by Navajo people and the development of new ceremonial symbolism. Aspects of Pueblo mythology and art, including that related to the katsina cult, were apparently added to traditional Navajo beliefs and practices. Schaafsma (1972:31–32) has written: "It is likely that the Navajo inclination to portray religious subjects in graphic form was an innovation inspired by the Puebloan tradition of wall and altar painting as well as by the prolific rock representations of ceremonial subject matter."

The Gobernador Representational Style shows supernatural beings known as *ye'i* (*Yeibichai*) that are prominent in Navajo mythology and

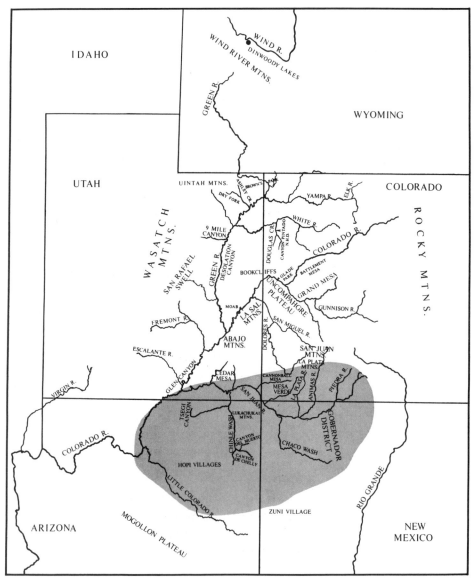

Map 9. *Region occupied by the Navajo including modern reservation lands in northeastern Arizona, southeastern Utah, and northwestern New Mexico. Navajo people
may have also occupied areas farther to the north. Associated rock art styles are dated
between approximately* A.D. *1700 and 1900.*

are ceremonially personated by masked dancers, and mythic heroes; "shields"; shield-figures; eagles and other birds; stepped "cloud" terraces and pyramids similar to those of Anasazi, Mogollon, and historic Pueblo art; corn plants; animals such as bison and horses with heart lines (an arrowlike line in the chest that is possibly a Great Plains symbol); and star ceilings or planetaria that show celestial symbolism painted on the roofs of overhanging cliffs and rock shelters (Plates 94, 95, 96, 97, and 98).

Painted images of equilinear crosses (stars), crescents, flowers, birds, and dragonflies have been placed on numerous ceilings using a variety of colors. In some cases very high rock ceilings (forty feet or higher from the ground) were used, and it appears that in some instances imagery was placed by shooting arrows armed with shaped yucca leaves or other plant fibers dipped in paint. Some crosses on high ceilings in Canyon del Muerto have ribbed impressions that resemble yucca leaves and dots in the center where an arrow point may have depressed the leaves (Plate 98).

Celestial subjects are part of Navajo mythology, and celestial symbolism is represented on the masks of *ye'i* and on other ceremonial paraphernalia, and in dry paintings using colored sand and other pigments (Newcomb and Reichard 1975; Reichard 1977). It is reported that planetaria in Canyon de Chelly National Monument were made as late as the early nineteenth century and continue to be ceremonially visited by modern Navajo singers (shamans or medicine men) on behalf of their patients (Schaafsma 1980:323).

Similarly, sites with sacred rock art in New Mexico continue to be used ceremonially, and at least one site is recognized to be a shrine or place of power. Schaafsma (1980) describes rock art at this shrine site located at the confluence of the Los Pinos and San Juan rivers (now inundated by the water of Navajo Reservoir). At the site, representations of supernatural beings, animals, corn, and other elements are dominated by two large white discs outlined and decorated with red. These "shields" are reported to represent the Twin War Gods. Navajo visits to the site were made "during times of crisis and were made to this place where certain important Navajo supernaturals were said to reside in order to read the 'Sands of Prophecy' located there where the rivers meet" (1980:310–311).

Navajo rock art and shrines are found at locations that also have Anasazi rock art, something that may have contributed to the significance of the places. Schaafsma (1980) reports that Navajo art in the Gobernador District frequently occurs with Rosa Style Anasazi art. One Navajo shrine in the Lukachukai Mountains of Arizona features symbolic associations between Navajo clay effigies and Basketmaker

Plate 94

Plate 95

Gobernador Representational Style rock art from the Gobernador District, northwestern New Mexico. Plate 94 shows red and white paintings representing supernatural beings, possibly deities associated with the Night Chant ceremony. Figure on the extreme left represents the ghaan'ask'idii, *Humpback God. Plate 95 shows petroglyphs including a corn plant, Humpback God, equestrians, and a horned mask. Plate 96 shows a white and red painted shield approximately 60 centimeters in diameter. Photographs by Glenn E. Stone.*

Plate 96

rock art (Jett 1982). A panel of Gobernador Representational Style petroglyphs near the Colorado-New Mexico state line recorded during this study occur in a rock shelter with remains of an Anasazi cliff dwelling and rock art (Figure 90).

In addition to the representation of heart lines, Great Plains influences in Navajo rock art are suggested by the representation of V-necked anthropomorphs and elongated feather headdresses. These are common traits of northwestern Plains art. The representation of shield-figures could have also been introduced to the Navajo by Great Plains groups. Northwest Plains peoples depicted V-necked figures and shield-figures after A.D. 1200–1300 (Keyser 1977). Of course, the Anasazi and historic Pueblo also used the shield-figure motif and may have introduced or encouraged its use among the Navajo. This influence is suggested by the use of shields to represent the War Twins. Comparable mythic heroes also figure prominently in historic Pueblo ceremonies (Stevenson 1904; Stephen 1969).

Themes of Gobernador rock art are warfare, moisture or rain, corn, and fertility. Warfare symbolism (frequently associated with rain symbolism) may be related as much to ceremonial battles involving cosmic and mythological forces as to actual human warfare. While the Navajo raided and fought various Indian groups and the Spanish and may have used warrior symbolism in this context, interpretations of modern images in dry paintings suggest it is associated with battles involving gods that are invoked to aid humans in battles against disease and drought. Such circumstances are seen to signify an individual's loss

Gobernador Representational Style rock paintings in Canyon del Muerto, Canyon de Chelly National Monument, Arizona. Plate 97 shows delicately painted supernaturals approximately 20 centimeters in length. Colors are red, black, and white. Plate 98 shows a star ceiling with paintings of black crosses. Circular marks can be seen in the center of some crosses that may have been made by the points of arrows. Texture seen in some crosses and lines may be patterns of fibers such as yucca that were used to imprint the designs.

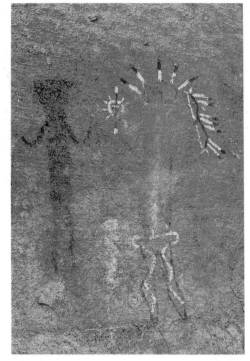

Plate 97

Plate 98

of harmony with nature. Human warfare may have fit this category as encounters with foreigners are seen as a source of illness.

According to Reichard (1977:14):

> The Navajo religion must be considered as a design in harmony, a striving for *rapport* between man and every phase of nature, the earth and the waters under the earth, the sky and the "land beyond the sky," and of course, the earth and everything on and in it. In order to establish and continue this *rapport* the beings which dwell in all these places must be controlled.

The myth of the Male Shooting Chant (symbolized by dry paintings) records the arming of the War Twins and an ensuing battle:

> To their garment he added hats of lightning and placed the lightnings in their hands, then went with them to test them in geography and to help them through their first encounter. They got as far as the middle of the sky and Sun was just beginning to ask them to name different parts of the earth when a black cloud came up out of the south and out of it strong lightning darted. This meant a fight and in it Rain Boy, Rain Girl, Hail Boy and Hail Girl, Water Boy and Girl, and Rainbow Boy and Girl were overcome by the Sun and his helpers (Newcomb and Reichard 1975:29).

Sacred subject matter exhibited in Gobernador Phase rock art continues to be represented in temporary dry paintings utilized in elaborate healing ceremonies as part of chants conducted by singers. Permanent sacred representations in rock art are believed to have not been made significantly after A.D. 1800 (Schaafsma 1980), although examples discussed below may be later. It is observed that sacred Navajo art involved the development of more abstract and geometric subjects over time (Schaafsma 1980:325). Later figures tend to be elongated with sharply defined angles, while earlier rock art forms are more stocky, rounded, and realistic.

Supernaturals presented in Gobernador Representational Style rock art have been discussed by Schaafsma (1980). These include the War Twins (Monster Slayer and Born-for-Water), Female God of the Night Chant, the *ghaan'ask'idii* (Humpback God), Mountainway sand painting people, and Shootingway people. In dry paintings, round heads generally denote male supernaturals, and rectangular heads denote female supernaturals. Females may wear *mantas* or off-the-shoulder dresses (worn by historic Pueblo women), and males wear kilts; both wear sashes. In dry paintings, goddesses wear sashes and kilts similar to those of the gods (Reichard 1977). The shapes of heads and types of clothing do not always conform precisely to these distinctions. Representations in some media show females with masks rounded on the top (Jett 1982).

Masks, headdresses, jewelry, and various paraphernalia related to supernaturals, such as arrows, "lightning" (zigzag lines), bows, plants, staffs, and rattles, are exhibited. Arms are generally uplifted at the elbow, and feet and calves of the legs may indicate the direction of movement (Schaafsma 1980:312).

Later, post-A.D. 1750–1800, Navajo rock art exhibits ceremonial dances and more secular subject matter, such as realistic equestrian battle scenes, horses, game animals, cars, trucks, and other modern materials. Particularly fine examples of such art are in Canyon de Chelly National Monument (Grant 1978), in Chaco Canyon (Schaafsma 1980), and at sites along the San Juan River in Utah (Plate 99).

ADDITIONAL CEREMONIAL ART OF THE NAVAJO

Petroglyphs similar to those of the Gobernador Representational Style are exhibited on the wall of a rock shelter in a tributary canyon to

Plate 99. *Detail of post-A.D. 1750–1800 Navajo rock paintings showing secular subject matter, including possible Spanish equestrians, people on foot, and game animals. Canyon del Muerto, Canyon de Chelly National Monument, Arizona.*

the Animas River in New Mexico, just south of the Colorado state line. The site also has the remains of a small cliff dwelling and white handprints of probable Anasazi origin. Navajo style representations include a pair of anthropomorphs with rounded heads, featherlike headdresses, and kilts and a third figure with a rectangular head and a kilt. All figures are pecked, and the kilts on two figures are decorated with dots. Generally, the figures are rounded and realistic rather than abstract and elongated, and may be contemporaneous with representations from the nearby Gobernador District to the east (Figure 90). The figures may represent *ye'i.*

An incised petroglyph from a nearby Animas River site may date from a later period. The petroglyph, which is very faint, shows an elongated and bent figure with a rectangular "head." The figure appears to wear a kilt and is similar to supernaturals, such as Rainbow Goddess, that border and enclose dry paintings (Reichard 1977:Pl. 14). This figure is abstract, elongated, and geometric in appearance. The figure is

Figure 90. *Detail of solid pecked petroglyphs from the Animas River drainage, northwestern New Mexico. These figures possibly represent Navajo* ye'i *or other supernatural personages.*

incised on sandstone bedrock in an open location, having no protection from the weather, and has been impacted by foot and vehicle traffic. Based on the form of the figure and the probable rate of erosion, it is possible that this petroglyph dates after A.D. 1800 (Figure 91).

An incised and pecked petroglyph of an elongated and bent figure similar to, but more complex than, the Animas River figure is present in the McElmo Creek drainage of extreme southwest Colorado (Figure 92). This petroglyph and an associated cloud-and-rain motif similar to that of historic Pueblo people (Stephen 1969) are located on the wall of a narrow slickrock canyon just above a pool. The sandstone walls of the canyon are subject to being flooded during rainstorms.

A black patina covers the surface on which the petroglyph is exhibited. Patina has been removed during the process of making the art, and reddish sandstone beneath the surface is exposed. The fact that the patina has not returned to the surface despite regular exposure to moisture suggests that the petroglyphs are relatively recent in origin or have been cleaned or reworked at some point. The petroglyphs have clearly been in place for some years, however, because erosion is evident. The edges of incisions are worn, and designs are blurred. It is difficult to estimate the age of the petroglyphs, but the condition suggests a date within the past one hundred years.

The bent figure and the cloud-and-rain symbol shown overhead are executed in outline with finely incised lines and pecked solid areas. The cloud-and-rain motif consists of a terraced pyramid of three semicircular "clouds" above descending "rain" symbolized by vertical lines. The body of the bent figure is highly angular and takes the form of a stepped pyramid similar to stylized "cloud terraces" that appear in Anasazi, Mogollon, historic Pueblo, and Gobernador Style art. The body is formed of parallel lines, and possible additional rain symbolism is shown below the apex of the triangle (and directly below the "rain cloud") by crosshatch and parallel descending lines.

The figure wears what appears to be a two-feather headdress and has a masklike head that has a flattened base or chin and rounded top. The "feathers" on the headdress are represented in a manner similar to those seen on paired figures in the Animas River drainage (Figure 90). The face is decorated by pecked and incised triangular and diamond-shaped designs. A decorated kilt and a sash are shown, and the feet have short descending fringelike lines. The figure holds two "lightning bolts" in uplifted hands, and long fringelike lines hang from the bottom of the bolts. A small image, possibly a snake, is pecked beside the "lightning."

On a low overhanging rock face above a tributary stream to the Uncompahgre River in west central Colorado is a red painting showing

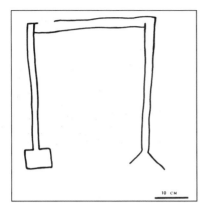

Figure 91. *Incised petroglyph from the Animas River drainage, northwestern New Mexico, showing a possible Navajo ye'i with a rectangular head and wearing a kilt. The image is heavily eroded, and drawing is probably incomplete. The basic form is similar to representations of supernatural beings in Navajo dry paintings or sand paintings.*

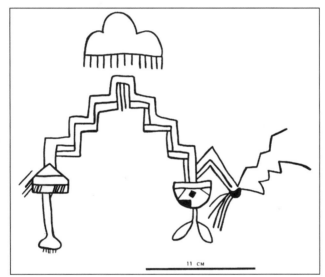

Figure 92. *Finely incised and solid pecked images showing a possible masked supernatural holding "lightning bolts" and wearing a kilt. A cloud and rain symbol appears above. These images are similar to representations in Navajo dry paintings. The petroglyphs occur near the head of a small canyon in the McElmo Creek drainage, southwestern Colorado.*

a humpbacked anthropomorph with a rounded head, flattened on top, and wearing a raylike (feather?) headdress (Plate 100). The figure holds a staff in the form of a triad and resembles representations of Humpback God (*ghaan'ask'idii*) that occur in Gobernador Representational Style rock art (Plates 94 and 95). Schaafsma (1980:317–318) notes that the god sometimes occurs as a single figure and at other times with a dance group, and she describes the representations as follows:

These ye'i wear mountain sheep horns, and their humps from which eagle feathers radiate are said to contain seeds and mist. The figure invariably carries a staff. This personage is regarded as either a deified mountain sheep or a guardian of the sheep, and is also defined as the "god of harvest, god of plenty, god of the mist" (Reichard 1950:443–44); he is frequently present in modern drypaintings.

Importantly, the representation differs from the Gobernador Style examples of Humpback God by the presence of the raylike headdress and the absence of mountain sheep horns and feathers on the hump. Also, the figure differs in other ways: the arms are shown extended and not uplifted, the feet do not obviously indicate a direction of travel, and the figure is less carefully executed than Gobernador Style art. However, given variations in Navajo art renderings and the lack of precise knowledge about many rock art subjects, it is possible that Humpback God or a related supernatural from Navajo religion is represented.

The Uncompahgre River painting occurs well north of the traditional Navajo homeland and modern reservation, although it is within an area where Navajo people have historically worked and traded. Certainly, the representation suggests a Navajo relationship, if not origin. It appears aboriginal in style. If not Navajo in origin, it may have been made by a Ute Indian living in the area prior to A.D. 1880, who was familiar with the art and myths of the Navajo.

Plate 100. *Possible Navajo representation of the* ghaan'ask'idii, *Humpback God, at a site in the Uncompahgre River drainage, west central Colorado. This figure is painted red and is approximately 40 centimeters in length.*

EASTERN SHOSHONI ROCK ART

Protohistoric and historic rock art styles of the northwestern Great Plains associated with Shoshonean groups have been described by Conner (1962), Conner and Conner (1971), Keyser (1975, 1977, 1984, 1987), Sundstrom (1984), and others. The art has been generally identified as representing ceremonial and biographic subject matter that has chronological and cultural significance. Eastern Shoshoneans in the study area may have made such art after A.D. 1500, the proposed time of arrival (Shimkin 1986).

CEREMONIAL STYLE ROCK ART

The Shield Bearing Warrior Style is dated between approximately A.D. 1300 and 1700 (Keyser 1977, 1987) and is seen as a division of Ceremonial Style art that is possibly related to vision quests (ritualized spiritual experiences sought by individuals among historic tribes of the Rocky Mountains, Great Basin Great Plains, and Columbia River Plateau). Ceremonial Style art may have earlier beginnings than the Shield Bearing Warrior Style. Vision quests are associated with puberty, warrior, and shaman rites and are reported to have taken place at sites believed to have power. Power sites include those in secluded locations and sites with rock art, and the making of rock art during vision quests has been documented (Lowie 1924; Teit 1930; Malouf 1961; Shimkin 1986). Images represented by vision seekers include their spirit helpers and manifestations of visions and dreams.

Keyser (1984:28) observes that art forms are rigid and feature individualistic images with intrinsic importance.

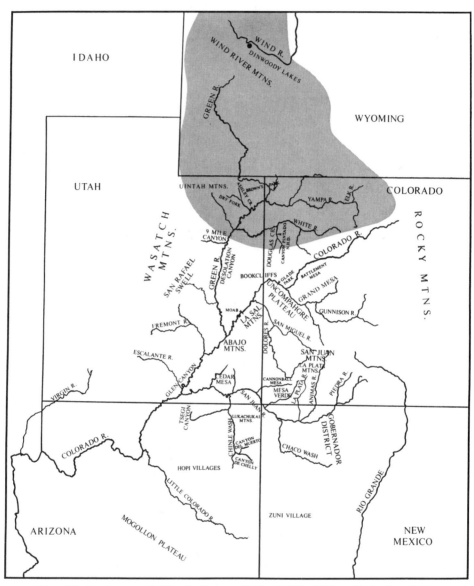

Map 10. *Region occupied by the Eastern Shoshoni (Wind River Shoshoni and Co-manche-Shoshoni) including modern reservation lands in west central Wyoming. It is likely that Eastern Shoshoni visited surrounding areas to raid and trade for goods such as horses and guns. Associated rock art styles are dated between approximately A.D. 1300 and 1850.*

The Shield Bearing Warrior style comprises a constellation of associated motifs, including shield bearing warriors, V-necked humans, boat form animals, and vulvaforms. . . . Shield Bearing Warrior style petroglyphs usually occur as small groups of human and animal figures shown in stiff, symbolic postures and stylized relationships. Yet, these glyphs are well made, with firm, bold incisions, creating carefully designed motifs. The result is an individualistic, highly stylized, static, well-executed art form that apparently functions in a magico-religious context.

Ceremonial Style art is expressed as pecked petroglyphs and rock paintings as well as incised petroglyphs (Wormington 1955; Hendry 1983; Sundstrom 1984). Anthropomorphs are featured elements and generally have rectangular bodies, often with upraised arms. Particularly striking examples of incised and painted Ceremonial art occur at Castle Gardens in western Wyoming (Hendry 1983:172–177), in the vicinity of the Wind River Shoshoni Reservation.

A few representations of shield-figures and anthropomorphs in the western Colorado area are stylistically consistent with Ceremonial Style art, particularly with the Shield Bearing Warrior Style. The elements occur in the northern portion of the study area, in the Yampa River drainage. This region is historically associated with the Eastern Shoshoni as well as with the Ute (La Point 1987), but rock art styles associated with the Ute do not include elements of this type.

Four painted shield-figures are found in a shallow rock alcove overlooking the upper Yampa River valley (Plate 101; Figures 93 and 94). One shield-figure is painted green with red details. This occurs with a hand print and a smaller shield-figure, both of which are red. A third red shield-figure has been scratched after being painted. All three shield-figures have legs exhibited. The fourth shield-figure is a red-painted shield that is outlined only on the right side. Three parallel lines, possibly representing feathers, protrude from the semicircular outline. A small rounded head with a long neck is shown above the shield, and a vertical row of dots extends the length of the shield below the head. The left side of the shield is decorated with a vertical row of solid triangular forms and a line. No legs or other appendages are shown. Other images in association with the shield-figures include an anthropomorph holding hooplike devices and an equestrian figure wearing a headdress and holding a shield and lance.

Elements at a second site in the upper Yampa River drainage that are consistent with Ceremonial Style art of the northwestern Plains include a white-painted anthropomorph with a rectangular body and

Plate 101. *Ceremonial Style (Shield Bearing Warrior Style) red painting at site 5RT6, near the Yampa River, northwestern Colorado. This figure has been heavily scratched, possibly by a later artist. Figure is approximately 25 centimeters in length.*

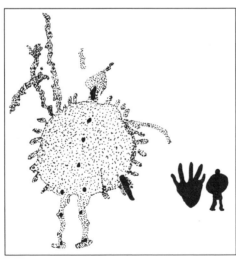

Figure 93

Figure 94

Plains Ceremonial Style rock art (Shield Bearing Warrior Style) attributed to the Eastern Shoshoni at site 5RT6, in the Yampa River drainage, northwestern Colorado. Stippled areas indicate green paint, and solid areas indicate red paint. Painted handprint in Figure 93 is life-size; shield-figure in Figure 94 is approximately 45 centimeters in length.

upraised arms; a petroglyph of a masklike face with a headdress; quadrupeds, including a petroglyph of a "supplicating" bear and deer or elk petroglyphs and paintings; combination red-painted and petroglyph shield-figures; and a pecked and incised rectangular anthropomorph with upraised arms (Figures 95 and 96).

Additional rock paintings and petroglyphs appear at this site located on a cliff at the top of a ridge. Other rock art at the site includes stick-figure anthropomorphs, figures that appear to wear robes, rows of sticklike shield-figures (with shields in outline), arrows, and quadrupeds. Rows of sticklike shield-figures (possibly Ute in origin) superimpose Ceremonial Style anthropomorphs.

A third upper Yampa River site exhibits a single incised anthropomorph with an elongated rectangular body decorated with vertical lines, a rounded head, and upraised arms. The figure appears to hold a staff, and a similar "staff" is adjacent. A headdress and feet may be present; the figure is very faint due to weathering. The site is situated on a mountain slope, and the petroglyph occurs on the side of a darkly patinated boulder.

Other examples of Ceremonial Style art are found in Dinosaur National Monument on the lower Yampa River and occur in the vicinity of a number of panels of Fremont style rock art. Examples of

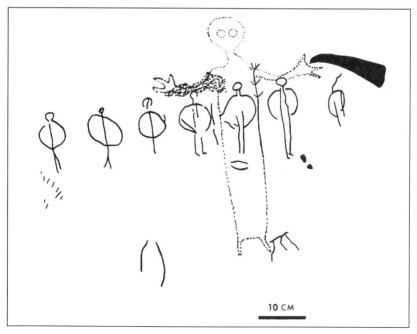

10 CM

Figure 95

10 CM

Figure 96

Details showing Ceremonial Style rock paintings and petroglyphs of possible Eastern Shoshoni origin superimposed by painted shield-figures of possible Ute origin at site 5RT345. Ceremonial Style art includes anthropomorphs with rectangular bodies and raised arms, a face or mask with a headdress and other attachments, a snake, a bear-like figure, and a quadruped, possibly a bighorn sheep or pronghorn. In Figure 95, the large anthropomorph shown in stipple outline is painted with a white claylike pigment; shield-figures and other solid lines and areas are painted red. In Figure 96, the large anthropomorph and other stippled elements are pecked; heavy stippling indicates more deeply pecked areas. Shield-figures and other solid lines and areas are painted red.

Ceremonial Style art at one site are a painted and pecked shield-figure with sticklike legs, a rounded head, and a shield shown in outline, and a painted and pecked anthropomorph with upraised arms who wears a headdress. These elements and others attributed to the Fremont occur inside a rock shelter (Burgh and Scoggin 1948:66–71; Fig. 45 and 47).

A second site exhibits a figure called Pat's Warrior, a painted anthropomorph with a rectangular body decorated by a vertical stripe and holding a shield and a "feathered" lance not unlike those seen in Fremont rock art (Figure 97). The head is not clearly visible, but a "feather" headdress is shown. Burgh and Scoggin (1948:71) assign Pat's Warrior to the historic period.

It is notable that all of the above sites with Ceremonial Style art are in secluded locations such as on high ridges, mountain slopes, and within rock shelters. Such locations support the possibility that Ceremonial Style art functioned as part of vision quests.

Between approximately A.D. 1625 and 1775, action scenes were added to Ceremonial Style art (Keyser 1987:45). For example, the subject matter included battle and hunting scenes, some showing equestrians and guns. This begins a trend toward art that shows realism and details of action in order to record actual events known as Biographic Style art.

Biographic Style Rock Art

After A.D. 1750, a Horse-Nomad culture developed in the northwestern Plains, and Biographic Style rock art dated after A.D. 1775

Figure 97. *Ceremonial Style red rock paintings in Castle Park on the Yampa River, northwest Colorado. Scale not available. Redrawn from Burgh and Scoggin (1948:Fig.47).*

(Keyser 1977, 1987) gradually replaced Ceremonial Style art. Biographic art is generally incised or drawn with charcoal and other pigments. Similar art is found in "winter counts" painted on hides, tipi paintings, and ledger book drawings of the same period (Mallery 1972; Keyser 1987). Early Biographic Style art is proposed to date between approximately A.D. 1775 and 1830–1850. Representations in early Biographic Style art are stylized and resemble those of Ceremonial Style art, while late Biographic Style art dated after A.D. 1850 shows the influence of Euro-American art traditions that emphasize naturalism.

Keyser (1977:52) describes Biographic Style art as depicting "secular events important in the lives of individual warriors or important to the history of an entire group." In contrast to Ceremonial rock art, Biographic Style art is realistic and fluid, and shows integrated action scenes involving animals, humans, weapons, and tipis. Detailed battle and horse-raiding events and hunting scenes are shown as well as those involving sexual exploits and ceremonies or dances. The art is seen as rudimentary picture-writing in which aesthetics were secondary to the communication of an event.

Keyser (1987) discusses a lexicon for Biographic Style rock art based on studies of ledger book drawings. This lexicon enables scenes to be "read" by the identification of meanings inherent in motifs and artistic conventions. The lexicon involves the recognition of horses and horse accoutrements, weapons and accessories, tracks (direction of movement), wounds, tense (past or future), posture and weapon placement, relative numbers, and ethnic dress, and speech and name glyphs.

One site in western Colorado is identified as exhibiting Biographic Style art that is subject to interpretation using the lexicon developed by Keyser (1987). The site occurs in the Book Cliffs within a small rock shelter located in a tributary canyon to the Colorado River. Six panels of drawings in red and black pigments are exhibited and show horses and riders (some with shields and lances), shield-figures, rectangular anthropomorphs, tracks, tipis, rifles, arrows or lances, shields, and a variety of abstract linear forms. Rock art at the site is reported by Mahaney (1986).

Rock art at this site is remarkably similar to early, pre-A.D. 1830–1850, Biographic Style art from the northwestern Plains, and portions of it can be "read." The most detailed panel shows a battle scene involving equestrians (some with shields and lances) and foot soldiers, some of which are shield-figures (Figure 98). The scene is divided into sections by the use of encircling lines. A number of dashed lines indicate that equestrians came from the lower right (north) and battled individuals associated with tipis (crossed lines) on the left (south) side of the panel. Some appear to have moved farther south as indicated by

Figure 98. *Panels of Biographic Style red drawings of probable Eastern Shoshoni origin at site 5GF1339, west central Colorado. The scene appears to record details of specific individual and group battles and types of weapons. Equestrians and warriors on foot are shown.*

a few dashed lines at the far left, but apparently other equestrians and foot soldiers moved west after reaching the tipis.

Near the top (west) of the panel, a circular line encloses imagery that appears related to two groups of tipis shown below. The three areas are connected by solid and dashed lines. This may indicate that occupants of the tipis were involved in events isolated in the enclosed area. The imagery shows a shield-figure with a cross design on the shield that appears to be fighting with another shield-figure with two lines decorating the shield. The latter may have dismounted to do battle because a horse stands behind. The shield-figures are connected by two long lines or lances, and neither appears to have been injured because they remain standing.

A nearby figure without a shield appears to have been shot by an arrow directed by another unmounted figure and is falling backward. A mounted figure is shown near the bottom of the circle and is connected to various forms.

Elsewhere on the panel to the south, a foot soldier near the tipis appears attached to a rifle aimed toward him, and an arrow is situated just in front of his head. This may have been shot by a nearby equestrian.

A vertical row of nine rifles, and possible lances represented by lines, are "stockpiled" and appear in the upper right (northwest) of the panel. Dashed lines and hoof prints apear to extend from the weapons into the previously described enclosed area. The rifles are directed at three anthropomorphs wearing headdresses that appear to be falling backward with outspread arms. One figure has a bowlike image attached to the shoulder that may represent a name glyph or power symbol. These figures are larger and more detailed than most figures represented in the panel, and may represent important individuals, possibly victims of a battle.

More detailed representations of rifles appear in the lower left of the panel. One of these resembles a flintlock and shows the cock, cockscrew, and frizzen (Keyser 1987). These depictions and unidentified images that occur with them are not clearly associated with the battle scene.

A separate panel to the right of the battle scene shows some of the same representations, but elements are less detailed and interrelated. Represented are equestrian figures, tipis, a shield-figure, rifles, a variety of lines, and a relatively large anthropomorph. In the upper left of the panel is a group of tipis with a rifle directed toward them.

The large anthropomorph wears a headdress and is shown with arms raised. The figure is broad and may represent a shaman or other ceremonial personage wearing a robe. The right arm of the anthropomorph superimposes a horse with rider, and two other equestrians and various unknown images are grouped around the figure. Based on size and appearance, this figure is impressive and is clearly intended to dominate the panel. Whether subjects of this panel are associated with the narrative of the nearby battle scene is unknown.

Rock art at this site is likely to be a record of an actual raid (possibly for rifles) that took place in the vicinity of the site or possibly in the wide valley of the Colorado River located a few miles to the south. Ethnic dress indicates that the battle involved Indian groups, possibly the Ute and Comanche-Shoshoni, and not Euro-Americans. Ute bands occupied the Book Cliffs area, and Eastern Shoshoni were in the area during the late 1700s (Grady 1984).

UTE
ROCK ART

It is likely that most historic aboriginal rock art identified in western and Colorado eastern Utah is of Ute origin. Bands of Ute Indians occupied much of the area at the time of historic contact and may have been there for two or more centuries prior to that period. Based on sites from the Uncompahgre Plateau in west central Colorado, Buckles (1971) has described two styles of Ute rock art, Early Historic Ute Indian Style and Late Historic Ute Indian Style. The styles are associated with the historic aboriginal period. Rock art of the following period, the Reservation Period, is characterized by Ute Representational Style rock art in the Ute Mountain Ute Reservation of southwest Colorado.

Following historic contact, Utes were making rock art that is stylistically distinctive as well as rock art that appears imitative of earlier art. Imitative art is apparent at west central Colorado sites, where Uncompahgre Style images have been "copied," and at Newspaper Rock in east central Utah, where details of a probable Anasazi figure have been copied. Creasman (1982:7) has observed imitative rock art (a shield-figure) of possible Ute origin in Cañon Pintado.

Ute informants have reported that they imitated older figures "just for fun" (Heizer and Baumhoff 1962:222), and Fewkes reports that the Ute added red paint to Anasazi rock art at Hovenweep ruins (Wenger 1956). Given the mobility of the historic Ute, it is possible that imitated elements occur as widely separated forms; that is, earlier and contemporaneous art seen in Utah may have been reproduced on the Uncompahgre Plateau in Colorado. In such a manner, style attributes and symbolism of a variety of cultures may have been incorporated by the Ute. Similar processes of assimilation involving less mobile cultures are likely to have happened during the long prehistoric period and provide one explanation for shared motifs.

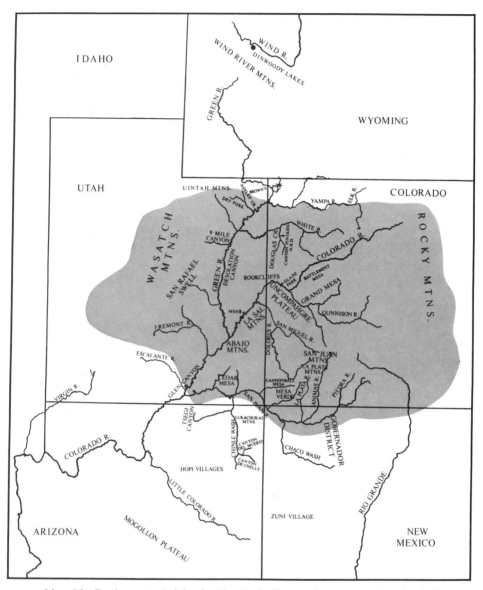

Map 11. *Region occupied by the Ute, including modern reservation lands in northeastern Utah and southwestern Colorado. Equestrians ranged far beyond the boundaries indicated on the map for purposes of trade and to raid for horses and other goods. Associated rock art styles are dated between approximately* A.D. *1600 and 1950.*

ABORIGINAL PERIOD

Early Historic Ute Indian Style

A.D. 1600 to 1830

Buckles (1971) has confined his style classification to art depicting and in association with known historic subject matter, such as horses, tipis, and guns. Early Ute Indian Style rock art is dated from the time the Ute began to use the horse, approximately A.D. 1640 (Smith 1974:19–20), until 1830 when contact between Utes and Euro-Americans became routine due to the establishment of trading posts in the western Colorado area.

Early Ute art includes petroglyphs and rock paintings and drawings. Petroglyphs are solid pecked, stipple pecked, and incised; most appear to have been made with stone tools. The art occurs throughout western Colorado and eastern Utah. The majority of documented sites in Colorado are in the west central region and in the White River-Douglas Creek area of northwest Colorado. In southwest Colorado, early rock art is reported from the vicinity of Cannonball Mesa. Utah sites occur in the Uinta Basin, the Book Cliffs, and in the Colorado River and San Juan River drainages.

Site locations and situations are diverse. For example, sites are located in deep semiarid sandstone canyons and on forested mountain slopes; rock art is found beneath overhanging boulders, inside limestone caves, and on prominent cliff faces. Certainly, the use of such diverse places by the Ute is understandable given their domain of mountains and plateaus and the mobility of their life style. Alpine cave sites in western Colorado are particularly interesting because only Ute style rock art has been found there. Paintings and drawings appear on interior as well as exterior walls of caves. Interior art is difficult to see without artificial lighting, and it is likely that fire light was used when the art was being made.

A number of sites that exhibit Ute rock art also exhibit other rock art styles. This is evident in west central Colorado, northwest Colorado, and in the Book Cliffs of Utah. In addition, examples of Early Ute Indian Style petroglyphs are superimposed on other styles, including Uncompahgre Style, Barrier Canyon Style (Plate 22), Ceremonial Style art (Figures 95 and 96), and Fremont style art. As in the case of Navajo rock art of the Gobernador District, it is possible that existing rock art sites and imagery had particular significance to the Ute. Apparent imitation of existing art by the Ute lends support to this proposal.

Subject matter of early Ute art includes anthropomorphs on foot and mounted ones. Shield-figures are also shown. Body forms range from sticklike to rounded and rectangular, and have few details. Anthropomorphs are frequently shown with arms out to the side and less often with arms hanging down. Males are identified based on the presence of phallic symbolism and such activities as hunting and warfare. Females are less obviously illustrated in early Ute art, although vulvalike forms are exhibited at some sites.

Other representations are horses; abstract images found in association with equestrians that may represent possible power symbols; quadrupeds, including elk and deer, bighorn sheep, and bison; birds; bows and arrows; shields and lances; a bolalike device, possibly a *poggomoggon* (rawhide-covered stone with a wooden handle or a string handle tied to the wrist [Stewart 1976]); abstract linear images; horse tack; tool grooves; hand prints (some including arms); and animal tracks, including bear paw prints and cloven hoof tracks. Probable bear tracks are common, and are shown as footlike forms and as stylized tripartite images similar to those of the Uncompahgre Style.

A few subjects may represent supernatural beings or people in ceremonial dress. These could include shamans known to have conducted curing and other ceremonies among the Ute (Smith 1974; Stewart 1976). Three sites in west central Colorado and one in northwest Colorado show figures of this type. Two sites occur in the lower Gunnison River drainage. One of these sites shows petroglyphs of four figures with upraised arms. Two are wearing brimmed hats or visor-type headdresses; one has a circle head, and the fourth figure has an earlike headdress. Two figures hold some sort of devices. A nearby figure also wears an earlike headdress (Figure 99).

Figure 99. Solid and stipple pecked petroglyphs of probable Ute origin showing figures wearing headdresses or hats. These figures occur near Early Ute Indian Style equestrian forms at site 5ME158, near the lower Gunnison River, west central Colorado. Anthropomorph on upper right is approximately 20 centimeters in length.

A second lower Gunnison River site shows a panel with petroglyphs of a horse and rider with shield, a bear paw print with long
claws, an anthropomorph with a horned headdress that appears to be
"walking," and a relatively large upright bearlike form. This last figure
has exaggerated clawlike hands and feet and is phallic; a headdress may
be present. The figure is impressive and appears to symbolize the
power of a bear, but it is not clear that it actually represents a bear. Such
ambiguity may be intentional insofar as it may represent a mythic personage or even a shaman dressed in a bear robe (Plate 102). Stewart
(1976:280, 317, 333) reports that bear shamans among the Ute wore
bearskins in war, impersonated bears, and were believed to have been
visited by bears. Koch (1977:44–45, 154) illustrates a George Catlin
painting of a Blackfoot medicine man wearing the entire skin of a bear
and states that bear ceremonialism, including that of bear cults and
classes of bear medicine men, occurred among the Utes as well as Indians of the Great Plains.

A site on the Colorado River near the Utah state line shows three
anthropomorphs wearing headdresses. One figure has an earlike headdress, four "arms," and decoration on the right side of the body. A second figure has no arms and wears a floppy fringelike headdress. A third
figure has a similar floppy headdress with a pointed "cap" in the center.
This figure has arms held out to the side.

Plate 102. *Early Historic Ute Indian Style petroglyphs at site 5ME232, west central
Colorado, showing a paw print, a horned anthropomorph, and a bearlike figure that
may represent an anthropomorph in disguise or may symbolize powers of the bear.*

A northwest Colorado site near the Yampa River exhibits two panels of red paintings that have ceremonial symbolism (Figures 100 and 101). One panel shows people that appear to wear robes or dresses, shield-figures, an equestrian, and a figure with a "feather" headdress. The panel may represent a dance or other type of ceremony.

A second panel shows equestrians, shield-figures, and a figure wearing a headdress (possibly with personal power symbols). Art at this site has narrative themes associated with Late Historic Ute Style rock art, but the overall abstraction of the images suggests that it dates from an earlier period.

Panels of Ute art are frequently crowded with images, and formal and thematic groupings are present. Themes of Early Ute rock art noted by Buckles (1971) include group aggression (battle or raid scenes), individual prestige (indicated by power symbolism and details of dress and material goods), and buffalo and other hunting. He suggests that these indicate that rapid culture change took place during the early historic period. Horses and related materials are obviously important to the Ute based on their frequent representation, and they are integral parts of thematic representations. Ceremonialism as indicated by site locations and settings, as well as by subject matter, is also a theme of Early Ute rock art.

Narrative is implied in some Early Ute Indian Style hunting and raiding or battle scenes, but "compositions" are generally not highly detailed and are loosely controlled. While panel groupings appear to have biographic content, truly narrative story lines like those of the Plains Biographic Style are not obvious. Panels have the appearance of having been added to over time. Differences in representations suggest that more than one artist was involved, possibly during a series of visits to the sites. This is noticeable at both open petroglyph sites and at mountain painted cave sites.

At an upper Colorado River cave site, crowded scenes and entire panels situated in the narrow confines of the cave exhibit a variety of workmanship and subject matter. Additionally, both Early and Late Ute rock art styles are present (Plate 103). This information, in combination with the dimly lit interior of the cave, strongly suggests that the site served as a shrine that was visited periodically. Other locations with less obvious characteristics may have also served as shrines.

Anthropomorphs and quadrupeds are often linear and highly abstract, with little attention to detail other than what is decorative and possibly symbolic of personal power and social status. For example, sticklike and triangular-bodied anthropomorphs exhibit headdresses, shields, and weapons; horses and game animals are frequently realistic in form, with emphasis on movement, antlers, humps, and horns.

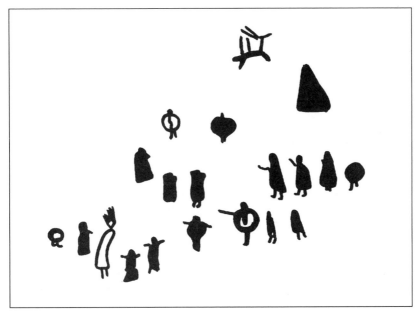

Figure 100

Figure 101

Early Historic Ute Indian Style red rock paintings at site 5RT90, near the Yampa River, northwestern Colorado. Figure 100 *appears in part to show a ceremony.* Figure 101 *shows equestrians, shield-figures, and a figure with a headdress and possible personal power symbols. Panel in* Figure 100 *is approximately one meter square; panel in* Figure 101 *is approximately three meters in length. Adapted from a field sketch by Sherri Hansen and Lynette Logan.*

Plate 103. *Early Historic Ute Indian Style rock paintings at site 5GF2, in the upper Colorado River drainage, north central Colorado. Paintings are black, yellow, and red and are situated inside a cave in a mountainous location. The detail shows early style equestrians and bison. Lines extending from the heads of the horses probably represent feathers. The central horsemen appear to carry shields.*

Quadrupeds, especially horses, tend to be unnaturally elongated and may be disproportionately larger than riders. Horses are shown wearing saddles, and feathers that probably decorated bridles and forelocks are frequently exhibited. A particularly clear example of a high pommel saddle is painted at a west central Colorado cave site, and "feathered" bridles are exhibited at sites throughout that region (Plate 103).

The abstract nature of Early Ute art with regard to anthropomorphs is well illustrated in the case of shield-figures displayed in horizontal rows. Sites in Colorado and Utah show rows of painted and pecked shield-figures with linear forms. The bodies, appendages, and occasional headdresses are composed of lines, and shields are represented by circles. Some rows have more than twenty such shield-figures, including very abstract representations composed of vertical lines with circles (Figures 95 and 96). More elaborate and detailed shield-figures of probable Ute origin occur in the Book Cliffs of Utah.

Equestrian forms are common in Early Ute art. In some instances, both horse and rider are represented by simple grooves or pecked and painted lines with no details provided. These may be very early representations, as both equestrian and horse forms in later styles are generally more realistic. More commonly, stick-figures and triangular-shaped riders are shown on elongated horses. Some early Ute style rock art is elaborate despite its abstract nature. An example is a painted equestrian figure from the Book Cliffs area of Utah. This triangular-shaped rider wears a trailing headdress and rides a highly abstracted horse (Plate 104). As noted above, riders may hold shields and lances, and wear feather headdresses; details of horse tack as well as bridle decorations, possibly feathers, are sometimes shown. Buckles (1971) observes that the overall lack of detail and realism is evidence that individualism is not stressed in Early Ute Indian Style art.

Bison and other game animals are frequently shown far larger than the equestrians who pursue them (Figures 102 and 103; Plates 103 and 105). Buckles (1971) suggests that this may reflect the awe felt by early Ute mounted hunters. It may also indicate the relative importance of the game animals as suggested by more detailed and realistic depictions. An example of relative size between hunters and "bison" is a lower Gunnison River hunt scene involving small abstract equestrians, a bear paw print, and a relatively large "bison" that resembles a large spotted beetle (Figure 103). This may be a very early depiction based on the abstractness of the equestrian figures and the "bison."

Other hunt scenes in western Colorado and eastern Utah have

Plate 104. *A variety of Early Historic Ute Indian Style rock paintings in the Book Cliffs area of east central Utah. Paintings are in red, white, and yellow, and show an abstract figure with a red and white trailing headdress riding an abstract yellow horse. These figures are superimposed by small white equestrians.*

Figure 102. *Early Historic Ute Indian Style petroglyphs at site 5ME163, near the lower Gunnison River, west central Colorado. All elements are solid pecked. Ute representations show a small sticklike rider following a row of quadrupeds and a stylized bear paw print. These elements superimpose earlier Uncompahgre Style elements shown in outline. The Ute-style paw print and some of the quadrupeds may imitate the earlier forms.*

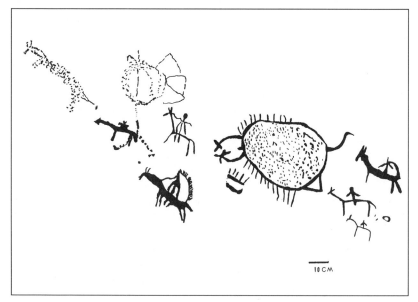

Figure 103. *Solid and stipple pecked Early Historic Ute Indian Style petroglyphs at site 5ME159, near the lower Gunnison River, west central Colorado. The large insect-like form possibly represents a bison being pursued by small sticklike equestrian figures.*

similar themes of animals much larger than horses and riders. This is seen in petroglyphs of a small hunter following larger and more realistic bighorn sheep at a site near the lower Gunnison River. A stylized bear paw print is also represented. In this case, the hunt scene superimposes earlier Uncompahgre Style petroglyphs (Figure 102). Another hunt scene, painted in black and gray, in the lower Dolores River canyon shows a single tiny horseman facing a much larger bison.

Large bison with lowered and turned heads are shown in a carefully executed petroglyph panel in the San Juan River drainage of Utah (Plate 105). This panel shows a row of bison being pursued by small equestrian hunters. One of the hunters is in association with an unidentified image that possibly represents a personal power symbol. Buckles (1971:1083) identifies a bird near an anthropomorph as a possible power symbol, and other possible examples occur in Early and Late Ute Indian Style art (Figures 101 and 104).

An elaborate hunt scene (possibly in combination with a battle or raiding scene) is painted and drawn in black and red on the walls of the second chamber of a cave in the upper Colorado River drainage (Plate 103). The site was discussed above as a possible shrine location that was visited periodically. The hunt scene supports that conclusion insofar as it appears to have been composed by various artists. Bison appear to have lowered heads and are surrounded by crowded equestrian figures that have a variety of forms. Some figures show such details as shields and "feathered" bridles and forelocks, while others are simple

Plate 105. *Early Historic Ute Indian Style petroglyphs at a site in Montezuma Canyon, southeast Utah. Large image on upper left may represent a power symbol. Note that bison heads appear to be lowered.*

Figure 104. *Late Historic Ute Indian Style solid and stipple pecked petroglyphs at site 5DT53, near the lower Gunnison River, west central Colorado. Abstract image in lower center may represent a personal power symbol.*

Plate 106. *Detail of Early and Late Historic Ute Indian Style petroglyphs at site 5ME101, lower Gunnison River drainage, west central Colorado. The more abstract early style art is in the lower part of the panel. The upper portion has more realistic representations including a battle scene that appears to involve shield-figures, riflemen, and equestrians with lances. A figure on the left has apparently been shot and has dropped a rifle. Shield-figure in upper center is approximately 35 centimeters in length.*

sticklike forms. Nearby equestrians are larger and more realistic and may date from a later period. Charcoal drawings at a northwestern Colorado site show Early Ute Style equestrian and possible bear hunting scenes that appear to have narrative qualities (Figure 105).

Late Historic Ute Indian Style

A.D. 1830 to 1880

Late Ute Indian Style rock art has pronounced continuities with earlier art but shows the influence of an Euro-American art tradition that emphasizes controlled compositions, realism, and naturalism in life forms (Buckles 1971). Abstraction and simplicity of form seen in earlier art, especially in anthropomorphic representations, is generally missing, although figures are often stylized. Subject matter of the Late Ute Style is similar to the earlier, but with some additional subjects. It includes anthropomorphs, decorated shields, shield-figures, horses and equestrians, tipis, bears, trees, and animal tracks.

Anthropomorphic and zoomorphic subjects show motion, realistic physical attributes, and details of clothing, tack, decoration, and life-

Figure 105. *Early Historic Ute Indian Style black (charcoal) drawings at site 5MF435, northwestern Colorado. These images show an equestrian figure and possible bear hunting scenes with a narrative quality. Equestrian figure is 24 centimeters in length. Redrawn from a field sketch by J.J. Lischka.*

styles. Figures are rarely naturalistic, but are clearly more realistic than those of the previous period.

Late historic Ute Indian Style panels are frequently crowded, and some elements appear to have been fit into spaces between other imagery. The impression that Late Ute Style art is crowded is enhanced by situations where Early Ute and other styles of rock art appear on the same panels. Buckles (1971) notes similarities between late Ute art and contemporaneous art of Plains Indians. He suggests that Plains culture influenced the Ute to express individualistic subjects.

Themes of the Late historic Ute Indian Style are male prestige, individualism, and aggression. The horse remains an important aspect of this art. Ceremonialism is suggested in Late Ute rock art by increasing emphasis on long trailing headdresses and other elaborate dress. Biographic attributes are clearly present in some late art, as in the earlier art. A few examples of narrative art with story lines occur, but compositions are much less complex and structured than Plains Biographic Style art. Two examples are found in the lower Gunnison River drainage of west central Colorado.

One example is a painted scene showing four realistic and detailed equestrians wearing distinctive and long trailing headdresses that are typical of those worn by Indians of the Great Plains and the Ute (Figure 106). These figures surround a shield-figure that may represent an

Figure 106. *Detail of Late Historic Ute Indian Style gray rock paintings and incised and pecked petroglyphs at site 5DT1, near the lower Gunnison River, west central Colorado. Paintings are gray and show four equestrians with trailing headdresses surrounding a shield-figure. The scene may record an actual event between mounted and foot warriors. Redrawn from Buckles (1971:Fig. 145).*

30 CM

enemy warrior. One rider and his horse are both spotted with paint. Raylike "feathers" protrude from the oval shield, and a symbol that resembles a bird track or trident decorates the center and is possibly a power symbol for the warrior.

Interestingly, a similar shield with raylike "feathers" is exhibited at the upper Colorado River cave site showing the elaborate bison hunt. This shield is circular and is painted and drawn with yellow, red, and black pigments. The center is decorated by a spokelike design, and "feathers" and fringelike lines are attached to the outside. The diameter of the shield is approximately sixty centimeters, and it superimposes an Early Historic Ute Indian Style horse and rider.

Another example of Late Style narrative art on the lower Gunnison River shows a battle scene involving petroglyphs of equestrians, one of which carries a shield and lance. Three shield-figures are shown, one of which brandishes a rifle, one who carries a lance and wears a headdress, and one who appears to have been shot and is falling backward. Also exhibited is a man shooting a rifle at a fallen man whose rifle appears to be falling, and a hunter who aims an arrow at a relatively large deer or elk. More abstract Early Ute Indian Style art occurs on the same panel (Plate 106). Another battle scene, painted black, occurs near the Colorado River in west central Colorado. This small scene shows a realistic equestrian and a rifleman (Figure 107).

Nonbiographic narrative art is also found in Late Ute Style art. This art appears to be illustrative of Ute mythology and occurs in the Uncompahgre River drainage at a site where numerous panels of prehistoric and historic petroglyphs are exhibited. One panel shows three bears in climbing poses; two are shown climbing trees (Figure 108). A third bear is the most detailed and has an open mouth and paws that

45 CM

Figure 107. *Late Historic Ute Indian Style black rock paintings at site 5ME1356, near the Colorado River, west central Colorado. The scene shows a realistic equestrian and a rifleman and may record a shooting incident.*

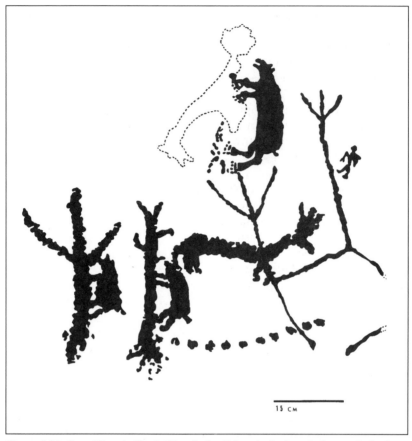

Figure 108. *Late Historic Ute Indian Style solid and stipple pecked petroglyphs show-ing "climbing" bears and a "walking" anthropomorph. The elements occur at site 5MN5, in the Uncompahgre River drainage, west central Colorado. Note that the paws of the uppermost bear are paw-print-like, similar to those seen in Uncompahgre Style rock art. A similar scene appears in a Ute painting about the Bear Dance leg-end made prior to A.D. 1900 (Buckles 1971:1072-1073).*

are in the form of paw prints (similar to depictions in Uncompahgre Style art). Buckles (1971:1072-1074) reports that the imagery is "duplicated in a painting of Ute Bear Dance by an Uncompahgre Ute Indian . . . The painting is said to depict a scene in the Bear Dance leg-end." The painting is dated approximately 1900. The imagery is con-sistent with the content of a Northern Ute legend that relates that a hunter "saw a bear dancing back and forth to a pine tree, and on his return home the hunter taught his people to do the dance" (Smith 1974:221).

More common than narratives in Late Historic Ute Indian Style rock art are groupings of figures, some with formal and thematic associations. Such art may have had biographic content. Smaller groupings appear to relate to a single individual or family, while larger groupings may describe groups such as war or hunting parties. Buckles (1971) illustrates examples of both in petroglyphs and paintings from the eastern slope of the Uncompahgre Plateau. The rock art shows groupings with realistic equestrians, tipis, and shields. Wenger (1956) illustrates a lone naturalistic equestrian figure with a tipi from the White River-Douglas Creek area of northwest Colorado. A very realistic and highly detailed tipi is carefully incised and painted at another White River site (Plate 107).

Of special interest are petroglyphs on the eastern slope of the Uncompahgre Plateau in the vicinity of a probable Ute campsite. The campsite is just across a drainage from the Harris Site, a previously discussed rock shelter with abstract groove petroglyphs. The pecked petroglyphs show the torso of a human wearing a top hat and an elongated but realistic horse figure (Figure 109). It is presumed that the two images are contemporaneous and were intentionally placed side by side. The human is significantly larger than the horse. This is unusual and may indicate the importance of a particular individual.

The face is not visible, but the neck is indicated. A circle appears in the chest of the figure, and the shoulders are rounded. It is possible that a cape or robe is signified, although the imagery is not explicit.

Plate 107. *A finely incised and painted tipi from site 5RB106, in the White River drainage, northwestern Colorado. The tipi is painted yellow and white and is 10 to 20 centimeters in length. The degree of detail suggests that the image dates from the late aboriginal period or the reservation period.*

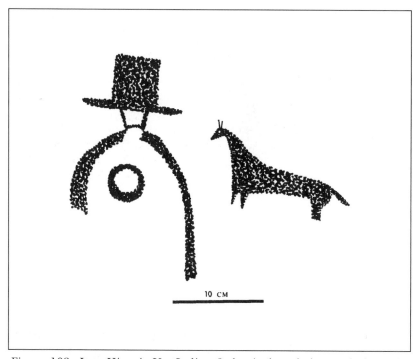

10 CM

Figure 109. *Late Historic Ute Indian Style stipple pecked petroglyphs at site 5MN3446, west central Colorado. Imagery shows an anthropomorph with rounded shoulders wearing a tall hat and a chest decoration, and an elongated horse. The circular chest decoration may represent jewelry, and the rounded shoulders may indicate a cape or robe. Photographs from the late 1800s show Ute males wearing tall hats, pendants, and capes (see Plate 108). Drawn from a photograph by Bill Harris.*

While the top hat may be of Euro-American origin, the figure probably represents a Ute Indian wearing this type of hat. Photographs from the late 1800s show Utes wearing similar hats (Plate 108). Artifacts in association with the campsite, such as blue-and-white drawn glass seed beads and a decorative chain from a nineteenth-century Spanish bit suggest a Ute presence, and a date associated with a Winchester .45–70 spent cartridge indicates that the site was used sometime after April 1879 (Horn 1989:C1).

Large panels of elaborately painted and drawn equestrians and shields occur in the Book Cliffs of Utah. These occur near panels of Fremont and Barrier Canyon Style rock art, as well as near examples of earlier Ute style art. At Thompson Wash, relatively large white-and-red anthropomorphs are shown standing near large "feathered" and decorated shields surrounded by smaller equestrians. One anthropomorph wears leggings (Plate 109). At another Book Cliffs site, a realistic horse

Plate 108. *Ute men wearing traditional and European style clothing, including top hats and capes at the Denver Expositions in 1882. A Ute with a top hat and cape may be represented in a petroglyph at site 5MN3446. William Henry Jackson photograph, courtesy of the Denver Public Library Western History Collection.*

Plate 109. *Detail of Late Historic Ute Style rock paintings in the Book Cliffs area of east central Utah. Elements are white and red and include a figure wearing leggings, shields, and a small but carefully detailed equestrian. The figure with the facial features on the left may date from the reservation period, post-A.D. 1880.*

and rider painted yellow and red occur with geometric abstract designs.

A well-known Late Historic Ute Indian Style petroglyph site is Newspaper Rock in Indian Creek Canyon, Utah, north of the Abajo Mountains (Plate 110). Late Style petroglyphs appear on a darkly patinated cliff with Early Historic Ute Indian Style petroglyphs and with others attributed to the Anasazi. Late Ute Style art superimposes some earlier art, and appears to imitate a prominent Anasazi figure located near the top of the panel.

Late Ute Indian Style imagery shown at Newspaper Rock includes equestrians, animal "pelts," and broad-shouldered anthropomorphs with headdresses. In one instance, a rider appears to be shooting an arrow at a deer or elk. Footprints and bear paw prints are numerous. On the right side of the panel, more than thirty large and small paw prints ascend the cliff. Quadrupeds shown at the site include horses, deer or elk, bighorn sheep, bison, and possibly bear. Shieldlike designs, bowlegged anthropomorphs, including one wearing fringed "leggings," or chaps, and many abstract linear images also occur.

The bowlegged figure with the "leggings" or chaps is part of an interesting grouping (Plate 111). The figure is surrounded by various subjects, including quadrupeds and equestrian figures, and all may have been intentionally placed in that position. Surrounding figures are not all consistent in workmanship, and it is possible that most, if not all, were present when the figure was pecked. The bowlegged figure wears a tall headdress, and long, wavy snakelike images are attached to both sides of the head. An abstract design, is directly over the headdress, and a bear paw print is beside the head on the left. This may be a power symbol. The figure holds what may be a quirt in the left hand. Keyser (1987:68) discusses and illustrates similar devices from Plains Biographic Style rock art and ledger art. The bowlegged figure provides an interesting and rare example of art combining aboriginal subjects and themes with Euro-American subject matter. Representations of tall headdresses, snakes, paw prints, and "power symbols" are traditional in aboriginal art from the prehistoric period to the historic, as demonstrated in this volume. Similar subject matter is exhibited throughout the western Colorado and eastern Utah areas. On the other hand, the quirt and possible chaps appear to represent material influences derived from Euro-Americans. This subject and various images at Newspaper Rock illustrate the changing nature of Ute culture after 1800. The variety in workmanship, subjects, and themes suggest that the Ute were experimenting with a number of ideas.

Despite contact with Euro-American culture, Ute rock art retains a decidedly aboriginal in subject and form. It is apparent that significance was placed on the horse and related materials, such as trailing headdresses, shields, and decorated bridles, but Ute rock art rarely indicates a concern with Euro-American life-styles or belief systems. In the Reservation Period, this pattern changes with regard to life-style, but certain rock art traditions, as well as cultural and symbolic traditions, endure into modern times.

Plate 110

Plate 111

Early and Late Historic Ute Indian Style petroglyphs at Newspaper Rock State Park, Utah. Plate 110 is an overview of Newspaper Rock with its variety of elements. Note the heavily patinated figures at the top center of the panel that are probably Pueblo II-III Anasazi in origin and contrast with the more recent and lightly patinated Ute petroglyphs. Plate 111 shows a detail of an anthropomorph that appears to wear fringed leggings or chaps and holds a quirtlike object similar to those appearing in late Plains rock art.

RESERVATION PERIOD

Between approximately 1900 and 1950, Jack House, the last traditional chief of the Weeminuche band of the Utes, and other Ute Indians made rock art in Mancos River Canyon and tributary canyons of the Mesa Verde. The rock art is preserved in the Ute Mountain Tribal Park on the Ute Mountain Ute Reservation in southwest Colorado. Stylistically consistent examples of Ute art in the vicinity of the Uintah and Ouray Reservation in northeast Utah have been reported by Castleton (1978). Other examples in the White River-Douglas Creek area of northwest Colorado are presumed to have been made by Utes following establishment of the Uintah and Ouray Reservation.

Mancos Canyon art is of particular interest because it is concentrated in an area known to have been continuously occupied by the Weeminuche band after the onset of the Reservation Period in 1880, and it is identified with the artistic efforts of a known individual with strong traditional ties. Chief Jack House was an important social and spiritual leader of the Weeminuche, a conservative band that avoided contact with outsiders for several years after occupying the reservation. Because of these factors, it is possible to study modern Ute rock art in the context of a continuous tradition that is three to four hundred years old.

Ute Representational Style

A.D. *1880 to 1950*

The Ute Representational Style is primarily based on examples from Ute Mountain Tribal Park. Many examples are believed to have been made by Chief Jack House between 1900 and 1950. However, other individuals are reported to have made rock art in Mancos Canyon during work projects of the 1930s, and it appears to duplicate the style of Jack House, who lived and raised cattle and probably made rock art in the canyon prior to that time (Bowman, personal correspondence).

A large panel of rock art is located on an overhanging cliff behind the site of a hogan owned by Chief House (Plate 112). His name and a date of 1947 appear on the panel. The art appears to have been created over a period of time since some elements look more recent than others, and the workmanship varies considerably. Some rock art panels in Mancos Canyon are signed by Jack House, but dates do not appear. His initials and a date of 1906 are on a rock near a panel of petroglyphs. Other rock art has symbolism that suggests Chief House is the

Plate 112. *Details of Ute Representational Style rock paintings, drawings, and petroglyphs from the Jack House hogan site, Mancos Canyon, Ute Mountain Tribal Park, Colorado. These were probably painted by Chief Jack House. Scale increments: 10 centimeters.*

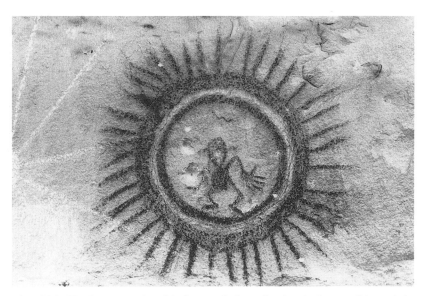

Plate 113. *Ute Representational Style petroglyphs and rock paintings possibly made by Chief Jack House, Ute Mountain Tribal Park, Colorado. This image may symbolize Chief House, whose name was "Hand in the Sun." Scale increments: 10 centimeters.*

artist. An example is a painting showing a human with exaggerated hands within a sunlike representation. This is likely to symbolize Chief House, whose Ute name was "Hand in the Sun" (Plate 113).

Rock art locations within the canyons of the Mancos River drainage include boulders along canyon floors, cliff faces, and rock outcrops. Some sites are near the top of steep canyons. All of the art is easily visible when approached and lacks the seclusion of some earlier Ute rock art. However, in a manner similar to earlier styles, Ute Representational art is frequently crowded. This is particularly obvious at the Jack House hogan site, where figures are shown side by side and above each other. Ute Representational art commonly occurs at sites with Anasazi rock art and may superimpose it. This also continues a pattern noted for earlier Ute rock art styles.

The Ute Representational Style includes rock paintings and drawings and petroglyphs; combination forms also occur. Petroglyph techniques are pecking, abrasion, scratching, and incising. Some show evidence of the use of metal tools, but others appear to have been made with stone tools. Entire figures may be incised in outline and have incised, pecked, and painted interiors. In some cases, fine incisions are used to add details to painted art. The pigments used are reported to be sheep (wool marking) dyes that were distributed to the Ute by the U.S. Government (Bowman personal correspondence). It is likely that charcoal and chalk provided additional pigments. Colors include blue, red, yellow, white, and black.

Generally, the style is realistic in the Euro-American tradition, and much of it is finely detailed. It can be seen as the culmination of a trend in earlier Ute rock art styles toward realism. Overall, given constraints of the media, the style is not unlike that illustrating western American subjects in publications of the late 1800s. A few highly abstract forms composed of dots and lines occur in Ute Representational Style art, but they are rare (Plates 114 and 115).

A few representations of what appear to be male and female dancers or other ceremonial subjects are more abstract than other anthropomorphic images. These figures are also relatively small. They are formed of scratched lines with painted faces, eyes, and body decorations, a technique that gives them a vague and almost supernatural appearance that may be intentional. The presumed male figures wear trailing and upright "feather" headdresses, and females wear dresses, some with jewelry. There is a similarity between these representations and dancers shown in late Navajo art (Schaafsma 1980), and the expressions may be related given the proximity between the Navajo and Ute reservations. One highly visible panel shows a female with a decorated face wearing a red dress beside a red handprint and a "sun"

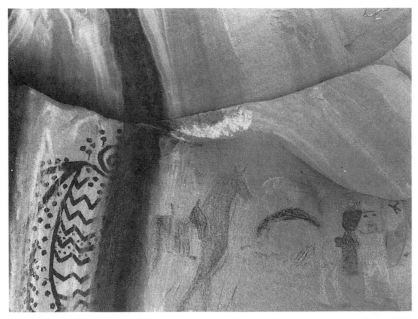

Plate 114

Plate 115

Details of Ute Representational Style polychrome rock paintings and rare abstract images, possibly made by Chief Jack House, at Ute Mountain Tribal Park, Colorado.

that superimposes part of a row of small scratched and painted figures (Plate 116). The large female has three red dots on the face that may represent ceremonial paint.

The Ute Representational Style features humans and equestrians, but horses are also important individual subjects (Plates 112, 114, and 115). In contrast to horses, humans are stiff and stylized in appearance. Earlier Ute rock art styles had similar distinctions. Humans are frequently near life-size and are shown full-face, in profile, and from the rear. Full-face torso views are common, especially of women with long hair that wear dresses and possibly shawls. The Jack House hogan site has seven or more of these painted representations, and they are found painted and pecked elsewhere in the tribal park (Plate 116). Rear views show male figures wearing pants with jeanlike pockets, chaps, boots with high heels, and broad-brimmed hats. On one panel, a similarly clad figure is shown with full and partial representations of three horses and a longhorn cow. Above the figures are carved the words, "J H Cowboy," presumably in reference to Chief Jack House. It is apparent that artists of the canyon were experimenting with drawing figure forms. In particular, variations in the skill with which naturalistic rear views and three-quarter views are depicted can be seen from one site to another.

Plate 116. *Ute Representational Style combination rock paintings and scratched and abraded petroglyphs. The woman shown wears facial paint. Tiny figures appear above and beneath the sunlike image. Scale increments: 10 centimeters.*

Portraiture is suggested for a few humans who have detailed facial features. In some cases, facial features are carefully sculptured. Traditional clothing, such as breast plates (Plate 117) and feather headdresses, are shown. Photographs of Ute males show them wearing bone breastplates and feather headdresses (Plate 118) that were reportedly used for ceremonial occasions (Marsh 1982). Cowboy attire is shown in great detail and includes articles described above as well as spurs. Hats and boots are also depicted as individual items.

Drawings of women are generally less detailed and individualistic and more stylized than males. To my knowledge, they are shown with full-face views only. This contrasts with males who are shown full-face, in profile, and from the rear. This may indicate that the representations served a symbolic role rather than representing certain individuals.

Horses and equestrians are relatively large forms and frequently approach half life-size. Sometimes only the heads of horses and other large animals are shown. Usually horses are shown in profile, but at least two examples have full-face views. Horse images are incised and painted in a variety of colors; some are spotted, while others have blazes on their faces. They are usually naturalistic in form, more so than other animals. Some show movement, such as running with the tail uplifted and bucking. Saddles and other horse tack are shown in great detail on equestrian figures, and saddles are also depicted as individual items (Plates 112, 114, and 115).

Plate 117. *Details of Ute Representational Style rock paintings, drawings, and petroglyphs from the Jack House hogan site, Mancos Canyon, Ute Mountain Tribal Park, Colorado.* Plate 117 *appears to show a figure wearing a traditional feather headdress and a bone breastplate.*

Animals, such as longhorn cows, bison, mules, rabbits, birds, and
deer, are also depicted in Ute Representational Style art. One interesting panel shows incised horses, a mule, a rabbit, two or three human
faces, and a hand that reaches for the horn of a saddle. A stylized eagle
with spread wings and tail is represented at the Jack House hogan site.

Additional subject matter are geometric abstract images, such as
large, bold red-painted designs composed of lines, dots, and spirals.

Plate 118. *Ute men wearing bone breastplates and feather headdresses, c. 1899.
Photograph courtesy of the Denver Public Library Western History Collection.*

They make an interesting contrast to adjacent art that represents horses and equestrians (Plates 114 and 115). The abstract designs may have been inspired by nearby Anasazi petroglyphs of spirals, dots, and lines.

Paintings and drawings of buildings also occur. A particularly interesting example is identified by writing as a mission school. The building is painted red and has white windows. Flags fly on either side of the building, and a group of incised and painted people stand in front.

Themes of Ute Representational Style art are traditional dress and ceremonies, possibly the Bear Dance; horses as symbols of value, prestige, and beauty; cowboy culture; personal recognition; and the art itself. This last theme, art for art's sake, is indicated by the abundance of art in the canyon, the variety of techniques employed, the number and types of subjects, the detailing of designs, and the use of various perspectives. It is assumed that most of the themes objectify the ideas of Chief Jack House, and the rock art greatly enriches our understanding of this individual and other Ute artists who were influenced by his work.

From the abundant rock art record, it is clear that traditional Ute ceremonies and symbolism continued to have importance after the establishment of the reservation and the change in lifestyle. Related to this is the continued importance of the horse and material culture associated with the horse. It is also clear that Euro-American cowboy culture became an important aspect of Ute social identity. Cowboy culture and livestock herding clearly provided a way in which many traditional Ute values expressed in earlier art, such as individualism, male prestige, mobility, the use of horses and equipment, and concern for personal attire, could function for a society that had undergone drastic change.

APPENDIX:

Numerical list of rock art sites used in this study, by state.

Colorado

County codes:

DT	Delta	ME	Mesa	MV	Mesa Verde
EA	Eagle	MF	Moffat	RB	Rio Blanco
GF	Garfield	MN	Montrose	RT	Routt
GN	Gunnison	MT	Montezuma	SM	San Miguel

5DT1	5ME163	5ME538	5MF610
5DT4	5ME164	5ME540	5MF685
5DT53	5ME165	5ME591	5MF756
5DT54	5ME167	5ME592	5MF758
5DT64	5ME168	5ME677	5MF948
5DT68	5ME175	5ME687	5MF1277
5DT355	5ME213	5ME696	5MF1753
5EA317	5ME214	5ME705	5MF2685
5GF72	5ME217	5ME706	5MF2691
5GF168	5ME223	5ME718	5MF2705
5GF304	5ME227	5ME724	5MN5
5GF305	5ME228	5ME725	5MN72
5GF331	5ME231	5ME729	5MN73
5GF332	5ME232	5ME730	5MN388
5GF333	5ME237	5ME735	5MN439
5GF339	5ME238	5ME778	5MN440
5GF342	5ME239	5ME792	5MN443
5GF418	5ME240	5ME830	5MN868
5GF518	5ME241	5ME841	5MN1186
5GF609	5ME247	5ME862	5MN2341
5GF619	5ME250	5ME886	5MN2777
5GF742	5ME279	5ME905	5MN2929
5GF931	5ME328	5ME935	5MN2930
5GF1339	5ME329	5ME1057	5MN3195
5GN928	5ME332	5ME1356	5MN3249
5ME1	5ME354	5ME1551	5MN3299
5ME10	5ME398	5ME1552	5MN3300
5ME13	5ME450	5ME3768	5MN3446
5ME27	5ME454	5ME4502	5MN3450
5ME76	5ME455	5ME4520	5MN3451
5ME79	5ME457	5ME4997	5MT2216
5ME80	5ME458	5ME5105	5MT2381
5ME88	5ME459	5ME5259	5MT2387
5ME94	5ME460	5MF289	5MT2405
5ME98	5ME462	5MF353	5MT2412
5ME101	5ME465	5MF354	5MT2414
5ME158	5ME468	5MF435	5MT4489
5ME159	5ME505	5MF436	5MT4491
5ME161	5ME526	5MF465	5MT4527
5ME162	5ME529	5MF492	5MT4549

5MT4554	5RB1046	**New Mexico**	42SA6967
5MT4555	5RB1607	LA 8970	42SA7736
5MT4556	5RB1849		42SA13797
5MT4619	5RB2497		42SA16825
5MT4656	5RB2498	**Utah**	42SA16826
5MT4726	5RB2717		42SV12
5MT4728	5RT6	County codes:	42UN40
5MT4370	5RT8	DA Daggett	42UN45
5MT4745	5RT47	EM Emery	42UN62
5MT4752	5RT90	GA Garfield	42UN88
5MT4777	5RT118	SA San Juan	42UN178
5MT4779	5RT120	SV Sevier	42WN6
5MT4809	5RT345	UN Uintah	42WN7
5MT5340	5RT698	WN Wayne	42WN8
5MT6811	5SM9		42WN9
5MT7491	5SM10	42DA14	42WN103
5MT7580	5SM14	42EM65	42WN149
5RB83		42GA1536	42WN155
5RB85		42GA2094	42WN178
5RB86	**Mesa Verde**	42SA48	42WN181
5RB92	**National Park**	42SA1448	42WN182
5RB95	MV 684	42SA1449	42WN184
5RB106	MV 687	42SA1450	42WN185
5RB222	MV 990	42SA1452	42WN187
5RB245	MV 1320	42SA1459	42WN188
5RB249	MV 1370	42SA1486	42WN190
5RB252	MV 1421	42SA1518	42WN191
5RB274	MV 1450	42SA1614	
5RB279	MV 1527	42SA1629	
5RB372	MV 1890	42SA1631	**Wyoming**
5RB489	MV 2198	42SA1638	County codes:
5RB698	MV 2201	42SA1776	HO Hot Springs
5RB820	MV 2210	42SA3589	SW Sweetwater
5RB827	MV 2703	42SA3711	
5RB851	MV 2469	42SA5263	48HO4
5RB890	MV 3572	42SA6801	48SW88

BIBLIOGRAPHY

Aikens, C. Melvin
1966   Virgin-Kayenta Cultural Relationships.
      University of Utah, *Anthropological Papers* 79 (*Glen Canyon Series* 29),
      Salt Lake City.
1970   Hogup Cave. University of Utah, *Anthropological Papers* 93, Salt Lake
      City.
1978   The Far West. In *Ancient Native Americans*, Jesse D. Jennings, ed., pp.
      131–182. W.H. Freeman and Company, San Francisco.

Aikens, C. Melvin, and David B. Madsen
1986   Prehistory of the Eastern Area. In Handbook of *North American Indians,
      Great Basin* vol. 11, edited by Warren L. D'Azevedo, pp. 149–160. Smith-
      sonian Institution, Washington, D.C.

Amsden, Charles Avery
1949   *Prehistoric Southwesterners from Basketmaker to Pueblo.* Southwest Mu-
      seum, Los Angeles.

Anderson, Keith M.
1971   Excavations at Betatakin and Keet Seel. *The Kiva* 37(1):1–29.

Baars, Donald L.
1983   *The Colorado Plateau, A Geologic History.*
      University of New Mexico Press, Albuquerque.

Bard, J.C., F. Asaro, and R.F. Heizer
1978   Perspectives on the Dating of Prehistoric Great Basin Petroglyphs by Neu-
      tron Activation Analysis. *Archaeometry* 20(1):85–88.

Berry, Michael S., and Claudia F. Berry
1976   An Archaeological Reconnaissance of the White River Area, Northeastern
      Utah. *Antiquities Section Selected Papers* 2(4–8):4–42, Division of State
      History, Salt Lake City, Utah.

Beschel, Ronald E.
1961   Dating Rock Surfaces by Lichen Growth and Its Application to Glaciology
      and Physiography (lichenometry). In *Geology of the Arctic* vol. 2, G.O.
      Raasch, ed., pp. 1044–1048. University of Toronto Press, Canada.

Black, Kevin
1986   Mitigative Archaeological Excavations at Two Sites for the Cottonwood Pass
      Project, Chaffee and Gunnison Counties, Colorado. Prepared for the Na-
      tional Park Service by Metcalf Archaeological Consultants, Eagle, Colorado.

Bolton, Herbert E.
1972   *Pageant in the Wilderness: The Story of the Escalante Expedition to the Inte-
      rior Basin, 1776.* Reprint. Utah State Historical Society, Salt Lake City.

Bowman, Doug
1989   Personal correspondence with regard to rock art at the Ute Mountain-
      Tribal Park.

Bradley, John E., William R. Killam, George R. Burns, and Marilyn A. Martorano
1986   An Archaeological Survey and Predictive Model of Selected Areas of Utah's
      Cisco Desert. Utah Bureau of Land Management, *Cultural Resources Series*
      18, Salt Lake City.

Breternitz, David A.
1970   Archaeological Investigations in Dinosaur National Monument, Colorado-Utah, 1964–65. *University of Colorado Studies, Series in Anthropology* 17, Boulder.
compiler
1984   *Dolores Archaeological Program: Synthetic Report 1978–1981.* U. S. Bureau of Reclamation, Denver, Colorado.

Buckles, William G.
1971   *The Uncompahgre Complex: Historic Ute Archaeology and Prehistoric Archaeology on the Uncompahgre Plateau in West Central Colorado.* Ph.D. dissertation, Department of Anthropology, University of Colorado, Boulder.
1989   Petroglyphic Research and Ogam in Southeastern Colorado: Strategies for Resolving Controversies. In *Rock Art of the Western Canyons*, Jane S. Day, Paul D. Friedman, and Marcia J. Tate, eds., pp. 113–155. Colorado Archaeological Society Memoir 3, Denver Museum of Natural History.

Bunzel, Ruth L.
1932   Zuni Katcinas. In *Forty-seventh Annual Report of the Bureau of American Ethnology*, pp. 837–1108. U.S. Government Printing Office, Washington, D.C.

Burgh, Robert F.
1950   A Fremont Basket Maker House in Dinosaur National Monument. *Tree Ring Bulletin* 16:19–20.

Burgh, Robert F., and Charles R. Scoggin
1948   The Archaeology of Castle Park, Dinosaur National Monument. University of Colorado Studies, *Series in Anthropology* 2, Boulder.

Burton, Robert Jordan
1971   *The Pictographs and Petroglyphs of Dinosaur National Monument.* M.A. thesis, Department of Anthropology, University of Colorado, Boulder.

Callaway, Donald G., Joel C. Janetski, and Omer C. Stewart
1986   Ute. In *Handbook of North American Indians, Great Basin* vol. 11, Warren L. D'Azevedo, ed., pp. 336–367. Smithsonian Institution, Washington, D.C.

Cassells, E. Steve
1983   *The Archaeology of Colorado.* Johnson Books, Boulder.

Chappel Collection Data Base
n.d.   Public domain documents with drawings by Nancy Olsen. Dolores, Colorado: Anasazi Heritage Center.

Castleton, Kenneth B.
1978   *Petroglyphs and Pictographs of Utah, Volume One, the East and Northeast.* Utah Museum of Natural History, Salt Lake City.
1979   *Petroglyphs and Pictographs of Utah, Volume Two, the South, Central, West, and Northwest.* Utah Museum of Natural History, Salt Lake City.

Clarke, David L.
1968   *Analytical Archaeology.* Methuen and Co., London.

Cole, Sally J.
1984   Analysis of a San Juan (Basketmaker) Style Painted Mask in Grand Gulch, Utah. *Southwestern Lore* 50(1):1–6.

1985   Additional Information on Basketmaker Masks or Faces in Southeastern Utah. *Southwestern Lore* 51(1):14–18.

1987   An Analysis of the Prehistoric and Historic Rock Art of West-Central Colorado. Colorado Bureau of Land Management *Cultural Resources Series* 21, Denver.

1988   Ute Rock Art in Colorado. In *Archaeology of the Eastern Ute: A Symposium*, Paul R. Nickens, ed., pp. 102–143. Colorado Council of Professional Archaeologists *Occasional Papers* 1.

1989a   *Rock Art Evidence for the Presence and Social Significance of the Katsina Cult at 13th–14th Century Homol'ovi in the Central Little Colorado River Valley, Northeastern Arizona*. M.A. Thesis in Anthropology, Vermont College, Norwich University.

1989b   Iconography and Symbolism in Basketmaker Rock Art. In *Rock Art of the Western Canyons*, Jane S. Day, Paul D. Friedman, and Marcia J. Tate, eds. pp. 59–85. *Colorado Archaeological Society Memoir* 3, Denver Museum of Natural History.

1989c   Rock Art at 5ME2341, The Harris Site. In *The Harris Site Excavation*, pp. A1–A26. Colorado Bureau of Land Management, *Cultural Resources Series* 28, Denver.

Colton, Harold S.
1959   *Hopi Kachina Dolls With a Key to Their Identification*. University of New Mexico Press, Albuquerque.

Conetah, Fred A.
1982   *A History of the Northern Ute People*. Kathryn L. McKay and Floyd A. O'Neil, ed. Uintah-Ouray Ute Tribe, Utah.

Conner, Carl, and Richard W. Ott
1978   Petroglyphs and Pictographs of the Grand Junction District. Prepared for the Bureau of Land Management, Grand Junction, Colorado.

Conner, Stuart W.
1962   A Preliminary Survey of Prehistoric Picture Writing on Rock Surfaces in Central and South Central Montana. *Billings Archaeological Society Anthropological Paper* 2.

Conner, Stuart W., and Betty Lu Conner
1971   *Rock Art of the Montana High Plains*. The Art Galleries, University of California, Santa Barbara.

Copeland, Jim, and Gay A. Ives
n.d.   A Survey of Cliff Palace Wall Decorations and Kiva Designs. Manuscript on file at the Mesa Verde Research Center, Mesa Verde National Park.

Cordell, Linda S.
1979   Prehistory: Eastern Anasazi. In *Handbook of North American Indians, Southwest*, vol. 9, Alfonso Ortiz, ed., pp. 131–151. Smithsonian Institution, Washington, D.C.

1984   *Prehistory of the Southwest*. Academic Press, New York.

Creasman, Steven D.
1981   Archaeological Investigations in the Canyon Pintado Historic District, Rio Blanco County, Colorado: Phase 1, Inventory and Test Excavations. *Reports of the Laboratory of Public Archaeology* 34, Colorado State University, Ft. Collins.

1982   Rock Art of the Canyon Pintado Historic District. *Southwestern Lore* 48(4):1–13.

Creasman, Steven D., and Linda J. Scott
1987   Texas Creek Overlook: Evidence for Late Fremont (Post A.D. 1200) Occupation in Northwest Colorado. *Southwestern Lore* 53(4):1–16.

Daniels, Helen Sloan
1954   Pictographs. In *Basketmaker II Sites near Durango, Colorado,* Appendix A. Earl H. Morris and Robert F. Burgh. Carnegie Institution of Washington Publication 604.
1976   Adventures with the Anasazi of Falls Creek. *Occasional Papers of the Center of Southwest Studies,* Fort Lewis College, Durango, Colorado.

Dary, David
1989   *Cowboy Culture.* University Press of Kansas, Lawrence.

Day, Kent C.
1964   Thorne Cave, Northeastern Utah: Archaeology. *American Antiquity* 30(1):50–59.

Day, Kent C., and David S. Dibble
1963   Archaeological Survey of the Flaming Gorge Reservoir Area, Wyoming-Utah. University of Utah *Anthropological Papers* 65 (*Upper Colorado Series* 9), Salt Lake City.

D'Azevedo, Warren L., editor
1986   *Handbook of North American Indians, Great Basin* vol. 11, Smithsonian Institution, Washington, D.C.

Dean, Jeffrey S.
1969   Dendrochronology and Archaeological Analysis: A Possible Ute Example from *Southwestern Colorado.* Southwestern Lore 35:29–41.

Dewdney, Selwyn
1970   Dating Rock Art in the Canadian Shield Region. *Art and Archaeology* (*Occasional Paper 24*), Royal Ontario Museum, Toronto.

Dockstader, Frederick S.
1985   *The Kachina and the White Man.* University of New Mexico Press, Albuquerque.

Dolzani, Michael
1988   Rocking Around the Geomorphical Clock: Dating by the Rock-Varnish Method. *Mammouth Trumpet* 4(2).

Dorn, Ronald I., and David S. Whitley
1984   Chronometric and Relative Age Determination of Petroglyphs in the Western United States. *Annals of the Association of American Geographics* 74(2):308–322.

Eddy, Frank W., Allen E. Kane, and Paul R. Nickens
1984   *Southwest Colorado Prehistoric Context.* State Historical Society of Colorado, Denver.

Eliade, Mircea
1964   *Shamanism: Archaic Techniques of Ecstasy.* Bolligen Series 76, Princeton University Press.

Farwell, Robin, and Karen Wening
1985   The Pictured Cliffs Project. Museum of New Mexico, *Laboratory of Anthropology Note* 299, Santa Fe.

Ferg, Alan
1982   14th Century Kachina Depictions on Ceramics. In Collected Papers in Honor of John H. Runyon, edited by G.X. Fitzgerald, pp. 13–29. *Papers of the Archaeological Society of New Mexico* 7, Albuquerque.

Fetterman, Jerry
1976   Rock Art of the Mesa Verde Region. Paper submitted for Honors in Anthropology, University of Colorado, Boulder.

Fewkes, Jesse W.
1892   A Few Tusayan Petroglyphs. *American Anthropologist* 5:9–26.
1897   Tusayan Totemic Signatures. *American Anthropologist* 10(1): 1–11.
1901   An Interpretation of Katcina Worship. *Journal of American Folklore* 14:81–94.
1906   Hopi Shrines Near the East Mesa. *American Anthropologist* 8: 346–375.
1916   New Fire House, A Ruin Lately Excavated in the Mesa Verde. Smithsonian Institution, *Annual Report*, pp. 44–46, Washington, D.C.

Feyhl, Kenneth J.
1980   Tool Grooves: A Challenge. *Archaeology in Montana* 2(1):1–31.

Furst, Peter T.
1977   The Roots and Continuities of Shamanism. In *Stones, Bones, and Skin: Ritual and Shamanic Art*, pp. 1–28. The Society for Arts Publications, Toronto.

Gebhard, David S.
1951   The Petroglyphs of Wyoming: A Preliminary Paper. *El Palacio* 58(3): 67–81.
1966   The Shield Motif in Plains Rock Art. *American Antiquity* 31(5):721–732.
1969   *The Rock Art of Dinwoody, Wyoming*. The Art Galleries, University of California, Santa Barbara.
1972   Rock Art. In American Indian Art: Form and Tradition, pp. 26–33. E.F. Dutton and Company, Inc., New York.

Gebhard, David S., and Harold A. Cahn
1950   The Petroglyphs of Dinwoody, Wyoming. *American Antiquity* 15(3): 219–228.
1954   Petroglyphs in the Boysen Resevoir Area. In Archaeological Investigations in the Shoshone Basin of Wyoming, pp. 66–70. *University of Wyoming Publications* 18(1):1–70.

Gillin, John
1955   Archaeological Investigations in Nine Mile Canyon, Utah: A Re-Publication. University of Utah, *Anthropological Papers* 21, Salt Lake City.

Gleichman, Peter J., Susan Eininger, and Douglas D. Scott
1982   The Archaeology of the West End (San Miguel Resource Area). In Archaeological Resources in Southwestern Colorado, pp. 429–523, Colorado Bureau of Land Management, *Cultural Resources Series* 13, Denver.

Gooding, John
1986   Personal correspondence with regard to tree-ring dates for Tabeguache
        Cave I.

Gooding, John, and William Lane Shields
1985   Sisyphus Shelter. Colorado Bureau of Land Management, *Cultural
        Resources Series* 18, Denver.

Gordon, E. Kinzie, Kris J. Kranzush, Donna J. Knox, Victoria E. Keen, and Craig
A. Engleman
1983   A Cultural Resources Inventory of Texas-Missouri-Evacuation Creeks,
        Colorado. Colorado Bureau of Land Management, *Cultural Resources
        Series* 15, Denver.

Grady, James
1980   Environmental Factors in Archaeological Site Locations, Piceance Basin,
        Colorado. Colorado Bureau of Land Management, *Cultural Resources
        Series* 9, Denver.
1984   *Northwest Colorado Prehistoric Context*. State Historical Society of Colo-
        rado, Denver.

Grant, Campbell
1967   *Rock Art of the American Indian*. Thomas and Crowell, New York.
1978   *Canyon de Chelly: The People and Rock Art*. University of Arizona Press,
        Tucson.

Grant, Campbell, James W. Baird, and J. Kenneth Pringle
1968   Rock Drawings of the Coso Range. Maturango Museum, *Publication* 4,
        China Lake, California.

Guernsey, Samuel J., and Alfred V. Kidder
1921   Basketmaker Caves of Northeastern Arizona. *Papers of the Peabody Mu-
        seum of American Archaeology and Ethnology* vol. 3(2), Harvard University,
        Cambridge.

Gunnerson, James H.
1969   The Fremont Culture: A Study in Culture Dynamics on the Northern
        Anasazi Frontier. *Papers of the Peabody Museum of American Archaeology
        and Ethnology* 52(2), Cambridge, Massachusetts.

Guthrie, Mark R., Powys Gadd, Renee Johnson, and Joseph J. Lischka
1984   *Colorado Mountains Prehistoric Context*. State Historical Society of Colo-
        rado, Denver.

Hauck, F.R.
1979   Cultural Resource Evaluation in Central Utah, 1977. Utah Bureau of
        Land Management, *Cultural Resources Series* 3, Salt Lake City.

Haury, Emil
1945   Painted Cave, Northeastern Arizona. *Amerind Foundation Publication* 3,
        Dragoon, Arizona.

Hayes, Alden C.
1964   The Archaeological Survey of Wetherill Mesa. National Park Service,
        Archaeological Research Series 7-A, Washington, D.C.

Hays, Kelley A.
1988a Human Figures on Anasazi Ceramic Vessels: Basketmaker III to Pueblo IV. Submitted as term paper for Anthropology 426, University of Arizona, Tucson.
1988b Life-form Designs on Homol'ovi Ceramics: Toward a Fourteenth Century Pueblo Iconography. Manuscript on file at the Arizona State Museum, Tucson.

Hebard, Grace Raymond
1930 *Washakie.* Arthur H. Clark, Cleveland.

Hedges, Ken
1985 Rock Art Portrayals of Shamanic Transformation and Magical Flight. In *Rock Art Papers* vol. 2 (*San Diego Museum Papers* 18), Ken Hedges, ed., pp. 83–94. Museum of Man, San Diego.

Heizer, Robert F., and Martin A. Baumhoff
1962 *Prehistoric Rock Art of Nevada and Eastern California.* University of California Press, Berkeley and Los Angeles.

Heizer, Robert F., and Thomas R. Hester
1978 Two Petroglyph Sites in Lincoln County, Nevada. In Four Rock Art Studies, William C. Clewlow, Jr., ed., pp. 1–44. *Ballena Press Publications on North American Rock Art* 1, Socorro, N.M.

Hendry, Mary Helen
1983 *Indian Rock Art in Wyoming.* Privately published by author.

Hewitt, Nancy J.
1980 Fiber Artifacts. In Cowboy Cave, Jesse D. Jennings, ed., pp. 49–74. University of Utah, *Anthropological Papers* 104, Salt Lake City.

Hobler, Phillip M., and Audrey E. Hobler
1978 An Archaeological Survey of the Upper White Canyon Area, Southeastern Utah. *Antiquities Section Selected Papers* 5(13), Division of State History, Salt Lake City.

Hodder, Ian
1982 *Symbols in Action.* Cambridge University Press, England.
1986 *Reading the Past.* Cambridge University Press, England.

Horn, Jonathon C.
1989 Analysis of Historic Artifacts from the Ute Component of the Harris Site (5MN2341). In The Harris Site Excavation, pp. C1–C4. Colorado Bureau of Land Management, *Cultural Resources Series* 28, Denver.

Hull, Frank W., and Nancy M. White
1980 Spindle Whorls, Incised and Painted Stone, and Unfired Clay Objects. In Cowboy Cave, Jesse D. Jennings, ed., pp. 117–127. University of Utah *Anthropological Papers* 104, Salt Lake City.

Hultkrantz, Ake
1986 Mythology and Religious Concepts. In *Handbook of North American Indians, Great Basin* vol. 11, Warren L. D'Azevedo, ed., pp. 630–640. Smithsonian Institution, Washington, D.C.

Hunt, Alice P.
1953   Archaeological Survey of the La Sal Mountains Area, Utah. University of Utah, *Anthropological Papers* 14, Salt Lake City.

Hunt, Charles B.
1967   *Physiography of the United States*. W.H. Freeman, San Francisco, California.

Hurst, C.T.
1940   Preliminary Work in Tabeguache Cave, 1939. *Southwestern Lore* 6(1):4–8.
1941   The Second Season in Tabeguache Cave. *Southwestern Lore* 7(1): 4–18.
1942   Completion of Work in Tabeguache Cave. *Southwestern Lore* 8(1):7–16.
1943   Preliminary Work in Tabeguache Cave II. *Southwestern Lore* 9(1):10–16.
1944   1943 Excavation in Cave II, Tabeguache Canyon, Montrose County, Colorado. *Southwestern Lore* 10(1):2–14.
1945   Completion of Tabeguache Cave II. *Southwestern Lore* 11(1): 8–12.
1946   The 1945 Tabeguache Expedition. *Southwestern Lore* 12(1):7–16.
1947   Excavation of Dolores Cave. *Southwestern Lore* 13(1):8–17.
1948   The Cottonwood Expedition, 1947, A Cave and a Pueblo Site. *Southwestern Lore* 14(1):4–19.

Hurst, C.T., and Lawrence J. Hendricks
1952   Some Unusual Petroglyphs Near Sapinero, Colorado. *Southwestern Lore* 18(1):14–18.

Huscher, Betty H., and Harold A. Huscher
1940   Conventionalized Bear-Track Petroglyphs of the Uncompahgre Plateau. *Southwestern Lore* 6(2):25–28.
1943   The Hogan Builders of Colorado. *Southwestern Lore* 9:1–92.

Irwin-Williams, Cynthia
1967   Picosa: The Elementary Southwestern Culture. *American Antiquity* 32:441–457.
1973   The Oshara Tradition: Origins of Anasazi Culture. Eastern New Mexico University, *Contributions in Anthropology* vol. 5(1), Portales.
1979   Post-Pleistocene Archaeology, 7000–2000 B.C. In *Handbook of North American Indians, Southwest* vol. 9, Alfonso Ortiz, ed., pp. 31–42. Smithsonian Institution, Washington, D.C.

Ives, Gay A.
1981   The Study of Anasazi Rock Art in the Dolores River Valley. Manuscript on file, Dolores Archaeological Progam archive, Anasazi Heritage Center, Dolores, Colorado.
1986   Rock Art of the Dolores River Valley. In *Dolores Archaeological Program: Research Designs and Initial Survey Results*, pp. 235–375. U.S. Bureau of Reclamation, Denver, Colorado.

Jeancon, Jean Allard
1926   Pictographs of Colorado. *Colorado Magazine* 3(2):33–45.

Jennings, Jesse D.
1953   Danger Cave: A Progress Summary. *El Palacio* 60(5): 179–213.
1957   Danger Cave. University of Utah, *Anthropological Papers* 27, University of Utah Press, Salt Lake City.
1964   The Desert West. In *Prehistoric Man in the New World*, Jesse D. Jennings and Edward Norbeck, eds., pp. 149–174. University of Chicago Press, Illinois.

1966   Glen Canyon: A Summary. University of Utah, *Anthropological Papers* 81. University of Utah Press, Salt Lake City.
1974   *Prehistory of North America.* McGraw-Hill, New York.
1978   Prehistory of Utah and the Eastern Great Basin. University of Utah, *Anthropological Papers* 98, Salt Lake City.
1980   Cowboy Cave. University of Utah, *Anthropological Papers* 104, Salt Lake City.

Jett, Stephen C.
1982   "Ye'iis Lying Down," A Unique Navajo Sacred Place. In *Navajo Religion and Culture: Selected Views,* David M. Brugge and Charlotte J. Frisbie, eds., pp. 138–149. Museum of New Mexico Press, Santa Fe.

Johnson, Alfred E.
1965   *The Development of Western Pueblo Culture.* Ph.D. dissertation, Department of Anthropology, University of Arizona, Tucson. University Microfilms, Ann Arbor, Michigan.

Jones, Anne Trinkle, and Robert C. Euler
1979   *A Sketch of Grand Canyon Prehistory.* Grand Canyon Natural History Association, Arizona.

Jorgensen, Joseph G.
1986   Ghost Dance, Bear Dance, and Sun Dance. In *Handbook of North American Indians, Great Basin* vol. 11, Warren L. D'Azevedo, ed., pp. 660–672. Smithsonian Institution, Washington, D.C.

Keyser, James D.
1975   A Shoshonean Origin for the Plains Shield Bearing Warrior Motif. *Plains Anthropologist* 20:207–215.
1977   Writing-on-Stone: Rock Art on the Northwestern Plains. *Canadian Journal of Archaeology* 1:15–80.
1979   The Plains Indian War Complex and the Rock Art of Writing-on-Stone, Alberta, Canada. *Journal of Field Archaeology* 6:41–48.
1984   The North Cave Hills. In Rock Art of Western South Dakota part 1, pp. 2–51. *Special Publication of the South Dakota Archaeological Society* 9, Sioux Falls.
1987   A Lexicon for Historic Plains Indian Rock Art: Increasing Interpretive Potential. *Plains Anthropologist* 32(115):43–71.

Keyser, James D., and George C. Knight
1976   The Rock Art of Western Montana. *Plains Anthropologist* 21(71):1–12.

Kidder, Alfred Vincent
1927   Southwestern Archaeological Conference. *Science* 68:489–491.

Kidder, Alfred V., and Samuel J. Guernsey
1919   Archaeological Explorations in Northeastern Arizona. *Bureau of American Ethnology Bulletin* 65, U.S. Government Printing Office, Washington, D.C.

Koch, Ronald P.
1977   *Dress Clothing of the Plains Indians.* University of Oklahoma Press, Norman.

La Point, Halcyon
1987   An Overview of Prehistoric Cultural Resources, Little Snake Resource

Area, Northwestern Colorado. Colorado Bureau of Land Management, *Cultural Resources Series* 20, Denver.

Leakey, Mary
1983 *Africa's Vanishing Art, the Rock Paintings of Tanzania.* Doubleday and Co., Garden City, New York.

Lewis-Williams, J.D.
1981 *Believing and Seeing: Symbolic Meaning in Southern San Rock Paintings.* Academic Press, New York.

Liestman, Terri
1985 Site 42UN1103: A Rockshelter in Dinosaur National Monument, Utah. *Midwest Archaeological Center Occasional Studies in Anthropology* 13.

Lindsay, La Mar W.
1976 Grand County: An Archaeological Summary. *Antiquities Section Selected Papers* 10, Division of State History, Salt Lake City.

Lipe, William D.
1978 The Southwest. In *Ancient North Americans*, Jesse D. Jennings, ed., pp. 420–493. W.H. Freeman and Company, New York.

Lischka, Joseph J., Mark E. Miller, R. Branson Reynolds, Dennis Dahms, Kathy Joyner-McGuire, and David McGuire
1983 An Archaeological Inventory in North Park. Colorado Bureau of Land Management, *Cultural Resources Series* 14, Denver.

Lister, Robert H., and Florence C.
1978 *Anasazi Pottery.* Maxwell Museum of Anthropology, University of New Mexico Press, Albuquerque.

Loendorf, Lawrence.
1986 A Radiocarbon Date at the Rochester Creek Site, Utah. *La Pintura* 12(3):8–9, 17–18.
1990 A Dated Rock Art Panel of Shield Bearing Warriors in South Central Montana. *Plains Anthropologist* 35(127):45–54.

Lowie, Robert H.
1924 Notes on Shoshonean Ethnography. American Museum of Natural History, *Anthropological Papers* vol. 20(2), New York.
1954 Indians of the Plains. *Anthropological Handbook* 1, The American Museum of Natural History, McGraw-Hill, New York.

Lutz, Bruce J.
1978 The Test Excavations of 5ME217: A Rockshelter in Mesa County, Colorado. Report prepared for Grand Junction District Bureau of Land Management, Colorado.

Madsen, David B.
1979 The Fremont and the Sevier: Defining Prehistoric Agriculturalists North of the Anasazi. *American Antiquity* 44:711–723.
1980 Fremont Perspectives. *Antiquities Section Selected Papers* vol. 7. Division of State History, Salt Lake City, Utah.
1989 *Exploring the Fremont.* Utah Museum of Natural History, Salt Lake City.

Madsen, David B., and Michael S. Berry
1975   A Reassessment of Northeastern Great Basin Prehistory. *American Antiquity* 40(1):82–86.

Madsen, David B., and Lamar W. Lindsay
1977   Backhoe Village. In *Antiquities Section Selected Papers* vol. 4(12), Division of State History, Salt Lake City, Utah.

Mahaney, Nancy
1986   Rock Art. In Colorado Department of Highways Prehistoric Cultural Resources Along State Highway 139, Loma to Douglas Pass, pp. 85–113. *Highway Salvage Report* 58, Denver.

Mallery, Garrick
1893   Picture-Writing of the American Indians. In *Tenth Annual Report of the Bureau of American Ethnology for the Year 1888–1889*, pp. 3–822. Government Printing Office, Washington, D.C.
1972   *Picture Writing of the American Indians.* 2 vols. Dover Publications, New York. Reprint.

Malotki, Ekkehart, and Michael Lomatuway'ma
1987   Maasaw: Profile of a Hopi God. *American Tribal Religions* vol. 11, University of Nebraska Press, Lincoln and London.

Malouf, Carling I.
1961   Pictographs and Petroglyphs. *Archaeology in Montana* 3(1):1–13.

Marsh, Charles S.
1982   *People of the Shining Mountains: The Utes of Colorado.* Pruett Publishing, Boulder, Colorado.

Marshack, Alexander
1977   The Meander as a System: The Analysis and Recognition of Iconographic Units in Upper Paleolithic Compositions. In "Form and Indigenous Art," *Prehistory and Material Culture Series* 13, Peter J. Ucko, ed., pp. 286–317. Australian Institute of Aboriginal Studies, Canberra.

Marwitt, John P.
1970   Median Village and Fremont Culture Regional Variation. University of Utah, *Anthropological Papers* 95, Salt Lake City.
1980   A Fremont Retrospective. *Antiquities Section Selected Papers* 7(16):9–12, Division of State History, Salt Lake City, Utah.
1986   Fremont Cultures. In *Handbook of North American Indians*, Great Basin, vol. 11, Warren L. D'Azevedo, ed., pp. 161–172. Smithsonian Institution, Washington, D.C.

McKern, W.C.
1978   Western Colorado Petroglyphs, Douglas D. Scott, ed. Colorado Bureau of Land Management, *Cultural Resources Series* 8, Denver.

Mesa Verde Museum
n.d.   Information on visit of Hopi medicine men to Mesa Verde National Park
n.d.   *Petroglyph Trail Guide*, Mesa Verde Museum Association, Mesa Verde National Park.

n.d.   *Mesa Verde Museum Exhibit Guide.* Chapin Mesa Archaeological Museum, Mesa Verde National Park.

Metcalf, Michael D., and Kevin D. Black
1988   The Yarmony Site, Eagle County, Colorado: A Preliminary Summary. *Southwestern Lore* 54(1):10–28.

Michaelis, Helen
1981   Willowsprings: A Hopi Petroglyph Site. *Journal of New World Archaeology* 4(2):3–23.

Miller, Wick R.
1986   Numic Languages. In *Handbook of North American Indians, Great Basin* vol. 11, Warren L. D'Azevedo, ed., pp. 98–106. Smithsonian Institution, Washington, D.C.

Molyneaux, Brian Leigh
1977   *Formalism and Contextualism: A Historiography of Rock Art Research in the New World.* Master's thesis, Department of Anthropology, Trent University, Petersburg, Ontario.

Morris, Earl H.
1924   Burials in the Aztec Ruin, The Aztec Ruin Annex. *Anthropological Papers of The American Museum of Natural History* vol. 26, parts 3 and 4, American Museum Press, New York.
1939   Archaeological Studies in the La Plata District, Southwestern Colorado and Northwestern New Mexico. *Carnegie Institution of Washington Publication* 533.
1951   Basketmaker III Human Figurines from Northeastern Arizona. *American Antiquity* 17(1):33–40.

Morris, Earl H., and Robert F. Burgh
1941   Anasazi Basketry, Basket Maker II Through Pueblo III, A Study Based on Specimens from the San Juan River Country. *Carnegie Institution of Washington Publication* 533, Washington, D.C.
1954   Basketmaker II Sites Near Durango, Colorado. *Carnegie Institution of Washington Publication* 604, Washington, D.C.

Morris, Elizabeth Ann
1980   Basketmaker Caves in the Prayer Rock District, Northeastern Arizona. *Anthropological Papers of the University of Arizona* 35, University of Arizona Press, Tucson.

Morss, Noel
1931   The Ancient Culture of the Fremont River in Utah. *Papers of the Peabody Museum of American Archaeology and Ethnology,* Cambridge, Massachusetts.
1954   Clay Figurines of the American Southwest. *Papers of the Peabody Museum of American Archaeology and Ethnology* 49(1), Cambridge, Massachusetts.

Munn, Nancy D.
1973   *Walbiri Iconography, Graphic Representation and Cultural Symbolism in a Central Australian Society.* University of Chicago Press.

Newcomb, Franc Johnson
1964   *Hosteen Klah, Navaho Medicine Man and Sand Painter.* University of Oklahoma Press, Norman.

Newcomb, Franc J., and Gladys A. Reichard
1975   *Sandpaintings of the Navajo Shooting Chant*. Dover Publications, New York.

Nichols, Deborah L., and F.E. Smiley
1984   A Summary of Prehistoric Research on Northern Black Mesa. In Excavations on Black Mesa, 1982: A Descriptive Report, Deborah L. Nichols and F.E. Smiley, eds., pp. 89–107. Southern Illinois University at Carbondale, *Center for Archaeological Investigations Research Paper* 39.

Nickens, Paul R., and Deborah A. Hull
1982   San Juan Resource Area. In Archaeological Resources of Southwestern Colorado, pp. 1–306. Colorado Bureau of Land Management, *Cultural Resources Series* 13, Denver.

Noxon, John, and Deborah Marcus
1985   Significant Rock Art Sites in the Needles District of Canyonlands National Park, Southeastern Utah. A report submitted to the National Park Service, Moab, Utah.

Olsen, Nancy
1985   Hovenweep Rock Art: An Anasazi Visual Communication System. University of California at Los Angeles, *Institute of Archaeology Occasional Paper* 14.

Ortiz, Alfonso
1979   Introduction. In *Handbook of North American Indians, Southwest*, Alfonso Ortiz, ed., pp. 1–4. Smithsonian Institution, Washington, D.C.

Pettit, Jan
1990   *Utes: The Mountain People*. Johnson Books, Boulder.

Pierson, Lloyd M.
1981   Cultural Resource Summary of the East Central Portion of the Moab District, 1980. Utah Bureau of Land Management, *Cultural Resources Series* 10, Salt Lake City. 1982a Arches National Park. In *Canyon Country Prehistoric Rock Art*, F.A. Barnes, pp. 182–185. Wasatch Publishers, Salt Lake City, Utah.
1982b   Moab Area. In *Canyon Country Prehistoric Rock Art*, F.A. Barnes, pp. 250–257. Wasatch Publishers, Salt Lake City, Utah.

Pilles, Peter J., Jr.
1975   Petroglyphs of the Little Colorado River Valley, Arizona. In *American Indian Rock Art*, Shari T. Grove, ed., pp. 1–26. San Juan County Museum Association, Farmington, New Mexico.

Plog, Fred
1979   Prehistory: Western Anasazi. In *Handbook of North American Indians, Southwest*, vol. 9, Alfonso Ortiz, ed., pp. 108–130. Smithsonian Institution, Washington, D.C.

Reagan, Albert B.
1931a   Additional Archaeological Notes on Ashley and Dry Fork Canyons in Northeastern Utah. *El Palacio* 31(8):122–131.
1931b   Collections of Ancient Artifacts from the Ashley-Dry Fork District of the Uintah Basin, With Some Notes on the Dwellings and Mortuary Customs of the Ouray Indians of the Ouray (Utah) Region. *El Palacio* 31(26): 407–413.

1933a   Anciently Inhabited Caves of the Vernal (Utah) District, With Some Additional Notes on Nine Mile Canyon, Northeast Utah. *Transactions of the Kansas Academy of Science* 36:41–70.

1933b   Indian Pictures in Ashley and Dry Fork Valleys in Northeastern Utah. *Art and Archaeology* 34(4):201–210.

1935   Petroglyphs Show That the Ancients of the Southwest Wore Masks. *American Anthropologist* 37(4):707–708.

Reed, Alan
1984   *West Central Colorado Prehistoric Context.* State Historical Society of Colorado, Denver.

Reed, Erik K.
1946   The Distinctive Features and Distribution of the San Juan Anasazi Culture. *Southwestern Journal of Anthropology* 2(3):295–305.

1948   The Western Pueblo Archaeological Complex. *El Palacio* 55(1):9–15.

Reed, Verner Z.
1896   The Ute Bear Dance. *American Anthropologist* 9:237–244.

Reichard, Gladys A.
1950   *Navaho Religion: A Study of Symbolism*, volumes 1 and 2. Bolligen Series 18, Stratford Press, New York.

1977   *Navajo Medicine Man Sandpaintings.* Dover Publications, New York, New York.

Rohn, Arthur H.
1977   *Cultural Change and Continuity on Chapin Mesa.* The Regents Press of Kansas, Lawrence.

Sackett, James R.
1977   The Meaning of Style in Archaeology. *American Antiquity* 42(3): 369–380.

Schaafsma, Polly
1963   Rock Art in the Navajo Reservoir District. *Museum of New Mexico Papers in Anthropology* 7, Santa Fe.

1971   The Rock Art of Utah. *Papers of the Peabody Museum of American Archaeology and Ethnology* 65, Cambridge, Massachusetts.

1972   *Rock Art in New Mexico.* State Planning Office, Santa Fe, New Mexico.

1980   *Indian Rock Art of the Southwest.* University of New Mexico Press (School of American Research), Albuquerque.

1985   Form, Content, and Function: Theory and Method in North American Rock Art Studies. In *Advances in Archaeological Method and Theory* vol. 8, Michael B. Shiffer, ed., pp. 237–277. Academic Press, New York.

Schaafsma, Polly, and Curtis F. Schaafsma
1974   Evidence for the Origin of the Pueblo Kachina Cult as Suggested by Southwestern Rock Art. *American Antiquity* 39:535–545.

Schaafsma, Polly, and M. Jane Young
1983   Early Masks and Faces in Southwest Rock Art. In Collected Papers in Honor of Charlie Steen, Nancy Fox, ed. pp. 11–34. *Papers of the New Mexico Archaeological Society*, Albuquerque.

Schroeder, Albert H.
1952   The Archaeological Excavations at Willow Beach, Arizona, 1950. University of Utah, *Anthropological Papers* 50, Salt Lake City.

Schroedl, Alan R.
1977   The Grand Canyon Figurine Complex. *American Antiquity* 42(2): 255–265.
1989   The Power and the Glory. *Canyon Legacy* 1(1):13–18.

Scott, Douglass D.
1981   Rock Art in the Gunnison Valley. *Southwestern Lore* 47(3):1–6.

Sharrock, Floyd W.
1966   An Archaeological Survey of Canyonlands National Park. University of Utah, *Anthropological Papers* 12 (*Miscellaneous Papers* 83), Salt Lake City.

Shimkin, Demitri B.
1986   Eastern Shoshone. In *Handbook of North American Indians, Great Basin* vol. 11, Warren L. D'Azevedo, ed., pp. 308–335. Smithsonian Institution, Washington, D.C.

Smith, Anne M.
1974   Ethnography of the Northern Utes. Museum of New Mexico, *Papers in Anthropology* 17, Santa Fe.

Smith, Gary, with Michael E. Long
1980   Utah's Rock Art, Wilderness Louvre. *National Geographic* 157(1): 94–117.

Smith, Howard N., Jr.
1980   Kiva Wall Paintings at Salmon Ruins. Paper presented to the Annual Meeting of the Archaeological Society of New Mexico, Santa Fe.

Smith, Watson
1952   Kiva Mural Decorations at Awatovi and Kawaika-a. *Papers of the Peabody Museum of American Archaeology and Ethnology* 37 (*Reports of the Awatovi Expedition* 5), Cambridge, Massachusetts.

Sowers, Ted C.
1939   Petroglyphs and Pictographs of Dinwoody. (Unpublished.) Archaeological Project W.P.A., Casper, Wyoming.

Stephen, Alexander M.
1969   *Hopi Journal of Alexander M. Stephen.* Two parts, Elsie Clews Parsons, ed. AMS Press, New York.

Stevenson, Matilda Coxe
1904   The Zuni Indians: Their Mythology, Esoteric Fraternities, and Ceremonies. In *Twenty-third Annual Report of the Bureau of American Ethnology*, U.S. Government Printing Office, Washington, D.C.

Stewart, Omer C.
1942   Culture Element Distributions: XVIII. Ute-Southern Paiute. *Anthropological Records* VI. University of California.
1966   Ute Indians: Before and After White Contact. *Utah Historical Society* 34(1):38–61.

1976   Culture Element Distributions: XVIII Ute-Southern Paiute. In *University of California Publications in Anthropological Records* 6, pp. 231–354, Reprint, Berkeley.
1982   *Indians of the Great Basin, A Critical Bibliography.* Indiana University Press, Bloomington.

Sundstrom, Linea
1984   The Southern Black Hills. In Rock Art of Western South Dakota, part 2, pp. 53-142, *Special Publication of the South Dakota Archaeological Society* 9, Sioux Falls.

Taylor, Dee C.
1957   Two Fremont Sites and Their Position in Southwestern Prehistory. University of Utah, *Anthropological Papers* 29, Salt Lake City.

Teit, James
1930   Salishan Tribes of the Plateau. In *Forty-fifth Annual Report of the Bureau of American Ethnology*, pp. 23–396. U.S. Government Printing Office, Washington, D.C.

Thompson, Richard A.
1979   A Stratified Random Sample of the Cultural Resources in the Canyonlands Section of the Moab District. Utah Bureau of Land Management, *Cultural Resource Series* 1, Salt Lake City.

Tipps, Betsy L., and Nancy J. Hewitt
1989   Cultural Resource Inventory and Testing in the Salt Creek Pocked and Devils Lane Areas, Needles District, Canyonlands National Park, Utah. *Selections from the Division of Cultural Resources* 1, Rocky Mountain Region National Park Service, Denver.

Titiev, Mischa
1937   A Hopi Salt Expedition. *American Anthropologist* 39:244–258.
1944   Old Oraibi: A Study of the Hopi Indians of Third Mesa. *Papers of the Peabody Museum of American Archaeology and Ethnology* 22(1), Cambridge, Massachusetts.

Toll, Henry Wolcott, III
1977   Dolores River Archaeology: Canyon Adaptations as Seen Through Survey. Colorado Bureau of Land Management, *Cultural Resources Series* 4, Denver.

Trick, Roger
1982   Hovenweep National Monument. In *Canyon Country Prehistoric Rock Art*, F.A. Barnes, pp. 240–243. Wasatch Publishers, Salt Lake City.

Truesdale, James A.
1989   Personal communication with regard to radiocarbon dates from Dinosaur National Monument.

Tucker, Gordon C.
1989   The Harris Site Excavation. Colorado Bureau of Land Management, *Cultural Resources Series* 28, Denver.

Turner, Christy G., II
1963   Petrographs of the Glen Canyon Region. *Museum of Northern Arizona Bulletin* 38 (*Glen Canyon Series* 4), Flagstaff.
1971   Revised Dating for Early Rock Art of the Glen Canyon Region. *American*

Antiquity 36:469–471. Ute Mountain Ute Tribe.
1985a   *Ute Mountain Utes: A History Text.* Ute Mountain Ute Tribe, Towaoc, Colorado.
1985b   *Early Days of the Ute Mountain Utes.* Ute Mountain Ute Tribe, Towaoc, Colorado.
1986a   *Ute Mountain Ute Government.* Ute Mountain Ute Tribe, Towaoc, Colorado.
1986b   *Ute Mountain Ute Stories, Games, and Noise Makers.* Ute Mountain Ute Tribe, Towaoc, Colorado.

Vastokas, Joan M., and Romas K. Vastokas
1973   *Sacred Art of the Algonkians: A Study of the Peterborough Petroglyphs.* Mansard Press, Peterborough, Ontario, Canada.

Wade, Nancy A.
1979   *Battleship Rock: An Experimental Archaeological Study.* Master's Thesis, Department of Anthropology, University of Colorado, Boulder.

Walker, Danny N., and Julie E. Francis
1989   Legend Rock Petroglyph Site (48H04) Wyoming: 1988 Archaeological Investigations. Report on file at Worland District Office, Bureau of Land Management and Office of the State Archaeologist, Wyoming.

Warner, Jesse
1984   An Analysis of Head Form and Head Gear of the Inverted Bucket Head Hunters. In *Utah Rock Art* vol. 3, edited by Cindy Everitt, Rex Madsen, and Phil Garn, eds., pp. 70–82, Utah Rock Art Research Association, Salt Lake City.

Weaver, Donald E., Jr.
1984   Images on Stone: The Prehistoric Rock Art of the Colorado Plateau. *Plateau* 55(2).

Wellmann, Klaus F.
1979   *A Survey of North American Indian Rock Art.* Akademischa Druck-und Verlagsanstalt, Graz, Austria.

Wenger, Gilbert R.
1956   *An Archaeological Survey of Southern Blue Mountain and Douglas Creek in Northwestern Colorado.* Master's thesis, Department of Anthropology, University of Denver, Colorado.

Wobst, Martin
1976   Stylistic Behaviour and Information Exchange. In University of Michigan Museum of Anthropology, *Anthropological Papers* 61:317–342.

Wormington, H.M.
1955   A Reappraisal of the Fremont Culture. *Denver Museum of Natural History Proceedings* 1, Colorado.

Wormington, H.M., and Robert H. Lister
1956   Archaeological Investigations on the Uncompahgre Plateau in West Central Colorado. Denver Museum of Natural History, *Proceedings* 2, Denver, Colorado.

Young, M. Jane
1985   Images of Power and the Power of Images: The Significance of Rock Art for Contemporary Zunis. *Journal of American Folklore* 98(387):2–48.

Zolbrod, Paul G.
1984   *Dine Bahane: The Navajo Creation Story.* University of New Mexico Press, Albuquerque.

INDEX